MORNING & EVENING
DEVOTIONAL

Whatever Is Lovely

BroadStreet
PUBLISHING

BroadStreet Publishing Group LLC
Savage, MN, USA
Broadstreetpublishing.com

Whatever Is Lovely A Morning & Evening Devotional

© 2018 by BroadStreet Publishing®

ISBN 978-1-4245-5747-9 (faux)
ISBN 978-1-4245-5748-6 (e-book)

Devotional entries composed by Janelle Anthony Breckell.

Design by Chris Garborg | garborgdesign.com
Edited by Michelle Winger | literallyprecise.com

Printed in China.

18   19   20   21   22   23   24   7   6   5   4   3   2   1

WHATEVER IS TRUE,
WHATEVER IS NOBLE,
WHATEVER IS RIGHT,
WHATEVER IS PURE,
WHATEVER IS LOVELY,
WHATEVER IS ADMIRABLE—
IF ANYTHING IS EXCELLENT
OR PRAISEWORTHY—
THINK ABOUT SUCH THINGS.

PHILIPPIANS 4:8 NIV

Introduction

• • • • •

We know from Scripture that we should think about things that are lovely, good, and pure. But how do we find this in a world that appears to be unraveling at the seams?

This morning and evening devotional will encourage you to spend the beginning and end of your day with God, experiencing his goodness and being refreshed in his presence. From the time you wake up, until the time you fall into bed at night, let your mind dwell on all that is excellent, and give thanks to your Creator who has blessed you with so much.

Remember the greatness of God as you continually fix your eyes on his truth.

A Blank Canvas

In the beginning, God created the heavens and the earth. The earth was without form and void, and darkness was over the face of the deep. And the Spirit of God was hovering over the face of the waters.

GENESIS 1:1-2 ESV

In the beginning God created all things from a blank canvas; the possibilities were endless! Does the thought of a new year create excitement or apprehension about the unknown possibilities and opportunities?

A blank canvas can be a good opportunity to dwell on what you really want to do this year and think about how God can use your personality, skills, and talents. As you head into your day allow yourself to explore what God has in store for you and let him fill you with encouragement for the year ahead.

Father, I want to thank you for a new year, for a new day. Thank you for the opportunity to start again in many areas of my life. Give me courage for today and for the year ahead.

God said, "Let there be light," and there was light. And God saw that the light was good. And God separated the light from the darkness. God called the light Day, and the darkness he called Night. And there was evening and there was morning, the first day.

<small>GENESIS 1:3-5 ESV</small>

In the beginning there was darkness, but God brought the light. The light was the beginning of the rest of God's magnificent creative work.

Have you been able to see God in your circumstances today? Have you seen his light in areas that you have kept in the dark? Think about God's goodness for you today and the hope that his light in your life will bring about more wonderful things for you this year.

God, I bring areas of darkness to you in my life and in the life of those around me, and I ask for your light to shine. Bring hope where I see none and restore life to my soul.

Where do you need to see God's light in your life this year?

Imago Dei

God said, "Let us make man in our image, after our likeness.
And let them have dominion over the fish of the sea and over the
birds of the heavens and over the livestock and over all the earth
and over every creeping thing that creeps on the earth."

GENESIS 1:26 ESV

God created you in his image. Have you ever pondered what this really means? God intended for you and the rest of humanity to demonstrate what he is like to the rest of the world; to display the goodness of the Creator and to represent his name. That's a big task.

Remember that it isn't what you strive to do, it's who you are, so be encouraged today that you are representing your Creator just by being you.

God, it seems like a really big thing to be bearing your image, but I thank you that you created me and you love me as I am. I pray despite my imperfections I would still be able to reflect you in my life toward others today.

God created man in his own image,
in the image of God he created him;
male and female he created them. And God blessed them.

GENESIS 1:27-28 ESV

Was your day full of peace and love or have you had moments of quarrelling and tension? No matter what way it went, you are loved by God and his grace allows you to continue to be like him.

An image in ancient days were idols made from human hands with no life in them. We are a different image from any manmade thing because the God of this universe breathed life into us. We are alive, just as he is alive.

God, I need you to breathe new life into areas of my life where
I am not fully representing the person you have created me to be.
I choose to look ahead to the renewal that is going to take place in
my heart and in my life.

What area of your life do you feel you need to reflect God more?

Very Good Work

The heavens and the earth were finished, and all the host of them. And on the seventh day God finished his work that he had done, and he rested on the seventh day from all his work that he had done.

GENESIS 2:1-2 ESV

It must have taken a lot of energy for God to create this universe, this world, and the complexity that is humanity. God also planned rest into his creative work. After he had finished his very good work he rested.

As you go through your day, your various working activities will require energy from you. Think about God's intention for rest after hard work; he knows what is best for us. Take a few moments to rest from your very good work.

God, I thank you for the day ahead. I ask for your energy to get some very good work done. I pray that you would give me moments of rest so I can be restored to do more work that will bring glory to you.

God blessed the seventh day and made it holy, because on it God rested from all his work that he had done in creation.

GENESIS 2:3 ESV

At the end of a long day it's easy to feel a little down because your energy has been depleted.

You may have had very little time for yourself today, but now you have a moment to sit and reflect on the goodness of God with the idea that he wants you to be here right now and rest in him. God took a whole day out of his work to rest.

God, I thank you for this moment of rest, this time to be restored by reflecting on being like you and resting like you did. I pray for your strength; I pray for great sleep so I am ready to face another day.

What day can you take this week that will allow you to have time to rest?

Hiding

They heard the sound of the LORD God walking in the garden in the cool of the day, and the man and his wife hid themselves from the presence of the LORD God among the trees of the garden.

GENESIS 3:8 ESV

It would have been a hard day for Adam and Eve, the day they were deceived and made the choice to disobey God. They were so ashamed that they hid, although they must have known that they would be found.

We all know what shame feels like, when we have committed wrong toward someone else. We want to run from our problems and not face those we have hurt, and yet the truth cannot escape us. Can you face your day with boldness, knowing that truth and owning up to your mistakes is better than hiding?

Jesus, I am going to need your help today to make sure that I don't hide from my mistakes, and to know that your presence is always there, not to condemn, but to give me grace.

The LORD God called to the man and said to him, "Where are you?" And he said, "I heard the sound of you in the garden, and I was afraid, because I was naked, and I hid myself."

GENESIS 3:9-10 ESV

Were there any mistakes or arguments in your day that made you feel like covering up or hiding? We aren't often very good at taking ownership of our wrongdoings, and sometimes we think that ignoring them is the easiest way out.

Perhaps you have been hurt by someone and are waiting for them to apologize. Whatever the wrongdoing, notice that God is all about restoration. In the garden, it was God who went to find Adam and Eve. He didn't wait for them to come out from hiding; he sought them out. Don't be afraid, and don't hide. God will always seek to restore relationship with you and with others.

God, there is a lot of brokenness around me, and sometimes I just want to carry on and try to hide from my own sin. Thank you for your forgiveness, for your grace, and for restoring relationship with me.

What relationship do you need God to restore to you? If you need forgiveness, approach God—he is for you, not against you.

Colorful Promises

*God said, "This is the sign of the covenant that I make between me
and you and every living creature that is with you, for all future
generations: I have set my bow in the cloud, and it shall be a sign
of the covenant between me and the earth."*

GENESIS 9:12-13 ESV

Rainbows are beautiful wonders of nature that bring joy
to those fortunate enough to see them. They come from a
combination of rain and sun, and it is easy to see why God put
such a beautiful reminder in the sky of his goodness.

Your day may be filled with some pain and some joy.
Remember that the combination of different aspects can
be turned into a beautiful reminder of God's promise to
remember his children and to show them his lovingkindness.

*Father, I need your lovingkindness in my life today. Whether I
experience rain or shine, or a little of both, I pray I would see your
beauty working in and through me.*

> *"When I bring clouds over the earth and the bow is seen in the clouds, I will remember my covenant that is between me and you and every living creature of all flesh. And the waters shall never again become a flood to destroy all flesh."*
>
> Genesis 9:14-15 ESV

It grieves God's heart to see his children in pain. It is good to remind ourselves that while we do not understand the ways of God, we believe in his goodness and knowledge of his creation to know what is best for the world.

When the waters of life seem to be rising higher and higher, don't panic. God has made a promise to keep you from drowning. Trust in him.

God, after a long day I am feeling overwhelmed. Help me to remember your promise to always be with me and to help me get through each and every day. Give me rest as I go to bed and give me hope for a new day.

What pressure are you feeling today that is causing you anxiety? Think of the rainbow that God put in the sky and remember that his promises are for you.

The Good Portion

Abram said to Lot, "Let there be no strife between you and me, and between your herdsmen and my herdsmen, for we are kinsmen."

GENESIS 13:8 ESV

Abram and his nephew Lot had been on a long journey together to reach the land that God had promised them. When they got there, Abram had a choice to make; there was good land and there was very good land. Abram chose peace over greed and gave the very good land to his nephew. As a result, God blessed Abram abundantly.

You may have some choices to make today that will require you to give up something that seems very good for the sake of someone else. Let God bless you as you practice generosity.

Thank you, God, for the many blessings of this life. I pray that if an opportunity comes today to be generous to someone else that you would remind me of your generosity toward me.

"Is not the whole land before you? Separate yourself from me.
If you take the left hand, then I will go to the right,
or if you take the right hand, then I will go to the left."

GENESIS 13:9 ESV

Have you had to put aside your need or desire in order to benefit someone else today? Or did you lose the opportunity because you didn't want to give it up?

Either way God is still on your side and will be with you whether you are an Abram or a Lot. Allow God to continue to work on gifting you with a generous spirit.

God, I don't always get it right and I am particularly challenged to have to give up opportunities for the benefit of those around me. I pray you would remind me of your love and immeasurable goodness so I will have the desire to give more to others.

In what ways do you find it hard to be generous toward others? Is it money, patience, or a better opportunity? Allow yourself to be challenged to give more.

Righteous through Faith

Abram said, "Behold, you have given me no offspring, and a member of my household will be my heir." And behold, the word of the LORD came to him: "This man shall not be your heir; your very own son shall be your heir."

GENESIS 15:3-4 ESV

It sounds a little bit like Abram was complaining when he reminded God that he had been given no offspring. Does this sound like your complaints at times?

What are you praying for that you feel like God has not given you, yet? Be encouraged by the Lord's response to Abram and know that God will answer you in his time.

God, there are things in my life that I am still waiting for and sometimes I feel as though you have neglected my desires. I choose to trust you today, and submit my desires to you, knowing that you care enough to answer me.

He brought him outside and said, "Look toward heaven,
and number the stars, if you are able to number them." Then he
said to him, "So shall your offspring be." And he believed the LORD,
and he counted it to him as righteousness.

This is the famous place in the Bible where we understand
that it isn't about what we say or do that saves us, rather, it is
what we believe. Abram and Sarah would have undoubtedly
felt skeptical that God would give them as many descendants
as the stars in the sky as they wrestled with having even one
child in their old age.

What God says is truth, and his Word did not come back void.
Somewhere along the line, Abram chose to believe and his
heart of belief, God said, made him righteous.

God, as I ponder your amazing miracle for Abram and Sarah, I see
your goodness and truth. I pray that you would do miraculous things
in my life, and that I would have the faith to believe in your Word.

What do you need to believe God for tonight?

Well Pleased

Jesus came from Galilee to the Jordan to John, to be baptized by him. John would have prevented him, saying, "I need to be baptized by you, and do you come to me?" But Jesus answered him, "Let it be so now, for thus it is fitting for us to fulfill all righteousness." Then he consented.

MATTHEW 3:13-15 ESV

Jesus didn't just come to the world to show us perfection, he also came to show us a new way of life. Of course he didn't need to be baptized, he was God. He chose, however, to model what our righteousness was all about.

John baptized Jesus to represent how our old life can die with Christ and rise again. You will probably be challenged in some way today, to put behind your old self and to live in the new life Jesus has given you. Are you up for this challenge?

Jesus, thank you for showing me that you made a way for me to live a better life. I know you don't require perfection, so I ask that you remind me, as I face challenges today, to be a person of the new life you demonstrated to us.

When Jesus was baptized, immediately he went up from the water, and behold, the heavens were opened to him, and he saw the Spirit of God descending like a dove and coming to rest on him; and behold, a voice from heaven said, "This is my beloved Son, with whom I am well pleased."

MATTHEW 3:16-17 ESV

When you get to the end of the day you can feel a sense of accomplishment knowing that you achieved a few things and simply got through the day without any major catastrophe.

Sometimes you may have even gone that one step above and remembered to show love in some way to someone around you—you lived in the new life that Christ has given you. Well done. Let yourself be encouraged that the Father says these same words to you, just as he did to his beloved Son: "Child, I am well pleased with you."

Father, sometimes I feel as though I don't deserve your praise. Thank you that you have a different view. Thank you that you see me with love and acceptance and that simply because I am your child, you are well pleased with me.

Can you imagine these words being just for you? Reflect on your day and let God show you the heart attitude that he was well pleased with.

Hard to Resist

Again, the devil took him to a very high mountain and showed him all the kingdoms of the world and their glory. And he said to him, "All these I will give you, if you will fall down and worship me."

MATTHEW 4:8-9 ESV

The world can offer a lot of great things. Careers offer success, relationships offer security, and riches can provide comfort. Nothing is inherently wrong with having these things, unless they are used for our own glory.

In the world, people want to glorify themselves. This is what the devil was after, too. He wanted to be worshiped. Thankfully, Jesus knew that the kingdoms of this world were nothing like the kingdom of God. He chose something greater. Are you able to resist the temptation of the world today?

God, thank you that you understand the temptations in this world. Please strengthen me for the day ahead and remind me that your kingdom is better than all the false glory that may come my way.

Jesus said to him, "Be gone, Satan! For it is written, "'You shall worship the LORD your God and him only shall you serve.'" Then the devil left him, and behold, angels came and were ministering to him.

MATTHEW 4:10-11 ESV

There are many pressures in the day to serve things other than God's kingdom. Have you found yourself tempted to buy something new but not needed? Have you booked another beauty appointment because you feel like you can't show anyone your flaws? Did you say yes to just one more thing that you don't have time for because you didn't want to look bad by saying no?

We need to reassess our decisions in light of who we are serving—is it God, or humans? The Bible says we should only worship the Lord our God. Tell the devil who is boss and let God minister to you as you resist temptation.

God, I am sorry for becoming distracted with desiring the things of this world. Help me to say no to temptation and worship only you. Minister to me now as I rest in your presence.

What is drawing you away from worshiping God and him alone?

Jesus Heals

Jesus was going throughout all Galilee, teaching in their synagogues and proclaiming the gospel of the kingdom, and healing every kind of disease and every kind of sickness among the people.

MATTHEW 4:23 NASB

It is hard to understand how and when God heals his children. Have you prayed for healing recently and haven't got any better? Do you know someone around you that is unwell and not recovering? It can be disheartening when you are sick, or see others that you care about not improving.

Our faith does not need to be great, but through our belief in Jesus, we can also acknowledge our belief in the miracles that he performed. Jesus showed us that what we think is impossible is not impossible with God.

Jesus, I pray for healing in my life and in the life of those who are unwell around me. I know you cared for others and had compassion to heal, but I also recognize that sometimes you don't answer us exactly how we want. Help me to trust that you are always good, no matter what.

News about him spread as far as Syria, and people soon began bringing to him all who were sick. And whatever their sickness or disease, or if they were demon possessed or epileptic or paralyzed—he healed them all.

MATTHEW 4:24 NASB

Sometimes healing doesn't come, and we need to trust that God is still faithful and gracious. He will restore perfect health to us in eternity.

We may have to wait for healing and we may never really know why. But let us still be encouraged today to believe in a God of miracles, and pray with all our might that he will bring healing to the sick.

God, I do trust that you are faithful and gracious. I believe there are times that you have healed me, or those around me, and I believe that you have also kept me safe in times I wasn't even aware of. Thank you for your enduring love.

Are you praying for healing for yourself or someone else? Can you see God's goodness in that situation?

Empty but Blessed

"Blessed are the poor in spirit, for theirs is the kingdom of heaven. Blessed are those who mourn, for they will be comforted."

MATTHEW 5:3-4 NIV

There are days where you might wake up a little more sluggish, with a little less energy and positivity about the day. That can feel kind of empty, a gap you're hoping to fill.

The great thing about the God you serve is that in him, you can be complete. He can be that gap-filler. As you sit with him, his light begins to burn brighter.

God, lift me up this morning. It's hard to get out of bed and sometimes I feel anxious or worried about the day ahead. Give me energy and strength to face another day.

"Blessed are the meek, for they will inherit the earth. Blessed are those who hunger and thirst for righteousness, for they will be filled."

MATTHEW 5:5-6 NIV

On this particular day, meet God in dependence. Come to him even when you don't feel like it. Present your helplessness and emptiness to him and he will bless you and fill your gap with warmth, joy, peace, care, and love.

As you spend time with God tonight, allow him to speak to you and rest knowing you were transformed and filled on one of the hardest days. He is faithful and loving no matter our circumstance or feeling.

I'm glad to be here in your presence tonight, God. It is a struggle for me to just sit down and think about you when my mind is so full of other things. As I seek you, let the things of this earth grow dim in the light of your glory.

Have you seen the fruit of this promise on one of your rough days?

Salt and Light

"You are the salt of the earth. But what good is salt if it has lost its flavor? Can you make it salty again? It will be thrown out and trampled underfoot as worthless."

MATTHEW 5:13 NLT

You are blessed simply because you believe in Jesus and have eternal life. When Jesus was speaking to the disciples, he wanted them to know that this very good thing that they had received needed to be shared.

There is no point to a life in Christ if we lose the one thing that makes us different from the world. God wants you to display a life that shows how wonderful salvation is. Can you be like salt in an otherwise bland world today?

Jesus, thank you that you blessed me with the gift of salvation. Let my words and heart attitude toward activities and people be an expression of this gift so I don't just blend in with everyone else. Let my life be that point of difference that makes people wonder why I have peace and joy.

"You are the light of the world—like a city on a hilltop that cannot be hidden. No one lights a lamp and then puts it under a basket. Instead, a lamp is placed on a stand, where it gives light to everyone in the house."

MATTHEW 5:14-15 NLT

As you prepare yourself for bed tonight, the last thing you will probably do is turn out the lights. You need the light to see everything you are doing until then. You need the light to show you the way. There would be no point of turning on the light only to cover it up.

This is our journey of salvation. Jesus didn't want you to receive his light and then hide it. He wants you to shine brightly so others will also see the path to faith.

Father, as I reflect on those places where I have hidden my light, I thank you for your grace. I know that you understand and that you want to give me the boldness to live out my faith as brightly as I can. I pray that as I greet the light tomorrow, I would be ready to shine alongside it.

Where have you hidden your light lately? What situations make you want to hide instead of shine?

Love All

"You have heard the law that says, 'Love your neighbor and hate your enemy.' But I say, love your enemies! Pray for those who persecute you!"

MATTHEW 5:43-44 NLT

The ways of this world are different from the ways of the kingdom. Jesus made this clear by contrasting what the world says to do with your enemies and what Christ-followers should do. You probably have people in your mind that you see as a threat, or those who are unkind toward you. Sometimes we even get mocked for our faith, whether overtly or subtly. These are the very people who Christ asks us to love.

It's not easy to pray for those who have hurt you. Jesus understands this; he had to forgive all who brought him to his painful death on the cross. Allow Christ to be your strength as you practice goodness to those who have wronged you.

God, I need your help with loving my enemies. Give me your heart for them. Help me to see that everyone is loved by you, no matter what they do or say. I don't accept their wrong behavior, but I choose today to pray for their healing, forgiveness, and restoration.

> *"In that way, you will be acting as true children of your Father in heaven. For he gives his sunlight to both the evil and the good, and he sends rain on the just and the unjust alike."*
>
> MATTHEW 5:45 NLT

It can seem unfair that good people suffer and those seemingly less deserving prosper. Jesus wanted us to recognize the Father heart of God for all his children, even those who reject him.

God loves unconditionally and when we show impartiality for all his creation, even those who seem bad, we know that we are being the true children of God, imitating his love for all humankind.

Lord Jesus, forgive me for a heart that cannot always see your love for all people. Help me to love these people who feel like enemies. Give me the grace to change my ways.

Who are your enemies? Is there anyone that needs an extra measure of grace and forgiveness from you?

When You Pray

"When you pray, do not be like the hypocrites, for they love to pray standing in the synagogues and on the street corners to be seen by others. Truly I tell you, they have received their reward in full."

MATTHEW 6:5 NIV

Cherish the secret things. So much of our life is for others. Whether it is the requirement of jobs, keeping up relationships, or the programs we volunteer for, so much of our time and energy is spent on other people.

God wants our time. He wants it for us and for him. Maybe this will require a designated prayer closet, or a quiet place away.

God, I pray that I don't become religious with the way that I spend time with you. I want to engage with you at any moment of any day, and I don't need it to be loud and pretentious. Let me be genuine in my prayers to you today.

"When you pray, go into your room, close the door and pray to your Father, who is unseen. Then your Father, who sees what is done in secret, will reward you."

MATTHEW 6:6 NIV

Were you able to head to a quiet place with your Bible and journal tonight? You might be reading this with noise all around you.

However you get your time, your heavenly Father sees you. What a faithful gift that thought is; he sees you in secret and will meet you where you are.

God, I have this time with you right now. I know it's not much, but after a long day, it's all I have. Thank you that you see me. Thank you that we don't have to make a fuss about this time, but it's something that we can both enjoy without trying to let everyone else in on it.

Can you get away today in secret to pray? In secret, God will reward your heart. Make slipping away with him a daily routine.

Your Treasure

"Do not lay up for yourselves treasures on earth, where moth and rust destroy and where thieves break in and steal, but lay up for yourselves treasures in heaven, where neither moth nor rust destroys and where thieves do not break in and steal."

MATTHEW 6:19-20 ESV

Have you ever been sitting on a beach and watched a little child work tirelessly on an elaborate sand castle? These little children are unaware of the patterns of ocean waves and don't realize that as the day passes, their masterpieces will eventually be swept away by the swelling tide. All that work, all that concentration, all that pride, gone as the water erases the shore.

What castles are we building in our lives that could, at any moment, be simply erased? We must know what can last and what won't. There are temporary kingdoms and a kingdom that will never pass away. We have to recognize which one we are contributing to.

God, I want to build meaningful things for your kingdom. Give me the discernment to know what is truly of worth to you.

"Where your treasure is, there your heart will be also."

MATTHEW 6:21 ESV

If your work and your heart are invested in a heavenly vision, then what you have spent your life on will continue to matter for longer than you live.

Spend your time investing in the eternal souls of people, in the eternal vision of advancing God's kingdom, and in the never-ending truth of the Gospel. In these things you will find purpose and treasure that will never be lost.

Father God, I know that you have created my life with meaning and purpose. Help me to see how the gifts that you have given me matter in terms of eternity. Let me see the value of all my time, energy, and talent.

What are you putting your time, energy, and talents into? Are they being used for God's glory?

Under His Care

*"Look at the birds. They don't plant or harvest or store food in
barns, for your heavenly Father feeds them. And aren't you far
more valuable to him than they are? Can all your worries add a
single moment to your life?"*

When you wake up in the morning you can begin to feel
anxious about the day ahead. What will you wear? What
do you need to organize? Will you make it in time to your
important appointment?

Life is so full that we can feel overwhelmed with worry about
getting it all done, and getting it all done right. Jesus didn't
want us to feel like that. God cares for us and takes care of a
lot of the small things that we probably don't realize he has
had a hand in. Recognize his work in your life today, and head
into it with confidence.

*God, I need you right by my side today. Thank you for all the small
things that you take care of. Thank you that you are a Father who
loves to take care of me.*

"Why worry about your clothing? Look at the lilies of the field and how they grow. They don't work or make their clothing, yet Solomon in all his glory was not dressed as beautifully as they are."

MATTHEW 6:28-29

What is it about coming home after a long day that makes you want to change into something more comfortable? You may have already done that and are ready to relax.

Sometimes we need to be reminded that we even have this option. We are privileged that God not only looks after our basic needs but often blesses us with more than that.

Father, thank you for taking care of me. Thank you that not only do I have my basic needs met, but that you bless me with other beautiful things. Help me to express more gratitude for all my blessings.

What blessings are you thankful for? Where can you see God's provision in your life today?

Hope in the Storm

"All who listen to my instructions and follow them are wise, like a man who builds his house on solid rock. Though the rain comes in torrents, and the floods rise and the storm winds beat against his house, it won't collapse, for it is built on rock."

MATTHEW 7:24-25 TLB

Jesus didn't just give instructions on how to live so we could be nice people. There are nice people everywhere: believers and unbelievers alike. He gave us ways to live so we could walk through the storms with peace and joy in our hearts.

Our confidence is not in everything that is happening around us; it is in knowing that with Christ we have a new, eternal life. That knowledge is our solid foundation.

God, thank you for reminding me that a life lived your way is a life that is able to weather all kinds of storms that may come my way. Help me to live by your instructions and to be wise so I will always carry the hope of eternity in all circumstances.

"Those who hear my instructions and ignore them are foolish, like a man who builds his house on sand. For when the rains and floods come, and storm winds beat against his house, it will fall with a mighty crash."

MATTHEW 7:26-27 TLB

When we ignore God's ways, we also ignore the hope that he has placed in our hearts for his eternal kingdom. Forgetting to live with this eternal perspective means that even the smallest of storms can beat us down, making us feel discouraged and hopeless.

As you take this time to think about your day, reflect on whether you have been facing your challenges with hope or despair.

God, I have faced a few challenges this week and I know there are times when I have responded with despair and a lack of hope. Remind me that the knowledge of a new, restored life is the very thing that will keep my head above the water. Give me joy and peace in all circumstances.

How have you been responding to the storms of life this week?

He's the One

"Go and tell John what you hear and see: the blind receive their sight, the lame walk, the lepers are cleansed, the deaf hear, the dead are raised, and the poor have good news brought to them."

MATTHEW 11:4-5 NRSV

There were many people in Jesus' time who wanted to know if Jesus was truly the one they had been waiting for. Jesus had been prophesied about and although many wanted to believe he was the one, they still had doubts. Even John the Baptist asked if Jesus really was the one.

It is good to remind ourselves that Jesus really is the one that came to save us all from the curse of sin. He is our redeemer, he is the one who brought healing and salvation to the world. You might need that solid reminder today. Read this Scripture in faith—Jesus is the one.

Jesus, at times I have doubts about my faith and sometimes it seems like my life is taken over by a different reality. Restore my faith today so I can live out a life that is completely convinced that you are the one.

"Blessed is anyone who takes no offense at me."
MATTHEW 11:6 NRSV

It can be easy to have a day full of wondering where God is in the middle of it all. We can admit that sometimes this faith in Christ seems absurd. We feel a form of persecution in the world when we hear others laugh about Christianity or find a way to blame religion for all the wrong in the world.

To the world, the message of the cross is offensive. To those of us who believe, we find the message of Christ our true fulfilment because it is a message full of hope, peace, and joy.

God, sometimes I don't even understand why I believe all that I do about you. I know that you can handle my doubt, but I ask that you restore an unwavering faith to me so I feel blessed that I am living in the truth.

Have you had moments today or this week of feeling like your faith has taken a knock?

One in a Hundred

"What do you think? If any man has a hundred sheep, and one of them has gone astray, does he not leave the ninety-nine on the mountains and go and search for the one that is straying?"

MATTHEW 18:12 NASB

Regardless of how beautifully or how imperfectly your earthly father showed his love, your heavenly Father's love is utterly boundless. Rest in that thought a moment. There is nothing you can do to change how he feels about you.

It's easy to forget we are already perfectly loved. Our Father loves you more than you can imagine. And he would do anything for you. Remember that throughout your day.

God, thank you that you care so much about me. At times, I have been that one lost sheep and you have come to find me. Thank you for your love for me.

"If it turns out that he finds it, truly I say to you, he rejoices over it more than over the ninety-nine which have not gone astray. So it is not the will of your Father who is in heaven that one of these little ones perish."

MATTHEW 12:13-14 NASB

You might have had a rough day, or maybe a really good day. Remember that your heavenly Father has been loving you throughout all of your day.

Who do you love most fiercely, most protectively, most desperately here on earth? What would you do for them? Know that it's a mere fraction, nearly immeasurable, of what God would do for you. Spend some time thanking him for his great love.

Father, I know that you will always search me out, no matter where I try to go. Help me to stay close to you so I can always bring you joy. Let me rest in your care for me as I go to sleep.

Are there areas of your life that you feel lost? Let Jesus take care of those things.

Gathered Together

"I also tell you this: If two of you agree here on earth concerning anything you ask, my Father in heaven will do it for you."

MATTHEW 18:19 NLT

When was the last time you felt spiritually recharged from conversation or prayer with other Christians? Sometimes going to church or a Bible study seems like just another thing to add to your list of things to do.

Are you giving yourself an opportunity to be uplifted by other believers or to be an encouragement to those around you? Remember that God promises to be with you when you are gathered together in his name. Is there a gathering that you can commit yourself to this week? Make an effort to go so you can experience the rich rewards of fellowship.

Father God, sometimes I feel too tired to go to something else. Give me energy to say yes to something this week that I know will be good for me and good for others.

*"Where two or three gather together as my followers,
I am there among them."*

Matthew 18:20 NLT

God is a relational God. He knows that we need each other, and that life is better together. As a Christian, it is especially important to share time with other believers.

When we make time to pray together, study the Bible together, and share our faith stories, we can be supported, encouraged, and strengthened.

God, thank you for creating others in my life. I have so many wonderful friends and I really do love my family. Help me to encourage those who have faith and to be a witness of your love to those who do not.

Take a moment this evening to make a mental list of all the things you are involved in. Are these things encouraging you in your faith? Are they resulting in rewarding relationships?

The Burden of Riches

"If you wish to be complete, go and sell your possessions and give to the poor, and you will have treasure in heaven; and come, follow Me."

MATTHEW 19:21 NASB

If only I had more money! The thought runs through our minds frequently, and though we may actually have enough to be content with, we are often thinking about what we could do with more.

Wherever you stand financially, you probably have a goal of accumulating more wealth than you have now. But did you ever notice how the Bible seems to view earthly riches as actually getting in the way of our relationships with God and others?

God today I will probably have to deal with money. Help me to show integrity and generosity in paying bills, shopping, and even in earning money. Show me ways that I can be generous too.

When the young man heard this statement, he went away grieving; for he was one who owned much property.

MATTHEW 19:22 NASB

Wealth is rarely what we hope it is; the more we have, the more we have to lose. Jesus wanted the rich man to have a compassionate heart—one that was willing to give up what he had for the sake of the kingdom. To do this, he would have needed to give up the life that he was accustomed to.

Before asking God to bless you with wealth, ask him to bless you with a heart of giving.

Heavenly Father, thank you that you have given me more than enough. Help me to be content with what I have and to think more of others than myself. Bring generosity and compassion into my heart.

Are there areas where God is asking you to be more generous?

First and Greatest

One of them, an expert in the law, tested him with this question: "Teacher, which is the greatest commandment in the Law?" Jesus replied: "'Love the LORD your God with all your heart and with all your soul and with all your mind.'"

MATTHEW 22:35-37 NIV

The Pharisees were always trying to trip up Jesus. They wanted nothing more than to find fault with him—a reason to put him on trial or do away with him. So when they asked him which of all the commandments was the greatest, they were hoping that he would somehow fail to come up with the correct answer.

Instead, as usual, Jesus got it right. When we love the Lord our God with all our hearts, everything else falls into place. The other commandments are easy to follow.

God, I know that you desire relationship above everything else. Help me to love you and love others with all my heart.

> *"This is the first and greatest commandment. And the second is like it: 'Love your neighbor as yourself.' All the Law and the Prophets hang on these two commandments."*
>
> MATTHEW 22:38-39 NIV

Have you given all of yourself to him? Do you love the Lord your God with all your heart, all your soul, and all your mind?

Let the last of your walls crumble, and give him all of you tonight.

Jesus, it's hard to say that I love you with everything because I know the truth is that I so often get distracted by everything else. I know that you see my heart, and you know my desire is to love you with my entire being.

What do you need to give up so you can put God first?

It's a Mission

"Behold, the cry of the children of Israel has come to Me, and I have also seen the oppression with which the Egyptians oppress them. Come now, therefore, and I will send you to Pharaoh that you may bring My people, the children of Israel, out of Egypt."

EXODUS 3:9-10 NKJV

Have you ever felt as though God gave you a task that was way too big for you to handle? After Moses had seen God in the burning bush, he was asked to take the people of Israel out of the land of Egypt and away from the grips of Pharaoh. This was going to be an amazing victory for the Israelites, but it required a huge amount of effort on the part of Moses.

What has God put on your agenda for this day, for this week, for this year? Does it feel like it is too big for you? God wants to do amazing things through you.

God, today I feel overwhelmed at the thought of the mission that you have put before me. I know that there are good things ahead but I feel apprehensive. Give me boldness and clarity to approach this day with courage.

*Moses said to God, "Who am I that I should go to Pharaoh, and
that should bring the children of Israel out of Egypt?" So He
said, "I will certainly be with you. And this shall be a sign to you
that I have sent you: When you have brought the people out of
Egypt, you shall serve God on this mountain."*

EXODUS 3:11-12 NKJV

Moses was understandably afraid and cautious about the
mission God had set before him. Even after he had seen God
in a flame-filled bush.

We need to remember the amazing things God has already
done for us and know that he is with us to do more amazing
things. God never asks us to do things in our own strength;
he simply wants us to take part in what he has the strength to
accomplish.

*Jesus, thank you that as I think about what you've done in my life
I realize there have been wonderful small miracles and amazing
things along the way. As I spend time with you right now I pray
I would understand that your presence and power is what will
enable me to do great things.*

What is one truly amazing thing that God has done for you?

Push Through

Moses and Aaron went to Pharaoh and said, "Thus says the LORD, the God of Israel, 'Let my people go, so that they may celebrate a festival to me in the wilderness.'"

EXODUS 5:1 NRSV

There must have been a lot of fuss involved with Moses and Aaron being able to approach Pharaoh to deliver the simple but daring message to tell him to let the Israelites go.

In this life, we often face barriers that try to stop us from doing or saying the right things. You may be challenged with something like this today. Remember the boldness of Moses and his God-given ability to navigate the circumstances so he could be a part of God's plan for the entire nation.

God, as I navigate potentially difficult circumstances today, I pray you would remind me of the simple message of your love for me and your love for others. I ask I would be able to deliver this message despite all the things that may try to get in my way.

Pharaoh said, "Who is the L<small>ORD</small> that I should heed him and let Israel go? I do not know the L<small>ORD</small>, and I will not let Israel go."

<small>EXODUS 5:2 NRSV</small>

Even after successfully overcoming the obstacles and delivering the bold message from God, Pharaoh still said no to Moses and Aaron. This is the world that we live in.

We cannot control the response of those who do not love God; we cannot even control the response of those who do. God still has his way of getting things done even when we feel like the walls have been put up. Be encouraged this evening that your efforts are not in vain and that God will come through one way or another.

God, at times I feel discouraged because I don't feel like anything is happening with the things that you have asked me to do and the dreams I hold in my heart. I pray for those who have hearts against you; soften those hearts so your good work will prevail in this world.

In what ways have you seen God breakthrough in your life, despite the obstacles?

No Need for Jealousy

"You must not covet your neighbor's house. You must not covet your neighbor's wife, male or female servant, ox or donkey, or anything else that belongs to your neighbor."

EXODUS 20:17 NLT

What does it mean to covet your neighbor's things? In the times of the Bible the number of livestock that a neighbor owned showed their wealth. We aren't that different today. We may not admit when we are jealous of what other people have, but we certainly know the things that we want that we do not yet have.

Instead of coveting sheep or goats, it might be your friend's house, car, clothes, or job. It is a real challenge to be content with what you have when the world tries to sell you the idea that more is better. Try to avoid the temptation to want what other people have today and learn the habit of contentment.

God, it must have been an important commandment that you would include this idea of not being jealous of things in your top ten. Help me to be aware of my heart attitude; forgive me and give me a feeling of peace and thankfulness with what I do have.

When the people heard the thunder and the loud blast of the ram's horn, and when they saw the flashes of lightning and the smoke billowing from the mountain, they stood at a distance, trembling with fear.

EXODUS 20:18 NLT

What a tremendous sight it must have been when God delivered the Ten Commandments to Moses. Certainly the sound of thunder and the vision of lightning would have made an impact.

Perhaps today we have forgotten the dramatic importance of the commandments that God gave. They were commandments to ultimately protect the relationships between people and between the Creator and his creation. Take some time to remember or read through these commandments that were so important to the Israelites. They also have significance for us today.

God, I thank you that your Word isn't about rules but about relationship. I trust that you care about my relationship with others and with you. I pray for the grace to follow your commandments so I can have healthy relationships.

What things are you envious of in other people's lives? Are there areas that you are not satisfied with?

Ask for Favor

"Lord," he said, "if I have found favor in your eyes, then let the
Lord go with us. Although this is a stiff-necked people, forgive our
wickedness and our sin, and take us as your inheritance."

EXODUS 34:9 NIV

Even though Moses admits the sin and wrongdoing of the
people of Israel, he still requests God's favor, not only for
himself but for the people who would represent the way
forward for all humanity.

From day to day we may forget that we are part of this greater
plan and that God wanted us to be a part of his saving work.
Even though you can admit that you aren't perfect, ask God
for his forgiveness and be ready to receive his favor.

*God, I am most certainly not perfect. I know I will not have a perfect
day today but I ask for your favor. I know that your grace covers a
multitude of sins and I will need your grace to face the day.*

"I am making a covenant with you. Before all your people I will do wonders never before done in any nation in all the world. The people you live among will see how awesome is the work that I, the Lord, will do for you."

EXODUS 34:10 NIV

Got accepted Moses' request to bless his people; he set up a covenant that would allow amazing things for and through the Israelites.

We know that God did many miracles, but we also know that the people didn't always obey and fulfill their part in that covenant promise. God remained faithful and showed his loving kindness toward them over and over again.

God, thank you for being faithful even when I am not. I know you still want to do amazing things in and through my life. I ask for your forgiveness. Open my heart to your loving advice.

Where and how do you need God's favor in your life this week?

Admit It

"Suppose you make a foolish vow of any kind, whether its purpose is for good or for bad. When you realize its foolishness, you must admit your guilt."

LEVITICUS 5:4 NLT

Admit it. We've all said some pretty foolish things in our lifetime. You might be thinking of a time when you judged someone unnecessarily, or assumed one thing was happening when it actually wasn't. You may have made youthful promises that you certainly haven't kept.

Sometimes we have good intentions, other times we do not, but Scripture says when you realize your foolishness, it's time to admit your guilt.

God, I'm sorry for those foolish things that I have said and done. I know that you are gracious and kind and so I come to you with an honest heart, admitting my mistakes, knowing I am forgiven. Let me be a shining example of your love today.

"When you become aware of your guilt in any of these ways, you must confess your sin. Then you must bring to the LORD as the penalty for your sin a female from the flock, either a sheep or a goat. This is a sin offering with which the priest will purify you from your sin, making you right with the LORD."

LEVITICUS 5:5-6 NLT

It can be hard to reconcile the many types of offerings and specific procedures that the Israelites had to follow with a God of grace and mercy. It seems like a lot of rules and sacrifices in order to prove you were sorry.

What a relief that Jesus took all those requirements to the cross. Admitting guilt, however, remains an important step toward forgiveness and restoration. If you have stumbled today, realize your foolishness, admit your mistake, and make things right with God.

God, I rely on your grace tonight, ever thankful that I don't have to go through rituals or sacrifices in order to atone for my guilt. Forgive my foolishness and help me to be humble before you and before others as I go forward.

What mistake have you made recently that you need to admit?

Neighbors

> "Do not nurse hatred in your heart for any of your relatives. Confront people directly so you will not be held guilty for their sin."

LEVITICUS 19:17 NLT

It is interesting that it is your neighbors can be the ones to irritate you the most, from parking the car in the wrong place to making too much noise in the evening, we can get disgruntled pretty quickly.

The Bible doesn't tell us that we should accept wrongdoing, but it does warn us about the risk of sinning on account of your irritation. Most of the time, tolerance and gracious conversation seem to be the best approach.

God, I am sorry when I have been overly judgmental of my neighbors, whether they are my house neighbors or the people next to me at work. Give me grace as I recognize that I will also irritate people at times. Help me to display a good attitude toward others today.

"You are not to seek vengeance or hold a grudge against the descendants of your people. Instead, love your neighbor as yourself. I am the LORD."

LEVITICUS 19:18 NLT

Often when we do things that bother people, it isn't intentional. We may have forgotten to do something we were asked to do, made too much noise, or parked in the wrong space. When someone else does these things, however, we somehow think they were intentionally trying to bother us.

Remember that we are all made in the same way, and we all have our faults. That's why one of our greatest commandments is to love others as we love ourselves.

Jesus, I know that I don't do everything right and I know that I can be overly judgmental when I've been wrong—even if it's just a small thing. Help me to be a good neighbor and to act graciously toward those I live or work next to.

Have you been able to give someone an extra portion of grace today? Who in your life needs to experience a little bit of mercy?

Productivity

"If you follow my statutes and keep my commandments and observe them faithfully, I will give you your rains in their season, and the land shall yield its produce, and the trees of the field shall yield their fruit."

LEVITICUS 26:3-4 NRSV

God designed humanity to work in harmony with his creation. His commandments were not just to please him, but to allow his creation to prosper.

Even though we don't always follow God's ways, we have the opportunity to start each day new. God wants you to prosper today. He wants the absolute best for you, and all you need to do is to listen to his voice.

God, help me to hear your voice clearly today. I know that you intend the best for your creation, and I want to experience the blessing of your love and goodness today.

"Your threshing shall overtake the vintage, and the vintage shall overtake the sowing; you shall eat your bread to the full, and live securely in your land."

LEVITICUS 26:5 NRSV

It is amazing how busy this world gets during the day. Sometimes we feel like working is not very spiritual, yet God wants us to be productive so we can have a life full of blessing.

Whatever type of work you have done today, know that God is pleased with you. Your dedication to doing your part in this world is helping you to be a blessing to your family and to others. God wants you to feel secure in knowing that he will provide you with all that you need.

Dear God, at times it feels like the work that I do each day is worthless. Please give me a fresh perspective tonight as I reflect on your goodness and provision for me.

Reflect on the work that you have done today, and be encouraged that this is part of God's plan to provide for you.

The Call to Follow

As Jesus passed along the Sea of Galilee, he saw Simon and his brother Andrew casting a net into the sea—for they were fishermen. And Jesus said to them, "Follow me and I will make you fish for people."

MARK 1:16-17 NKJV

Simon and Andrew were just doing their ordinary job when Jesus called out to them. It wasn't like they were doing anything particularly special. Jesus must have known that they longed for significance in their lives. He put his call to them in their language. They knew that catching fish was sometimes difficult and that it required determination and strength.

This is what the Christian life is like for us. It is sometimes difficult. Think of Jesus calling out to you as your do your ordinary things today. He wants you to follow him into a life full of significance.

God, thank you for the call to follow you. Thank you that you give me that chance again and again. I am reminded today that I want to follow you, and I ask you to give me the strength and determination to share the good news with others.

Immediately they left their nets and followed him.

MARK 1:18 NKJV

The disciples responded immediately to Jesus' call to follow him. They must have known about Jesus and his ministry, and they were eager to be a part of God's work on earth.

In our busy lives we can be quick to dismiss Jesus' voice, or it can be drowned out in the noise of everything else competing for our time and energy. As you take some time this evening to stop and still your heart, listen for what Jesus wants to say to you, and commit to responding quickly.

Jesus, thank you for calling out to me. I know that there are times in the day that I find it hard to hear your voice, but I thank you for this time and for the words that you are speaking to me right now. I ask for a diligent heart to respond to your words tonight.

What can you hear Jesus speaking to you in this moment?

Moment of Solitude

In the morning, having risen a long while before daylight, He went
out and departed to a solitary place; and there He prayed.

MARK 1:35 NKJV

When do you find time to pray? Even if we are intentional and
passionate about prayer, the everyday activities in our life will
almost always take priority over time with God. It is often said
that prayer can happen at any time, and of course it does, but
is there value in setting aside a specific time to communicate
with God?

Did you ever realize that the notion of quiet times comes
from the example set by Jesus? We see in the Bible that Jesus
would get up before daylight and pray in a solitary place. We
are not often told what Jesus prayed about. It's not the content
that matters; it's the willingness to maintain our relationship
with the Father and seek his will. What better time to do this
than at the beginning of our day?

Jesus, I give you this time, now. Thank you for the opportunity to
spend some quiet time with you.

Simon and those who were with Him searched for Him. When they found Him, they said to Him, "Everyone is looking for You."

MARK 1:36-37 NKJV

Does this sound like you tonight, as you try to step away from the busyness of the day? Are people looking for you, pressing in on your alone time? Instead of trying to fit prayer into your busy day, pray before it gets busy, so you can cope with the pressures of life.

Were you able to give God some time in the early morning? Did you find a solitary place to hear from him? If not, fight for your time now. Be like Jesus and find the time and space to wait upon the Father.

Father, I know you are gracious and that you are not concerned with religious practice. Help me, however, to get into a good routine of introducing you into my morning and evenings so I am equipped to love you and to love others throughout my day.

How will you fit prayer time into your busy life?

Growing Seeds

"The kingdom of God is as if someone would scatter seed on the ground, and would sleep and rise night and day, and the seed would sprout and grow, he does not know how."

MARK 4:26-27 NRSV

The process of growth is an incredible wonder. We plant seeds, but we aren't really sure what is involved in making them grow. Science can tell us these days the amazing process of growth, but it's nothing that we do. We just wait for nature to take its course.

Jesus was describing God's kingdom like this. We don't have to worry about how things are going, we just need to trust that things are happening and that our faithfulness to God's work will result in sprouting and growth.

Thank you, God, that you take care of the growth in my life and in those things that I have committed myself to. There are times when I worry that nothing is happening. Give me the confidence to trust that you are doing great things.

"The earth produces of itself, first the stalk, then the head, then the full grain in the head. But when the grain is ripe, at once he goes in with his sickle, because the harvest has come."

MARK 4:28-29 NRSV

There are days that we rejoice because our waiting is finally over. You may remember a time when a prayer was answered, you achieved a goal, or a tough season had come to an end. We rarely know how God is working things out, but when he does, it is time to rejoice; the harvest has come.

Today may have been just another day of waiting but remember that God is working it out. Keep the faith and fight the good fight.

Father, you have given me times to rejoice in the past when I have seen things come to fruition. Give me patience to wait for signs of life in other areas where I have been waiting to see you breakthrough.

When do you see sprouts growing in your life? Have faith, the harvest is yet to come.

Quiet Places

The apostles returned to Jesus from their ministry tour and told him all they had done and taught. Then Jesus said, "Let's go off by ourselves to a quiet place and rest awhile." He said this because there were so many people coming and going that Jesus and his apostles didn't even have time to eat.

MARK 6:30-31 NLT

Life has so much going on that it can be exhausting. We have many demands, be it children, work, study, or other commitments. Even if you enjoy being around people, there are times when you need to go off by yourself and take some time out.

This day is likely to get busy for you, so take a quiet moment now and allow Jesus to refresh your soul.

Jesus, I need peace so I can approach the day with a serenity that only comes from knowing that ultimately you are in charge. Thank you for showing me that you understand what it is like to get weary and to need some time to rest.

They left by boat for a quiet place, where they could be alone.
MARK 6:32 NLT

The only real way to get some time to yourself and rest is to physically move yourself from one place to another. Where can you go right now that will mean you distance yourself from the demands of this world?

Jesus wanted to be alone for a while, and it is okay that you want that from time to time. You can't escape the demands of life, but you can let yourself get away, get quiet, and let God take control for a while. Listen to him speak, ask for his presence, and enjoy the peace.

God, I don't often get time to be alone and quiet. Thank you for a small window of opportunity this evening to rest. Let your presence give me peace and energize me for the demands that lay before me tomorrow.

When was the last time you were able to get away from it all and just be alone with Jesus? When could you do that again?

His Way

Then, calling the crowd to join his disciples, he said, "If any of you wants to be my follower, you must give up your own way, take up your cross, and follow me."

MARK 8:34 NLT

We get up in the morning with good intentions. We intend to work hard, we intend to be kind, and we intend to help others. Sometimes our good intentions succeed, but many times they don't.

We want to follow Jesus, but he asks that we follow him on his terms. It is not about our good intention, but about his way. As you approach your day, commit your ways to his ways, knowing that he needs you to surrender your desires to his.

God, my one true desire this morning is to follow you. I know that you care about the things that I want to accomplish today, but I also know that your calling on my life is more important. I know there are people who need to see your love today, so I submit to this greater purpose.

*"If you try to hang on to your life, you will lose it. But if you give up
your life for my sake and for the sake of the Good News, you will
save it. And what do you benefit if you gain the whole world but
lose your own soul?"*

MARK 8:35-36 NLT

You might have had times today where you were reminded of
your calling to follow Jesus. We get caught up in wanting so
many things that this world has to offer us, but it can make us
feel miserable if that is all we are chasing.

The world will disappoint, and we can lose our soul in the
process, but we will never regret surrendering our life to
Jesus and living out his mission to spread the good news.

*Jesus, I know that living for you means that I have to surrender my
own life to your plan and purpose. Help me to do this gladly and
with peace, knowing that I will only lose if I choose my own way.
Thank you for saving my life; give me the joy of knowing that your
way is best.*

Did you have the chance to share the love of Jesus today?
Pray for this opportunity again tomorrow.

Prayer of Faith

"If you can?" said Jesus.
"Everything is possible for one who believes."

MARK 9:23 NIV

When you pray, are you doing it in a spirit of boldness, expecting that God can change the circumstance? It's as if we are afraid to bother God with our requests so we speak tentatively, "Dear Lord, if it is your will, it'd be great if you could…" "Father, I know you have so many bigger things, but I'd love it if…."

Let's stop with faithless prayers. God knows your heart already. Believe that he can do what you are asking. There is no need for caution with the Father who loves you so dearly.

Father, I approach your throne of grace with boldness and ask that you make things possible because of my faith in you.

Immediately the boy's father exclaimed,
"I do believe; help me overcome my unbelief!"

MARK 9:24 NIV

Do you believe that God can make things possible in your life? We know that he's not a genie, granting every wish, but he is a good Father who wants the best for you.

Step out boldly in faith, beginning with your prayer life. Are you talking to God in a spirit of timidity? Ask him for help in overcoming your disbelief. Everything is possible for those who believe, so set your heart upon doing so.

Father God, thank you that you care about what is best for me.
I pray, in faith, that you would give me breakthrough in the areas
that I have been asking for your guidance, healing, and support.

What things feel impossible for you right now?
Boldly approach God to give you the possibilities.

First Last, Last First

He sat down, called the twelve, and said to them, "Whoever wants
to be first must be last of all and servant of all."

MARK 9:35 NRSV

Jesus always gets straight to the heart of the matter; being
first in this life doesn't count for much. The disciples were
having a discussion about who would be greater in God's
kingdom, and Jesus had to remind them that his kingdom
doesn't work like the world's.

To be great in God's kingdom means loving others first; it's
not about rising to the top above others. Carry this thought
with you into today and choose humility and kindness over
your idea of success.

Heavenly Father, we live in a world that tells me to put myself first
and to take care of my needs. Thank you for the reminder that
your kingdom is about serving others. Help me to approach this
day with an intention to bless others.

Then he took a little child and put it among them; and taking it in his arms, he said to them, "Whoever welcomes one such child in my name welcomes me, and whoever welcomes me welcomes not me but the one who sent me."

MARK 9:36-37 NRSV

God wants us to take notice of others. We can be quick to let our lives be influenced and filled with the popular people, and we can strive to be popular and to get noticed. It's important, however, to make an effort to show all people that they are significant and that they matter.

When we choose to look at people through God's eyes, we will see beauty and worth in those who need to feel beautiful and worthy. When we take the time to show love toward others, Jesus feels blessed by you.

Jesus, I know that you care about all people and show particular kindness to the people who society thought of as the least. Help me to see others as worthy to be cared for. I want these people to experience the kind of love that can only come from understanding your love.

Is there someone in your life that needs to be noticed, encouraged, and uplifted this week?

Small and Significant

People were bringing little children to Jesus for him to place his hands on them, but the disciples rebuked them. When Jesus saw this, he was indignant. He said to them, "Let the little children come to me, and do not hinder them, for the kingdom of God belongs to such as these."

MARK 10:13-14 NIV

Is your life so busy that you seem to overlook some small yet significant things? It might be jobs that you've promised to do, it might be children that need your attention, it might just be a friend who you should have called weeks ago. Take some time to consider what you're putting most of your energy into and ask whether you are neglecting some of the more important things.

The disciples thought that Jesus' teaching was more important than the children, and yet Jesus said, "Let them come to me." Jesus' heart is always for those who need him. Find time to do those small but important things today.

God, I am so grateful for the reminder that you care about the hearts of people rather than doing the seemingly spiritual or important stuff. Bring to mind the things I have been neglecting and need to pay attention to today.

"Truly I tell you, anyone who will not receive the kingdom of God like a little child will never enter it." And he took the children in his arms, placed his hands on them and blessed them.

MARK 10:15-16 NIV

Children may or may not be a part of your family life but we need to remember that they are the future of this world. Children need to be cared for, taught, and shown love so they can one day be the kind of adults that will respect this world and respect others.

We can pass on our faith to the children around us by being adults who show the love of Christ to them.

Heavenly Father, I thank you for the children of this world. I pray for those who are in physical need that they would find provision. I pray for those who need to be loved and cherished they would be surrounded by people who can show them love. I pray for those who need to know more about Jesus and ask that they would find faith. Let my heart be open to providing any or all of this to those children.

Think of the children that are in your life. Are you giving them the attention and love that they deserve?

The Father's Command

As Jesus was starting out on his way to Jerusalem, a man came
running up to him, knelt down, and asked, "Good Teacher, what
must I do to inherit eternal life?" "Why do you call me good?"
Jesus asked. "Only God is truly good."

MARK 10:17-18 NLT

We know that Jesus was perfect—without sin—so it seems
strange that he questioned someone calling him good. Jesus,
however, was always pointing toward the Father because
that's who he came to reveal.

Most of us know the Ten Commandments, the big ones,
at least. We know that we shouldn't kill, steal, or commit
adultery. There are more about not worshipping idols, not
swearing in the name of God, remembering the day of the
Sabbath, and not being envious. These commandments are
not just rules; they are life lessons, worth paying attention to
because they point us toward a relationship with the Father.

Heavenly Father, thank you for revealing yourself through Jesus'
life and his words. Thank you that you have shown me a good way
to walk. Let me keep your commandments throughout this day.

"To answer your question, you know the commandments: 'You must not murder. You must not commit adultery. You must not steal. You must not testify falsely. You must not cheat anyone. Honor your father and mother.'"

MARK 10:19 NLT

Sin is often disregarded in today's culture. We may be careful not to commit the "big" sins, but then we display anger toward others, judgment, lying, and comparison. We rarely get held accountable to these by our brothers and sisters.

We need to get on our knees in repentance and lay these sins at the cross. Let's be willing to ask forgiveness for all sin today.

Jesus, forgive me for the sins I haven't yet repented of. Forgive me for sins that I commit in secret that I have no accountability for. Forgive me for the sin that I don't want to let go of. Give me a fresh start as I begin again tomorrow.

What are you feeling convicted of this evening? Repent and know you are forgiven.

Riches

Jesus said it again: "Dear children, how hard it is for those who trust in riches to enter the Kingdom of God. It is easier for a camel to go through the eye of a needle than for a rich man to enter the Kingdom of God."

MARK 10:24-25 TLB

People who have a gained a lot in life also have a lot to lose. When Jesus asked a young wealthy man to give up his possessions, he simply couldn't do it. He had lived a good moral life, but he just wasn't prepared to let go of everything.

Our possessions and desire to succeed in life can sometimes hinder us from following Jesus with our whole hearts. Choose this day to approach your tasks, leisure, and responsibilities with a heart that is willing to let go of earthly things for the sake of his kingdom.

God, help me to avoid the trap of wanting more and more that this world has to offer. Help me to hold the things of this world loosely and to be prepared to let go of them if you ask me to.

The disciples were incredulous! "Then who in the world can be saved, if not a rich man?" they asked. Jesus looked at them intently, then said, "Without God, it is utterly impossible. But with God everything is possible."

MARK 10:26-27 TLB

The disciples got it wrong too. They had assumed that wealth was a sign that people had done things right and that good works was about how much you could give. How quick we are to forget that Jesus keeps telling us that his kingdom is about the heart.

It is God, and he alone, who saves us. It's not anything we can do. As you reflect on your day, were you able to give Jesus some room in your heart to move? Give yourself some grace as you understand that it's not about what you do, but about what God is doing in your heart.

Jesus, I give room for you to work in my heart right now. I let go of the compulsion to figure it all out on my own. I surrender those areas of my life that seem impossible and I ask you to be the one to make them possible. Thank you for the gift of salvation.

What things have seemed impossible in your life lately? With God, all things are possible.

Released in Prayer

"I tell you, whatever you ask for in prayer, believe that you have received it, and it will be yours."

MARK 11:24 NIV

It seems like most families and many circles of friends contain at least two people who aren't speaking to one another—and haven't for years. Perhaps you know someone. Perhaps you are someone in this situation. Occasionally, the offense itself is truly unforgivable: abuse, betrayal, or complete disregard.

Other times, and considerably more often, even the people involved admit the silliness of the quarrel and are no longer angry about it. But they're still angry with the person. The best thing we can do is pray for one another. If you know people who are fighting, pray for them. If you are the one involved in the argument, pray for forgiveness.

God, I ask for your forgiveness in an area that I am holding a grudge, or feeling upset with someone. I pray for restoration with that person.

"When you stand praying, if you hold anything against anyone, forgive them, so that your Father in heaven may forgive you your sins."

MARK 11:25 NIV

What do you gain when you hold onto bitterness? When you refuse to let go of anger, what benefit is it to you? While an offense may be unforgivable, no person is. Jesus proved that when he died for all of us.

Let us encourage one another, and ourselves, to believe what the Scriptures tell us. Tonight, open your hands and surrender your grudges, and ask the Father to refill you with peace.

God, thank you for reminding me that I need to surrender my heart to you and to ask for forgiveness. Thank you that I can forgive others, because you forgave me first.

Who needs your forgiveness, and what will you resolve to do about this tomorrow?

The Widow's Offering

Jesus sat down opposite the place where the offerings were put and watched the crowd putting their money into the temple treasury. Many rich people threw in large amounts. But a poor widow came and put in two very small copper coins, worth only a few cents.

MARK 11:41-42 NIV

How do you decide whether to give money to charity or a church? Do you consider whether it is a worthy cause, or if they have already asked too much, or if you just don't believe in supporting that particular issue?

Sometimes we can get too caught up in the "why should I?" that it delays us responding at all. Sometimes, we just need to give without question, and let God take care of the rest.

Jesus, I want a chance to put my skepticism to the test. Bring someone or something along my path today where I can give without reserve. Thank you that you always bless a cheerful giver.

Calling his disciples to him, Jesus said, "Truly I tell you, this poor widow has put more into the treasury than all the others. They all gave out of their wealth; but she, out of her poverty, put in everything—all she had to live on."

MARK 11:43-44 NIV

What would it take for you to decide to give all that you had? It seems almost absurd, possibly even unwise, for someone to give up everything, and yet this is what Jesus told the rich man to do in order to receive the kingdom of heaven.

Jesus doesn't ask us to give more or less than we have, but the reality is that accepting God's kingdom means a surrender of all that you have, all that you are. It's a challenging concept, but one worth considering. Talk to God about it, this evening, and let your heart settle on what he wants from you.

God, tonight I surrender my heart to you and ask that you would speak to me about what you want me to give more of. Help me to not hold onto my possessions so dearly, and give me the courage to give up things that I don't need.

What is God asking you to surrender tonight?

Sacrifice for All

As they were eating, Jesus took some bread and blessed it.
Then he broke it in pieces and gave it to the disciples, saying,
"Take it, for this is my body."

MARK 14:22 NLT

Jesus' body was broken for you, and it was broken for all. We can't keep the truth to ourselves; we have a mission to partner with God and continue the work that Jesus began which was to see everyone come to believe in him that they would all be saved.

It's hard to know where to begin in your day-to-day life with sharing the gospel. Perhaps it starts with reading up on the good news, or spending some time in God's presence, or maybe it's just going into the day with the intention of sharing that you are Christian. Whatever you do, do it with the heart of wanting to see those who don't believe come to understand that Jesus was broken that we might be made whole.

Jesus, present me with some opportunities today. Give me the eyes to see people who are broken that need the healing of your saving power.

He took a cup of wine and gave thanks to God for it. He gave it to them, and they all drank from it. And he said to them, "This is my blood, which confirms the covenant between God and his people. It is poured out as a sacrifice for many."

MARK 14:23 NLT

Understanding that people will be condemned if they don't believe should compel us to want to share the truth with those who are searching.

God made a promise to his people and to the world, that he would save them from death. This was at the cost of his own Son's life and the sacrifice of Jesus was the provision that we all needed to be set free. People need to hear of this freedom.

Lord God, I know that you don't want me to feel pressured to preach, but I also know that I can be better at sharing the source of my love and wisdom with others. Give me the words as I go into my day tomorrow.

Were you able to share any of your faith with someone today?

Preach the Gospel

Then he told them, "You are to go into all the world and
preach the Good News to everyone, everywhere."

MARK 16:15 TLB

When Jesus was leaving his disciples to ascend to heaven, he
gave them the mission to go spread the Good News of his life,
death, and resurrection.

This is the Good News that has reached you today, and will
continue to reach others as we all take part in sharing Christ
to the world around us. This mission is your call today. Let
yourself hear Jesus say to you right now, "Go and preach the
good news."

God, I sometimes struggle to even let people know that I am a
believer. The world can be tough on Christians. Help me to work
past my fear of what people will think of me. Remind me that
you are the best news anyone could receive today. Fill me with
boldness to declare your truth.

> *"Those who believe and are baptized will be saved.
> But those who refuse to believe will be condemned."*
>
> MARK 16:16 TLB

God doesn't ask us to be the one to change people's hearts.
That's his job. We are simply asked to share his good news
and the rest is between God and that person. What they do
with the truth is up to them. The Bible says that some will
believe and be saved. Others will not.

Some days you may not feel like you get the opportunity to say
anything about Christ; these are the days when perhaps it's
just better to live the way Christ would and let your actions
speak louder than words. Other days, you may just need
the Holy Spirit to fill you with boldness so you can proudly
declare the truth. Either way, be encouraged that sharing is
your job, and God will take care of the rest.

*God, I ask for the opportunity to speak your truth to people in my
life this week. As I go to sleep tonight I thank you for the good news
that has set me free. I want the same freedom to be experienced by
others in my life. Give me the boldness and wisdom to share your
Word with them.*

Who is on your heart to share the gospel with?

Stories of Old

"These commandments that I give you today are to be on your hearts. Impress them on your children. Talk about them when you sit at home and when you walk along the road, when you lie down and when you get up."

DEUTERONOMY 6:6-7 NIV

When God made a covenant with the people of Israel, it wasn't a book to be read. It was a story to be memorized through repeating and sharing. The stories of God are meant to be read and re-told, over and over again.

Don't let yourself get bored with the same story; instead, figure out how to repeat the truth of his Word as many times and in many ways as you can. Tell your kids, talk about it with your spouse, and think about it as you go for a walk. Start this day with a Bible story that is close to your heart.

God, thank you for the promises that you made to your people that are passed down through each generation and landing right here with me right now. Give me an opportunity today to think, talk, and reflect on your commandments and stories.

"Tie them as symbols on your hands and bind them on your foreheads. Write them on the doorframes of your houses and on your gates."

DEUTERONOMY 6:8-9 NIV

Our busy days can create a lot of stories to tell the people we live with about when we get home. Whether it is work, meeting with other people, or taking care of dependents, conversation with others is important.

God didn't want his commands to be a burden, he simply wanted them to flow out of our hearts toward other people. The symbolism of words on your hands and foreheads and doorframes is really just about God's Word being with you always. Take some time this evening to dwell on his words and let them sink deeper and deeper into your heart.

God, I know I am only scratching the surface of the things that I know about your Word and the stories of all the wonderful and mighty things you have done. I praise you because you have placed me in the middle of it all, as someone to carry your story forward. Give me the boldness to share your truth.

What words and commands of God are present in your heart right now? Who can you share these with?

Proving Character

*Remember how the LORD your God led you through the wilderness
for these forty years, humbling you and testing you to prove
your character, and to find out whether or not you would
obey his commands.*

DEUTERONOMY 8:2 NLT

We all experience seasons of wilderness. The Israelites could
have gone straight to the promised land but they doubted and
the result of that led them down a longer path. God didn't put
them there to make them suffer, but he allowed it to be an
opportunity to refine their character and to hear his voice.

Be encouraged if you are experiencing a type of wilderness
in your life. It doesn't matter so much how you got there, but
that you understand that God is with you, guiding you and
encouraging growth.

*Lord God, I'm sorry if I have been grumbling during the
wilderness. Thank you that you have always been good to me and
will always remain by my side. I need your encouragement today,
as I head into whatever is in store for me. Give me the strength and
continue to provide for me as only a loving heavenly Father can.*

*Yes, he humbled you by letting you go hungry and then feeding
you with manna, a food previously unknown to you and your
ancestors. He did it to teach you that people do not live by bread
alone; rather, we live by every word that comes from
the mouth of the LORD.*

DEUTERONOMY 8:3 NLT

The story of the Israelites wandering in the desert is pretty
well known. It is good to be reminded every now and then
that God is always in control. The Israelites thought they
knew what they needed to survive—bread. Yet God had a
different way of providing for them.

We can often try to ask or demand things from God that we
think we need in order to get through. But God may have
another way to provide, and we need to humbly give up our
own way to let God's way prevail.

*God, I am sorry for trying to control all my needs. I am so grateful
for the ways that you have provided for me in the past, and I
believe that you will continue to provide for me. Help me to trust
you and to allow you to lead me in the right path by your Word.*

What are you trying to control that you need to hand over to
God? Ask for his provision.

Foreign Compassion

"The LORD your God is God of gods and LORD of LORDS, the great
God, mighty and awesome, who shows no partiality and accepts
no bribes. He defends the cause of the fatherless and the widow,
and loves the foreigners residing among you,
giving them food and clothing."

DEUTERONOMY 10:17-18 NIV

From the very beginning, God showed himself as a God of
love. Though he chose the Israelites as the people group to
show himself through, he has always loved all people groups.
He has compassion on those in need.

What a beautiful God we have as king of our heart. You are
about to step into a world full of people in need today. As
an image bearer of this compassionate God, make it your
mission to show no partiality and to love those who need it
the most.

Father God, thank you for your compassion toward me. Thank you
for providing me with more than I need. Help me to be a helping
hand and compassionate heart to someone in need today.

> *"You are to love those who are foreigners,*
> *for you yourselves were foreigners in Egypt."*
>
> DEUTERONOMY 10:19 NIV

Were you able to show compassion and help someone in need today? We can be guilty of not noticing the needs of others around us, or to be so comfortable with our surroundings that we forget to look out for those who are feeling on the outside.

We all know what it is like to feel like a foreigner, whether a new school, job, or city. God doesn't want anyone to feel alone, which makes his call to attend to the fatherless and the widow all the more meaningful.

Jesus, I can certainly relate to feeling lonely. Help me to translate this empathy into an act of kindness and compassion for someone this week. Thank you for providing me with family and friendship. Allow me an opportunity to share the blessing of friendship with those who are feeling like foreigners.

Is there someone you need to journey alongside to help them feel a little less lonely?

Voices

"If there arises among you a prophet or a dreamer of dreams, and he gives you a sign or a wonder, and the sign or the wonder comes to pass, of which he spoke to you, saying, 'Let us go after other gods'—which you have not known—'and let us serve them,' you shall not listen to the words of that prophet or that dreamer of dreams, for the LORD your God is testing you to know whether you love the LORD your God with all your heart and with all your soul."

DEUTERONOMY 13:1-3 NKJV

In this present time, it is not necessarily our temptation to go after other gods in the sense of finding someone else to worship. Yet we are still faced with gods of this world, and plenty of temptation to draw near to them.

We love our phones, social media, clothes, house décor—the list is endless. You will be out in the world today with many things calling for your attention, time and money. Try to avoid those words that say, "Let's go after that," and instead direct your heart, mind, and soul toward the one true God.

God, I need you in my life more than anything else. Help me to go into my day with a clear and focused mind that is centered on what is most important.

*"You shall walk after the Lord your God and fear Him,
and keep His commandments and obey His voice;
you shall serve Him and hold fast to Him."*

DEUTERONOMY 13:4 NKJV

What kind of voices did you have calling out to you today? God didn't want you to obey his voice just because he is a ruler demanding things of his servants. The purpose of obedience is that you would flourish in your relationships with others and with God.

God's promise to his people was that if they listened to him, they would be blessed.

Father, I want to walk after you with my whole heart. Give me the grace to continue to follow your voice, to serve you, and to hold fast to your ways.

What voices seem to be taking over in your life? How can you overcome these voices and listen to your loving Father?

Open Your Hand

"If there is among you a poor man of your brethren, within any of the gates in your land which the LORD your God is giving you, you shall not harden your heart nor shut your hand from your poor brother, but you shall open your hand wide to him and willingly lend him sufficient for his need, whatever he needs."

DEUTERONOMY 15:7-8 NKJV

Whether we feel like we have little or much, God has given each one of us something to give. We often wonder how we might help someone who is in need, especially if we don't have a lot of money.

Sometimes we worry that what we give won't be what is needed, or that it won't be used well. It doesn't matter what you are able to give, the blessing is in having a generous heart.

God, if I come across a need today, whether it is poverty, ill-health, or just helping someone with a task, help me to give with a spirit of joy and generosity. Give me an opportunity to bless someone today.

*"You shall surely give to him, and your heart should not be grieved
when you give to him, because for this thing the Lord your God
will bless you in all your works and in all to which you put your
hand. For the poor will never cease from the land; therefore I
command you, saying, 'You shall open your hand wide to your
brother, to your poor and your needy, in your land.'"*

DEUTERONOMY 15:10-11 NKJV

The truth of this world is that it is not perfect yet. This means
that there will always be needs, hurts, and a sense of things not
being quite right. Be encouraged that God is at work until the
day that all creation is fully redeemed. He isn't finished yet.

In the meantime, he needs his children, he needs you, to be
a part of restoring those things that aren't quite right. Open
your hand, wide, to others, and the promise of his blessing
will be given to you.

*God, I know I can't fix everything in this world, but I know that you
have blessed me enough to be able to help where there are needs.
Continue to give me a heart that is compassionate and wise.*

What needs have you seen today that God could be prompting
you to help with?

Battles

*"When you go out to battle against your enemies, and see horses
and chariots and people more numerous than you,
do not be afraid of them; for the L*ORD *your God is with you,
who brought you up from the land of Egypt."*

DEUTERONOMY 20:1 NKJV

Life can be a battle sometimes. Waking up can be hard,
getting organized to get out of the door can be chaotic, and
facing all kinds of different personalities and conflicts in
your day can be challenging.

If your day is starting to look like this, remember that God
is with you. He wants you to remember that ultimately, he is
the King of Kings, and he is in control of all things. Don't be
afraid.

*God, I need to feel your presence by my side today. I feel all kinds
of challenges coming my way, whether from people around me,
or even the pressure that I put on myself. I surrender this to you,
this morning, and ask for peace of mind, knowing that you are in
control.*

"So it shall be, when you are on the verge of battle, that the priest shall approach and speak to the people. And he shall say to them, 'Hear, O Israel: Today you are on the verge of battle with your enemies. Do not let your heart faint, do not be afraid, and do not tremble or be terrified because of them; for the Lord your God is He who goes with you, to fight for you against your enemies, to save you.'"

DEUTERONOMY 20:2-4 NKJV

Sometimes conflict is inevitable. There are times when you have to stand up for yourself and stand up for the truth. Sometimes the battle is internal, we feel insecure, unloved, and alone, and yet these are lies from the enemy.

Remember that God's truth is stronger than anything you might be facing, and it is certainly stronger than any lies. Let his love and grace overcome evil thoughts or actions and let him fight for you and save you.

Jesus, I need your power to help me to fight those emotional or spiritual battles that I am on the verge of facing. Help me to recognize when I am giving in to fear and let me remember that you are with me, fighting for me.

What battles are you on the verge of facing this week? Remember that truth and love always win.

Proclaim His Name

"I will proclaim the name of the Lord;
ascribe greatness to our God!"

DEUTERONOMY 32:3 ESV

The start of a new day can mark a time for new beginnings
in your heart. As you make preparations for the day ahead,
remember the greatness of your God.

Take some time to read your favorite Scripture or listen to
some worship music. When you allow yourself to dwell on the
wonder of God, your lips can't help but proclaim his name.

Jesus, you are great and powerful and awesome. Thank you
for working in my life and for giving me a brand-new start this
morning. Give me an opportunity today to see your beauty and
wonder in the world around me. Give me the boldness to ascribe
this greatness to you, my Creator.

> *"The Rock, his work is perfect, for all his ways are justice.*
> *A God of faithfulness and without iniquity, just and upright is he."*
>
> DEUTERONOMY 32:4 ESV

Did you start your day with joy in your heart, only to find
that busyness, conflict, or stress crowded out that feeling?
Be encouraged that God will never let you down, even if the
world has.

Moses had the confidence to proclaim that all God's ways
are perfect, despite the years of wandering in the desert and
never entering the promised land. God is not deceitful, but
the world can be. Remind yourself of his faithfulness toward
you and rest in the knowledge that he will one day make all
things perfect again.

Faithful God, I hand over my disappointment, fears, and concerns
into your capable hands. I surrender to your will this evening and
ask for you to fill my heart with hope and trust that your works are
perfect and just.

As you reflect on the day that has just been, are you feeling
disappointed about anything in particular? Give this
disappointment to God and proclaim that he is faithful
and just.

Kingdom Worthy

The angel said to her, "Do not be afraid, Mary, for you have found favor with God. And behold, you will conceive in your womb and bring forth a Son, and shall call His name Jesus."

LUKE 1:30-31 NKJV

Here's the thing about Mary—she was an ordinary person, asked to do an extraordinary thing. There's no doubt she was worthy for the role, as the Scriptures say, she had found favor with God, and she was chosen to do one of the most significant acts of our Christian faith.

You may feel ordinary or insignificant in this life, but you are not. God sees your hard work, your diligence, and your ability to do great things for him. He has so much in store for you.

God, at times I feel insecure and unsure about my significance in life and even in my faith. I ask for you to restore my confidence in your grace, knowing that it is about what you can do through me rather than what I can do I my own strength.

"He will be great, and will be called the Son of the Highest;
and the Lord God will give Him the throne of His father David.
And He will reign over the house of Jacob forever,
and of His kingdom there will be no end."

LUKE 1:32-33 NKJV

Something so immeasurably great came through one obedient person. God used many people along the way to achieve his great plan of redemption, and he is still doing this today.

God wants to use you in this kingdom that has no end. You are already a part of eternity.

Jesus, thank you for reminding me that you are the great Son of the Highest, that you reign, and that your kingdom has no end. Thank you that I am significant because I am a special part of your kingdom. I receive your love. Help me to dwell on my worth through your eyes as I lay down to sleep tonight.

As you think over your day, can you see where God is using you right now? Can you dream about where he can use you in the future?

Full of Promise

"Blessed is she who has believed that the Lord would fulfill his promises to her!"

LUKE 1:45 NIV

When Mary, a virgin, was told that she was going to have a baby—the Son of God no less—she must have felt a huge range of emotions. If she was anything like us, she probably felt quite a bit of fear and trepidation. True to our human nature, she rushed to a trusted friend in whom she could confide.

The Scripture says that Mary was blessed, and indeed she was. She just had to remember the promise that God had given her and then be confident that he would fulfil it.

God, thank you that you are a God of wonderful promises. Thank you that you made promises to people long ago and that you are still able to make and keep promises now. Help me to be full of promise today.

"My soul glorifies the Lord and my spirit rejoices in God my Savior, for he has been mindful of the humble state of his servant. From now on all generations will call me blessed."

LUKE 1:46-48 NIV

What's the first thing Mary's friend and cousin Elizabeth says to Mary when she found out she was with child? That she was blessed. She believed that God would follow through on what he told her was true, and because of that she was endowed with divine favor.

This gift she would be given wasn't one she asked for, and she'd have to face a great deal of hardship because of it, but she believed that God was good through it all.

God, thank you that you still give us important things to do for your kingdom. Help me to recognize that I am blessed in all circumstances.

Are you looking for God's promises amidst your hardship? Believe that what the Lord says is true, and you too will find blessings in your life.

Liberty

"The Spirit of the Lord is upon me, because he has anointed me to proclaim good news to the poor."

LUKE 4:18-19 ESV

When Jesus, the long-awaited Messiah, revealed his deity to his family, his disciples, and the crowds, they were expecting a mighty king who would deliver them from their oppressors and establish his everlasting kingdom. What they got was a humble servant who dined with tax collectors and whose feet were cleansed by the tears of a prostitute.

Jesus wasn't exactly what they thought he would be. He was better. Jesus is the good news people have been waiting for.

Jesus, I know that you are good news for me. Help me to proclaim your good news to others around me. Give me boldness to say why I am full of hope and peace and life. Give me opportunities to share your love.

"He has sent me to proclaim liberty to the captives and recovering of sight to the blind, to set at liberty those who are oppressed, to proclaim the year of the Lord's favor."

LUKE 4:19 ESV

He came to bring salvation to those who were drowning in a sea of sin and sickness; those who were cast out and in need of holy redemption; those whom the religious leaders had deemed unworthy but whose hearts longed for true restoration. He came to redeem his people, but not in the way they expected.

Jesus delivers you from the bonds of sin and oppression through his death and resurrection and through your repentance from sin by faith. The Spirit of the Lord is upon you and he has anointed you. Proclaim this good news tonight; you have been set free.

Jesus, thank you that I am no longer trapped in sin. You have set me free.

Where have you experienced the freedom that you have in Christ?

He Is Willing

It happened when He was in a certain city, that behold, a man who was full of leprosy saw Jesus; and he fell on his face and implored Him, saying, "Lord, if You are willing, You can make me clean."

LUKE 5:12 NKJV

What faith and boldness this man with leprosy had. There is little doubt that he had heard of the miracles that Jesus could perform, yet there would have been many who doubted his power. This man, however, saw Jesus and immediately believed in God's power and expected to be healed.

You may have seen a lot of unanswered prayer that leaves you with doubts about what God can do, but faith is believing that if God is willing, he can make it happen.

God, let me have the kind of faith today that can expect good and powerful things to happen in my life and in others' lives. Fill my heart with hope and positive expectation about what you are going to do today and in the days ahead.

He put out His hand and touched him, saying, "I am willing;
be cleansed." Immediately the leprosy left him.

We have to ask Jesus for help, but we also have to wait for him
to respond. With great faith comes a great wait. Sometimes
it is quick, other times it is not. Be assured, as the Scripture
says that Jesus is always willing to work in your life.

It is interesting that the man is asking to become clean rather
than healthy, but Jesus makes him whole in every respect—
body, mind, and heart.

Jesus, give me faith to know that you are always willing to make
me whole. I ask for your wisdom to know when I am trying to see
your healing in one way, when really you are healing me in other
ways. Grant me great faith as I experience your great love for me.

What kind of healing are you asking for today? Allow him to
respond with his willingness to make you clean.

Kingdom for the Poor

*Jesus turned to his disciples and said, "God blesses you
who are poor, for the Kingdom of God is yours."*

LUKE 6:20 NLT

It doesn't matter whether you have material wealth or not,
you can experience poverty in so many other ways. Perhaps
you are waiting to find the love of your life and you feel lonely.
Maybe you have lost the love of your life and you feel void.

When we feel we have nothing left in life, God reminds
us that he will bless us with his kingdom. He wants you to
experience blessing in this life, but he also wants you to know
that his kingdom will fulfill everything you have ever wanted
or needed. It's yours.

*Thank you, heavenly Father, that you care about my state of mind
and heart. I have felt lonely and lost, and I have felt like I have
nothing in life. I don't always feel this way, but when I do, please
remind me of your Word—that you have a wonderful kingdom
waiting for me where I will experience joy and fulfilment.*

*"God blesses you who are hungry now, for you will be satisfied.
God blesses you who weep now, for in due time you will laugh."*

LUKE 6:21 NLT

It is easy to feel as though you are never satisfied. You may
be at the end of a long day, wishing you had accomplished
more or had done something more enjoyable. You may feel
miserable from all the pressures of life that seem to be
robbing you of your joy.

Remember again that Jesus wanted us to know that there
are times when you will feel dissatisfied, and that's okay.
There are times when you will weep until your tears run dry,
and that's okay too. He will restore joy to your life—let his
kingdom come.

*Jesus, bring me joy this evening despite moments of feeling
anxious or disappointed. I need your presence with me as I sleep,
reminding me of the many blessings you have brought and will
bring into my life.*

Are you dissatisfied or experiencing heartbreak right now?
Remember God has promised to bless you with satisfaction
and joy.

Love without Limit

"Love your enemies, do good to them, and lend to them without expecting to get anything back. Then your reward will be great, and you will be children of the Most High, because he is kind to the ungrateful and wicked."

LUKE 6:35 NIV

It's easy to feel compassion for those who suffer. You see the unfairness of it all—good people who are struggling with the pressures of what life has thrown their way. But what about those people who don't seem so good? The ones you look at and say, "Well, they deserve some suffering for all the wrong they've done."

It's tough to look into our hearts and find compassion for people like this, but the Bible tells us we must. Pray for a change of heart today. Ask your heavenly Father to soften your heart toward those who do you harm. Only then can you truly love your enemies the way he wants you to.

Father, soften my heart toward those who have wronged me. Change my heart to care more about your kindness than their unkindness.

"Be merciful, just as your Father is merciful."
LUKE 6:36 NIV

Our God is kind to the ungrateful and wicked; therefore, we must be too. Though it goes against our very nature to do good to those who have wronged us, it is expected of us. This requires nothing short of a heart change that can only come from the God.

Were you able to love those you have had struggles with today? Perhaps it is a difficult co-worker, or a bit of road-rage. Trust in God's grace to help you be more like him.

Jesus, there are definitely some people in my life that I feel treat me as their enemy. Give me the strength to be extra good to these people, so they might see your light shine through me.

Who are the people who feel like enemies today? How could you show them love?

Inside Out

"A good tree can't produce bad fruit, and a bad tree can't produce good fruit. A tree is identified by its fruit. Figs are never gathered from thorn bushes, and grapes are not picked from bramble bushes."

LUKE 6:43-44 NLT

What you are on the inside will come to light on the outside. People can be good at hiding some of their actions, behaviors, and thoughts, but eventually it comes out in some form. This is why Jesus used the analogy of a tree. We show our fruit whether we are conscious of it or not, and more often than not it comes from what we say.

As you begin to make plans for your day, let God work on your heart so you can continue to shine as the loving, gracious person that he created you to be.

God, help me to not have to hide my flaws and ugliness, but to instead submit these things to your wonderful grace and allow the love that you have placed in me to begin to shine on the outside so people can know who I really am.

> *"A good person produces good things from the treasury of a good heart, and an evil person produces evil things from the treasury of an evil heart. What you say flows from what is in your heart."*
>
> LUKE 6:45 NLT

What you see is what you get. While we never truly know a person's heart, the actions and words of others can be a good indication of where they are at. Remember it can also be an indication to others of where you are at.

Rather than trying to hide some of those things that you are ashamed of, why not expose them to the light of God so you can be made clean and begin to produce beauty again?

God, my heart can be pretty dark sometimes. Bring those dark things to light, and allow me to speak truth and love into those areas that are evil and full of lies. Help me to be a spokesperson of true life, which is a life lived in you.

What do you need to expose to God's light?

Saving Faith

"I tell you, her sins—and they are many—have been forgiven,
so she has shown me much love. But a person who is forgiven
little shows only little love." Then Jesus said to the woman,
"Your sins are forgiven."

LUKE 7:47-48 NLT

When we think of sin, we often get complacent about those sins that we regard as small or harmless. A white lie here and there, ignoring a prompt from the Holy Spirit, a harmless piece of gossip—these kinds of things don't exactly throw us on our knees at the mercy seat of Jesus.

This Scripture seems to be saying that acknowledging a great amount of sin is acknowledging our absolute dependence on Jesus for his saving grace. The woman in this Scripture recognized Jesus as the divine God, able to forgive, and this showed the trusting love that she had for her Savior.

God, I am sorry for my sins, whether great or small. I know that
you have the power to forgive my sins and I place my trust in you
as the God who provides true salvation. Let me have a heart of
forgiveness toward others today.

The men at the table said among themselves, "Who is this man, that he goes around forgiving sins?" And Jesus said to the woman, "Your faith has saved you; go in peace."

LUKE 7:49-50 NLT

There was a lot of confusion in that day about who Jesus really was. Many were expecting a different kind of Savior and often even Jesus' miracles weren't enough for people to believe that he was the true Messiah.

This woman had faith to accept the Savior, to love him, and to seek forgiveness. Her faith and love for Christ saved her.

Jesus, thank you for coming to earth to show humankind a different way to live and a different way to love. I acknowledge you as Lord and ask for your peace to be with me as I sleep, knowing that my faith and salvation is in you.

Do you need to restore your faith in Jesus? Acknowledge him as the true Christ, able to forgive all sin.

Stop Wailing

All the people were wailing and mourning for her. "Stop wailing," Jesus said. "She is not dead but asleep."

LUKE 8:52 NIV

Do you know who you really belong to? Your father and mother rightly claim you as their child, but do you recognize Jesus as the one who also calls you his child? He knows your coming and going, and your every inner working. You are his.

God is faithful to the deepest needs of your heart; he knows you full well! Where is he directing you today? Are you in need of healing? Of hope? Hear his voice and let your spirit be renewed.

Father, thank you that you call me your child. I need to hear your voice as a loving father today. Speak to me as I wait on you.

They laughed at him, knowing that she was dead. But he took her by the hand and said, "My child, get up!" Her spirit returned, and at once she stood up. Then Jesus told them to give her something to eat.

LUKE 8:53-55 NIV

How difficult it is to put our needs into the hands of the Father. Do we dare hope? Imagine watching a child die and feeling the despair of her absence, as the father of the girl in the story of Luke must have done. Then Jesus claims that she is only asleep.

Both the girl's father and Jesus love the child, and both can claim her as their daughter, but only Jesus commands her spirit and her life. His child hears his voice and obeys his command.

God, I am glad to know you as my Father. At times I forget to bring all my worries and fear to you. Help me to keep listening to you and to learn to obey your commands.

What do you need your Father to speak life into right now? Ask him, knowing how much he cares for you.

Follow Me

To another he said, "Follow me." But he said, "Lord, first let me go and bury my father." But Jesus said to him, "Let the dead bury their own dead; but as for you, go and proclaim the kingdom of God."

LUKE 9:59-60 NRSV

Obedience to Christ is both an awesome and challenging endeavor. Listening to the voice of God and obeying that voice isn't easy. God will ask us to do things that don't make sense, and his schedule will not always line up with our own.

It can be tempting for us to want our "ducks in a row" before we start following Christ into something. With our human agendas and preferences, we like to make sure we've crossed off our to-do lists before moving forward.

Jesus, as you lead me today, help me to obey. I don't always have to understand your ways, so help me to not find excuses or to procrastinate in the things that you are calling me toward.

Another said, "I will follow you, Lord; but let me first say farewell to those at my home." Jesus said to him, "No one who puts a hand to the plow and looks back is fit for the kingdom of God."

LUKE 9:61-62 NRSV

When God speaks to you and calls you to something, instead of telling him what you need to do first, obey without hesitation.

God isn't interested in the to-do lists of this world. He has a kingdom agenda with an eternal perspective. If you could see what he can see, you would never say, "Let me first..."

God, I admit that I am often anxious or wary of what you have put in front of me. Give me the confidence to move when you tell me to move. Give me faith that you are calling me into things that will be good for me and good for your kingdom.

What is God leading you toward? What does your heart feel compelled to do this week? This year?

Open Doors

"Keep on asking, and you will receive what you ask for. Keep on seeking, and you will find. Keep on knocking, and the door will be opened to you. For everyone who asks, receives. Everyone who seeks, finds. And to everyone who knocks, the door will be opened."

LUKE 11:9-10 NLT

It is hard to reconcile some of the promises in God's Word with our disappointment with things that we have asked for but haven't yet received. Jesus wouldn't have said these words if they were not the truth.

Perhaps you are waiting for an answer or are hoping for a miracle. Be encouraged that Jesus says we need to be persistent and resilient and that he is always willing to open the door to you so you can find him. When you allow Jesus into your life, you will receive all that you need.

Jesus, I ask for a resilient mind so I can keep asking, knocking, and seeking in faith that I will find what I need. I put my trust in you, knowing that you care for me and that you open the door to answer me. Encourage my faith in you as I head into my day.

"You fathers—if your children ask for a fish, do you give them a snake instead? Or if they ask for an egg, do you give them a scorpion? Of course not! So if you sinful people know how to give good gifts to your children, how much more will your heavenly Father give the Holy Spirit to those who ask him."

LUKE 11:11-13 NLT

It's a humorous picture that Jesus paints, of asking for one thing and getting something not only entirely different, but entirely unwanted. This is not the kind of father that God is. He not only wants the best for us, but he wants to give us the true desire of our heart.

We know that God is not a genie to give us anything that we want, so search your heart and ask him for those things that you truly desire. It may surprise you that when you spend time with him, your heart isn't after the superficial things of this world.

Holy Spirit, I give my heart's desires to you this evening. I know that you can discern what is right and what is selfish. I ask, in faith, that you bless me with the good gifts that I ask for.

What is on your heart to ask for God for tonight? Ask him now in faith.

Considered Surrender

"Suppose a king is about to go to war against another king. Won't he first sit down and consider whether he is able with ten thousand men to oppose the one coming against him with twenty thousand? If he is not able, he will send a delegation while the other is still a long way off and will ask for terms of peace."

LUKE 14:31-32 NIV

Surrender is offering what you have to someone else because you have considered your options and know that doing it your way would do more harm than good. Once you surrender something, you give up your ownership and your rights along with it.

What does a life fully-surrendered to Christ look like? It's holding nothing back from God, and surrendering every part to him. Full surrender to a holy God cannot be fabricated. God, the omniscient one, cannot be fooled by eloquent words or false commitment. Complete surrender to him can be nothing less than sincere, legitimate, full abandonment.

God, I don't know how to fully surrender myself to you, so instead hear my heart behind the words. I really want to have a life that is dedicated to you and even though I fail, I still want to give it all up for you. Give me a chance to show you that today.

"In the same way, those of you who do not give up everything you have cannot be my disciples."

LUKE 14:33 NIV

Being a disciple of Christ requires complete and total surrender of everything you have and everything you are. He is not asking you to give up anything that he wasn't willing to give for you. When he gave up the glory and rights of his heavenly throne, he surrendered more for you than you ever could for him.

Jesus never sold this life as being casual, simple, or inexpensive. But he did promise that the reward would be great.

Jesus, let me remember the rewards that I have for a life surrendered to you far outweighs any earthly treasure. I choose to serve you today and every day. Give me the strength and grace to pursue you with all my heart.

What is God asking you to surrender to him? Trust that he knows what is best for you.

When Others Fail

"Be on your guard! If your brother sins, rebuke him;
and if he repents, forgive him."

LUKE 17:3 NASB

There are few things worse than being unjustly wronged. It's not easy when you are hurt—especially by someone close to you. A deep part of each of us cries out for justice. It's a God-given trait, meant to call us to stand in the gap for the hurting, the widow, the orphan—it's our longing for true religion.

When we identify injustice, that longing rises up strongly. We feel pain, hurt, confusion, and pressure. And more than all of those emotions, we feel the deep need to see justice served. No matter how hard it is today to forgive someone who has hurt you, remember how much you have been forgiven. How can we extend any less grace than that which we have received?

God, give me the grace today to forgive those who have wronged me. I don't feel like these people deserve to be forgiven, and so I rely on your heart of love for them.

*"If he sins against you seven times a day, and returns
to you seven times, saying, 'I repent,' forgive him."*

LUKE 17:4 NASB

Forgiveness does not mean that you have to keep accepting
the same behavior over and over. It does not mean that you
have to continue to get hurt. God gives us wisdom to know
when to move on from something that is unhealthy and not
for our wellbeing.

Forgiveness is handing the hurt to God and leaving the
judgment to him.

*God, I need your wisdom in situations where I have been hurt, over
and over again. I know that you do not want me to be in harm's
way, and so I ask for a way through or a way out. I still choose to
forgive those who have wronged me and ask that you give me peace
in my heart.*

Who do you need to forgive today? Is God asking you to
remove yourself from harm?

Witnesses

*"Why are you frightened?" he asked. "Why are your hearts filled
with doubt? Look at my hands. Look at my feet. You can see that
it's really me. Touch me and make sure that I am not a ghost,
because ghosts don't have bodies, as you see that I do." As he
spoke, he showed them his hands and his feet.*

LUKE 24:38-40 NLT

We are so far from the events of Jesus' death and resurrection
that we may forget that there were many witnesses who
saw Jesus alive after his death. They were as shocked and
frightened as any of us would have been, seeing him walking
around again, not as a ghost, but a person with a body.

How wonderful that Jesus not only showed us how we can
live as humans, but how we will live as resurrected people.
Remember his hands and his feet as you go into your day and
rejoice because he has risen.

*Jesus, at times I doubt some of the stories, and yet my faith is
restored this morning as I read the account of those witnesses who
really did see your resurrected body. Thank you that my faith in
you gives me the same hope of resurrection.*

"Yes, it was written long ago that the Messiah would suffer and die and rise from the dead on the third day. It was also written that this message would be proclaimed in the authority of his name to all the nations, beginning in Jerusalem: 'There is forgiveness of sins for all who repent.' You are witnesses of all these things."

LUKE 24:46-48 NLT

It's part of our human nature to forget important details, especially when we are stressed, sad, or frightened. When Jesus had been put to death, it would have been hard to remember in the midst of the grief that he had said he would rise again.

It is important to remember that not only did his resurrection become true, but that his message would go to all the nations. We are witnesses to this truth as we see the message of Christ spread around the globe.

Father, thank you that I am a witness of your truth continuing to spread into the world, including filling my own heart and the lives of people around me. Help me to be a true witness to your life and light tomorrow and the rest of my days.

What important truths from God do you need reminding of? Be encouraged that God's Word will always prevail.

Courage

"Be strong and very courageous. Be careful to obey all the law my servant Moses gave you; do not turn from it to the right or to the left, that you may be successful wherever you go. Keep this Book of the Law always on your lips; meditate on it day and night, so that you may be careful to do everything written in it. Then you will be prosperous and successful."

JOSHUA 1:7-8 NIV

Joshua was the chosen one to lead the Israelites through to the promised land. Moses had taken them as far as he was allowed and now it was the next generation's turn. Although Moses had made mistakes, there was no doubt that God was with him wherever he went, and this same promise was given to Joshua.

The same promise is given to you. When you take the time to read his Word, when you listen to his voice, when you are careful to obey his ways, God's promise is that you will prosper.

God, give me courage to live your way. Help me to read more of your Word so I am constantly reminded of your ways. Your goodness is throughout Scripture, so I commit today to meditate on the truth of your Word.

*"Have I not commanded you? Be strong and courageous.
Do not be afraid; do not be discouraged, for the LORD
your God will be with you wherever you go."*

JOSHUA 1:9 NIV

When you have been dwelling on God's Word, it is much
easier to be strong and courageous. God's reminder to Joshua
was to remember his words and the promise that God made
to always be with him.

When you remember that God is with you, fear and
discouragement have no power. You may have had a rough
day today, or perhaps you are facing some anxiety about
upcoming decisions or responsibilities. You don't need to
face them alone because the Lord your God will be with you
wherever you go.

*God, I choose to be strong and courageous in my present
circumstances because I know your presence is with me. You are
here in the quietness of the evening and you will be with me in the
busyness of my day tomorrow.*

How does the truth of God's presence help you face any fear
and discouragement that you are experiencing?

Stones to Remember

*Those twelve stones, which they had taken out of the Jordan,
Joshua set up in Gilgal, saying to the Israelites, "When your
children ask their parents in time to come, 'What do these stones
mean?' then you shall let your children know, 'Israel crossed over
the Jordan here on dry ground.'"*

JOSHUA 4:20-22 NRSV

We have markers in our lives to remind us of special times
and events. We have photos and landmarks and even special
dates or smells that trigger our memory. It is important to
have ways to remember significant things in your life so you
can share the story with others.

For Joshua, setting up a pillar of stone was his way to mark
out a very important event that would be told over and over
again. Take some time today to think of the times when God
has done something special in your life. See if you can share
that story with someone.

*God, you have been good to me. I'm glad that I can say that
despite the things that haven't always gone right in my life,
because when I reflect on the past, I can see your hand in all of it.
Remind me to share these good stories with others.*

> *"The LORD your God dried up the waters of the Jordan for you until you crossed over, as the LORD your God did to the Red Sea, which he dried up for us until we crossed over, so that all the peoples of the earth may know that the hand of the LORD is mighty, and so that you may fear the LORD your God forever."*
>
> JOSHUA 4:23-24 NRSV

It is not always easy to share the wonders of God with people today. Our day-to-day life is filled with the ordinary, but important, things like work, kids, meals, study. At the end of your day today, you may wonder where the time went and where your opportunity to share God's story was lost.

Rest assured there will be more opportunities, and prepare for it by reading up on all the amazing things God has done for his people in the past—like drying up the water so the Israelites could walk through and be saved. He is mighty.

God, you are mighty and powerful. It doesn't always seem like you are going to part the waters for me, but I trust that you are always working in my life. Help me to be more responsive and attentive to your guiding hand.

How has God shown his power in your life? How can you mark these special times so you will remember them?

Sincere Serving

"Fear the LORD and serve Him in sincerity and truth;
and put away the gods which your fathers served beyond
the River and in Egypt, and serve the LORD."

JOSHUA 24:14 NASB

You might be able to remember the time when you were not a Christian or not following the ways of Christ. In Bible times, people served other gods because they wanted health, wealth, and all forms of prosperity.

Instead of serving stone idols, we can be lured into finding other ways to achieve prosperity—from beauty products to the pursuit of high paying jobs. God's ways direct us in different forms of prosperity like healthy relationships, healing, and strength of character. Serve the Lord in sincerity and truth; his ways will give you all you need.

God, I am so often drawn to the things that used to make me feel better and yet I recognize that some of these things are shallow and not truly fulfilling. I come to you now, in sincerity and truth, and choose to serve you to the best of my ability today.

"If it is disagreeable in your sight to serve the LORD, choose for yourselves today whom you will serve: whether the gods which your fathers served which were beyond the River, or the gods of the Amorites in whose land you are living; but as for me and my house, we will serve the LORD."

JOSHUA 24:15 NASB

It's important to understand that not everyone will choose to serve the Lord. We live in a world that has temptations that some will not be able to resist. We live in a world where we may be mocked for our decision to follow Christ.

It is important, just as Joshua did, to make a decision one way or another. Scripture says elsewhere, we cannot serve two masters. When you make the choice, be brave and bold about your choice to follow God.

God, I am sorry when I chase other things in this life that will not bring true joy into my heart. The truth is that I will only ever be satisfied with a choice to follow you. Give me peace as I go to sleep tonight, knowing that my decision remains to serve the one true God.

Are you tempted to serve other things in this world? Choose today who you will serve.

Not Again

"I brought you out of Egypt into this land that I promised to your ancestors, and I said that I would never break my covenant with you, if you, on your part, would make no peace treaties with the people living in this land; I told you to destroy their heathen altars. Why have you not obeyed?"

JUDGES 2:1-2 TLB

It can be heartbreaking to read the failure of Israel to remain faithful to God. It is like watching a movie where everything is going wrong and you want the characters to see that they are headed for disaster. Just when God sets them back on track, they choose to go back to their past mistakes.

We recognize this pattern in ourselves. There are times when we realize that we are making the same mistake again. God is calling you forward into his promises, don't go back.

God, you are so loving. I know that you saved your people because of this great love. I believe I am forgiven for my past mistakes, and I ask that you help me to move forward into the good things you have called me to do.

> *"Since you have broken the contract, it is no longer in effect, and I no longer promise to destroy the nations living in your land; rather, they shall be thorns in your sides, and their gods will be a constant temptation to you."*
>
> JUDGES 2:3 TLB

God doesn't punish, but he can't promise that we will be blessed if we continue to live our own way. Until God's final return, we know that the world will always offer us temptation that lures us away from him.

While it may seem an impossible mission, God's grace allows us to live a life that is not only in obedience to his will, but that will also allow us to prosper.

God, I know that I can be lured back to my old ways and things in the past. Be with me tonight as I rest and help me to look forward to a future that begins as I wake.

What are you being tempted to go back to? Remember God's promise and ask for his help to resist.

Wise Woman

Israel's leader at that time, the one who was responsible for bringing the people back to God, was Deborah, a prophetess, the wife of Lappidoth. She held court at a place now called "Deborah's Palm Tree," between Ramah ad Bethel, in the hill country of Ephraim; and the Israelites came to her to decide their disputes.

JUDGES 4:4-5 TLB

God used all people, regardless of gender and age. Deborah was clearly a very wise woman who was well regarded among the people. Scripture says she was responsible for bringing the people back to God; she was a hero in that day.

Wisdom and truth will always prevail over prejudice and wrong assumptions. Be encouraged this morning as you face the tasks of the day, that your decision making can honor God and change the hearts of people.

God, thank you for reminding me that you chose all kinds of people to lead and to do mighty things for you. I know that you have called me to be a person that speaks with truth and justice. Help me to speak to others with grace and wisdom today.

*Israel's population dwindled,
until Deborah became a mother to Israel.*

JUDGES 5:7 TLB

Deborah not only turned the people back to God, but she also
led the Israelites into battle and defeated their enemies.

It only took one person to turn the nation around and to
create change that would bring the nation peace for forty
years. A little bit of courage and wisdom can go a long way.

*God, I know that sometimes what I think are small things can
become great. Thank you that it is often little but good decisions
that change hearts or situations. I give you the battle that I am
facing right now and ask that you help me to have courage to
believe that it can change.*

What situations are you facing that you think you can
influence with wisdom and courage?

Reassurance

The angel of the Lord came and sat down under the oak in Ophrah that belonged to Joash the Abiezrite, where his son Gideon was threshing wheat in a winepress to keep it from the Midianites. When the angel of the Lord appeared to Gideon, he said, "The Lord is with you mighty warrior." "Pardon me, my Lord," Gideon replied, "but if the Lord is with us, why has all this happened to us? Where are all his wonders that our ancestors told us about when they said, 'Did not the Lord bring us up out of Egypt?' But now the Lord has abandoned us and given us into the hand of Midian."

JUDGES 6:11-13 NIV

How often have you had an encouraging word from the Lord, only to respond with your doubts and insecurities? Gideon had plenty of good reasons to be skeptical and yet God reassured him that he had provided him with enough strength to make it through.

It's in our nature to question why things happen the way that they do, but when God speaks, he wants you to be confident and trust that his Word is truth.

Jesus, I need to hear your reassuring voice today. At times, I doubt my ability to overcome obstacles or to share my faith, or to forgive wholeheartedly. Thank you that the strength of you dwelling within me is enough to do these things.

*The Lord turned to him and said, "Go in the strength you have
and save Israel out of Midian's hand. Am I not sending you?"
"Pardon me, my Lord," Gideon replied, "but how can I save Israel?
My clan is the weakest in Manasseh, and I am the least in my
family." The Lord answered, "I will be with you, and you will
strike down all the Midianites, leaving none alive."*

JUDGES 6:14-16 NIV

We compare ourselves to others when assessing our ability to
do something. Gideon felt like he was the least according to
family hierarchy and his birth order.

God has created each of us as a unique person and he doesn't
look at outward factors. Instead God looks at the heart and
will use anyone who is willing to trust that God can work
through them. It is not about you, but about your willingness
to let God work through you.

*God, I have been surrounded today by people and comparison is
everywhere. Protect my heart and mind from thinking less of myself
because of others. I am willing for you to work through me; be my
strength as I live in your Word and the life you have chosen for me.*

In what ways do you compare yourself to others? Can you
trust God to work through you?

False Trust

The LORD replied, *"When the Egyptians, the Amorites, the Ammonites, the Philistines, the Sidonians, the Amalekites and the Maonites oppressed you and you cried to me for help, did I not save you from their hands? But you have forsaken me and served other gods, so I will no longer save you. Go and cry out to the gods you have chosen. Let them save you when you are in trouble!"*

JUDGES 10:11-14

When you face trouble, hardship, or just need help, where do you turn to first? We have many things that promise to bring us just what we need from diet plans, self-help books, and the varied advice received from friends, social media, and television.

Even though we know that God is faithful, he is not often the one we seek out first. When we are really in trouble, it is only God who can help.

God, today I choose to seek you first. Help me to notice those things that are distractions to the real help and guidance that I need from you. I don't want to be like the Israelites and frustrate you with serving other things. Keep me on your true path.

> The Israelites said to the LORD, "We have sinned. Do with us
> whatever you think best, but please rescue us now." Then they got
> rid of the foreign gods among them and served the LORD.
> And he could bear Israel's misery no longer.

It is good to acknowledge when we have turned from God's
ways and need to set ourselves on the right path again.
Sometimes a little bit of purging goes a long way. Israel got
rid of the things that were getting in the way of their reliance
on God. They were lured into the temptation that they needed
more than God to help them in their distress.

An honest declaration of your sin will get you the right
response from God because he is merciful and loving and
doesn't want to see you suffer.

*Father, I acknowledge my sin before you this evening. I admit that
I don't always feel like you are enough and that I think that I need
other things in this world to fulfil me or to keep me happy. Thank you
that you rescue me in times of trouble. Help me to always trust you.*

What things can you get rid of in your life that are hindering
you from trusting God?

The Word, the Light

*In the beginning was the Word, and the Word was with God,
and the Word was God. He was with God in the beginning.
Through him all things were made; without him nothing
was made that has been made.*

JOHN 1:1-3 NIV

Jesus was the Word from the beginning, with God in the creation of this world, and the creation of humanity. Jesus had a hand in creating you. It's great to know of Jesus as he was on earth, but it's also important to remember where and who he was from the beginning.

Jesus not only can empathize with you from a human perspective, but he knows you inside out. Talk to him today as the person who knows you the best.

Jesus, thank you that you are a divine and human person and that you know me so well. As I go into my day today, help me to recognize your Spirit speaking to me and working in me. I love you, my Savior and my friend.

In him was life, and that life was the light of all mankind. The light shines in the darkness, and the darkness has not overcome it.

JOHN 1:4-5 NIV

Jesus created life and then he came to rescue the very thing he had created. We don't have to fear the darkness because Jesus is the light that came to overcome it.

As the darkness sets in this evening and you turn on lights so you can clearly see, remember Jesus, the light that came into this world so we could see the truth.

Jesus, thank you for coming to earth and saving humankind. Thank you that you are not only the light of this world but the light of my life. Help me to sleep with the peace of knowing that darkness has been overcome by your love.

What are the fears that threaten to surround you? Allow Jesus' light to expel all darkness.

Grace Realized

Of His fullness we have all received, and grace upon grace.

JOHN 1:16 NASB

Your day might be looking a little grim, with so many deadlines and things to get done. You might be wondering when you will get a day where you feel his blessing of time, peace, and fun.

Being a child of the Almighty gains us access to that blessed feeling every day, even when our circumstances are ordinary or even difficult. His love is so full, and his grace so boundless, that when his Spirit lives in us, even a flat tire can feel like a blessing. Our status as beloved children of the King guarantees it; we need only claim it.

Jesus, thank you that your grace is there to pick me up today, and to give me a day where I can experience the fullness of your love.

The Law was given through Moses;
grace and truth were realized through Jesus Christ.

JOHN 1:17 NASB

You know those days, the perfect ones? You looked great, you nailed an assignment, you said just the right thing and made someone's day. It's good upon good, blessing upon blessing.

Today might not have been that perfect day, but you can still bring home a perfect attitude. You aren't bound by rules and laws, you are walking in the freedom of his grace. You can choose to be thankful for God's fullness in your heart and in your life. Be gracious to yourself and to others this evening.

God, thank you that I take your grace with me each day. Thank you that even if today wasn't perfect, your love for me is.

Do you see God's grace poured out upon you today? Thank him for it.

Prepare the Way

"You yourselves know how plainly I told you, 'I am not the Messiah. I am only here to prepare the way for him.'"

JOHN 3:28 NLT

John the Baptist was a radical man with a fire in his belly to prepare the earth for the coming of Jesus. He didn't live for himself but was completely sold out on the message of the Messiah. He had a thirst for eternity and an agenda to bring glory to God.

Just as John was the voice in the wilderness preparing the way for Jesus to come the first time, we now are the voice crying out to ready the world for the second coming.

God, give me boldness to proclaim your name today, and in the days to come.

"It is the bridegroom who marries the bride, and the best man is simply glad to stand with him and hear his vows. Therefore, I am filled with joy at his success."

JOHN 3:29 NLT

In order for Jesus to have his rightful place in the hearts of the people, John knew he had to fade away. You cannot save the people you're preaching to. You can't rescue them from sin or keep them from hell. Only Jesus can do that. But you can prepare the way in their hearts for his presence.

Don't keep the glory of God shut up. Let it out and make him known, so when he comes, those who have known you will know who he is because you proclaimed him clearly.

God, sometimes it is hard for me to know how to proclaim who you are and what you are doing in this world. I know, however, that I am your image bearer and that I can be a reflection of you. Let me represent you well.

How can you deliver the message of Jesus that is relevant to the people in your life?

Believe in the Son

"God so loved the world that he gave his one and only Son, that whoever believes in him shall not perish but have eternal life. For God did not send his Son into the world to condemn the world, but to save the world through him."

JOHN 3:16-17 NIV

It is good to be reminded of the simple truth of the gospel. This verse is so well known because it sums up our faith so well. This was God's plan for the world, and his plan for you.

God loved you so much that he gave his Son, Jesus. When you believe in him, you have eternal life. It's a great thought to take into your day. Let the hope of eternal life give you the perspective you need to face today's challenges.

God, thank you for reminding me that there is hope of eternal life with you. Thank you that as a believer, I am no longer condemned to death, but I am saved. Remind me of this amazing grace today.

"Whoever believes in him is not condemned, but whoever does not believe stands condemned already because they have not believed in the name of God's one and only Son."

JOHN 3:18 NIV

It really is as simple as believing. We can often approach this faith with the idea that we need to be better people. Sometimes we expect others to be better, to do better, to live more of a righteous life. It's important that we live in God's ways, but more importantly is our faith in Jesus. This belief is what saves us, and what saves every other person.

When you love God, you will be better—not through your effort, but through the revelation of love that God shares with you because you believe.

Lord Jesus, I am sorry when I have expected the wrong things from other people or become self-righteous about my faith. Thank you that all you require from my heart and that of others, is a belief that you are the Son of God and that you came to save us. Thank you that I am made righteous through this belief.

What expectations do you have of yourself and others? How do they relate to belief in Jesus Christ?

From the Heart

"The time is coming—indeed it's here now—when true worshipers will worship the Father in spirit and in truth. The Father is looking for those who will worship him that way."

JOHN 4:23 NLT

When was the last time you gave yourself over fully to a time of worship? Not just singing along to the words in church, not just bowing your head in prayer, but letting yourself be completely consumed by the presence of the Lord?

Take some quiet time today to allow his mighty presence to wash over you. Revel in the time that you have with him, worshiping him in whatever way feels natural to you. You'll discover that he is indeed worthy of your adoring reverence.

God, I worship you with my whole heart this morning. Give me time in my day to reflect on how truly wonderful you are.

> *"God is Spirit, so those who worship him must worship in spirit and in truth."*
>
> JOHN 4:24 NLT

True worship is quite different than just singing along. We serve a God who is awesome and powerful. He is deserving of our utmost devotion. When we discover just how amazing he is, we know that he is worth our full praise.

People can talk about worshiping God, and show all kinds of outward devotion, like lengthy prayers, hands in the air, or intense biblical debate. But God is after the heart, that's why he made it known that there are true worshippers and false worshippers.

God, I know that sometimes I compare myself to other people who seem to be more spiritual than me, or who like to "worship" more than I do. Thank you for confronting me with the truth, that it isn't about the songs that I sing, or the way I show my worship, but that you care about a heart that is directed to you. I give you my heart's attention tonight.

How will you worship in truth this week?

Ripe

"My food," said Jesus, "is to do the will of him who sent me and
to finish his work. Don't you have a saying, 'It's still four months
until harvest'? I tell you, open your eyes and look at the fields!
They are ripe for harvest."

JOHN 4:34-35 NIV

Food is a necessary part of our existence. Sometimes it feels
like we eat to live and live to eat. Jesus explains that doing
the will of the Father is necessary and fulfilling. He says that
unlike the crops that we wait for, we do not need to wait for
souls that need saving, they are already ready.

Jesus wants us to know that there are many still waiting to
hear and receive the gospel.

*Jesus, help me to see salvation as a necessary part of my calling
as well. Thank you that you have involved me in your plan for
humanity and that you want me to share my faith. Give me
boldness to help reap what has been sown.*

"Even now the one who reaps draws a wage and harvests a crop for eternal life, so that the sower and the reaper may be glad together. Thus the saying 'One sows and another reaps' is true."

JOHN 4:36-37 NIV

Jesus needs both those who are willing to sow seeds and those who are bold enough to reap when the harvest is ready. God needs to use all gifts to achieve his purpose.

Whether you are quietly showing kindness to a neighbor or boldly declaring the gospel to unbelievers, God can and will use you. We need to appreciate one another and the different ways that God uses us to build his kingdom.

God, thank you that you place all kinds of believers in the field and that we all have different ways of contributing to your kingdom. Help me to rise up to the calling to share my faith in big or small ways.

Is God asking you to sow or reap this season?

Into the Fold

"I am the good shepherd. I know my own and my own know me, just as the Father knows me and I know the Father; and I lay down my life for the sheep."

JOHN 10:14-15 ESV

In Jesus' day there were many shepherds. It is interesting that sheep would learn their shepherd's voice and only follow the voice they know.

When you follow Jesus, you are both known by him and you know his voice. We know that a shepherd diligently watches over his sheep to keep them from harm. Well, Jesus not only does that, but he also gave his life for us. He gave his life for you.

Jesus, you are my good shepherd. I feel blessed because I am known by you. Help me to know your voice better so I can follow closely in your footsteps and be safe from harm.

"I have other sheep that are not of this fold. I must bring them also, and they will listen to my voice. So there will be one flock, one shepherd."

JOHN 10:16 ESV

Not only did Jesus have followers of that day, but he knew and wanted there to be so many others that would come into his fold.

God has always had a heart for all people and does not discriminate between people groups, race, gender, or age. We are all one people in Christ.

God, I have so many people on my heart that I want to come to know you. I ask your Holy Spirit to move in the lives of these people so they would accept that you are the one true God who cares about their lives. I commit them to you tonight, in your precious name.

Who can you pray for today that needs to come into the fold of the good shepherd?

Jesus Wept

> When Jesus saw her weeping, and the Jews who had come along
> with her also weeping, he was deeply moved in spirit
> and troubled. "Where have you laid him?" he asked.
> "Come and see, Lord," they replied.
>
> JOHN 11:33-34 NIV

In telling the story of Lazarus' death and resurrection (see John 11:1-46), take some time this evening to reflect on why these words are set apart and given their own verse. Take some time to reflect on the humanity of Jesus and how he deeply cared for others.

Are you able to imagine Jesus openly weeping with Mary and Martha? As you reflect on your day, have you shared in the emotions of those around you?

God, I thank you for all the different people who you have placed in my life. Thank you for all the range of emotions that we can feel, even for emotions of grief. Remind me of your presence in everything that I feel, and help me to share in the joys and pains of others today.

Jesus wept.

JOHN 11:35 NASB

In the shortest verse in the Bible, but also among the most beautiful, Jesus saw how his dear friends were hurting and was moved to tears. He knew he was about to take their pain away by raising Lazarus to life again, but in that moment, their pain was his pain—and it broke his heart.

When someone we love is in pain, their ache becomes our ache. We cry openly with our newly jobless neighbors, recently bereaved friends, freshly disappointed children. Tears come easy when your heart is surrendered to the Holy Spirit, because they are his tears. He hurts when we hurt.

God, thank you for sharing in my pain. Help me to have that same compassion for the people around me this week.

How have you felt Jesus' affection for you today?

Divine

Jesus cried out and said, "Whoever believes in me, believes not in me but in him who sent me. And whoever sees me sees him who sent me."

JOHN 12:44-45 ESV

It was one thing to believe and follow Jesus as a man doing amazing miracles with great teaching, but Jesus made it clear that he was sent by God and that he was the Son of God.

Believing in Jesus for us means that we can know the Father by understanding who Jesus was and is. The Holy Spirit is our helper to reveal all of this to us, so be encouraged that when you believe in the acts and character of Christ, you are beginning to understand the heart of the Father.

Father God, thank you for sending your Son, Jesus, into the world so we could see who you are. Help me, Holy Spirit, to understand more about you.

"I have come into the world as light, so whoever believes in me may not remain in darkness. If anyone hears my words and does not keep them, I do not judge him; for I did not come to judge the world but to save the world."

JOHN 12:46-47 ESV

Jesus came to earth because it was the will of the Father. He did not come in the way the Jews had expected—with a sword to destroy all their enemies. He came to save and bring people from darkness to light.

This is our responsibility too, as imitators of Christ. We are not here to judge others, but to give them the message of love and salvation. When we come home from a hard day at work, with the kids, or at school, we may forget about the light that we carry inside of us. Don't hide it. Keep it burning brightly for all to see.

God, help me to remember your words and to keep them in my heart so I am always ready to share the light of your life with others.

Who are the people in your life, or in the outside world that need to see the light, rather than hear about judgment?

Acts of Humility

When he had washed their feet and put on his outer garments and resumed his place, he said to them, "Do you understand what I have done to you? You call me Teacher and Lord, and you are right, for so I am. If I then, your Lord and Teacher, have washed your feet, you also ought to wash one another's feet. For I have given you an example, that you also should do just as I have done to you."

JOHN 13:12-15 ESV

Jesus showed just how great his love was by doing the job that was reserved for a lowly servant. He was revered by his disciples as a great teacher and yet he gladly showed the disciples his affection through an act of humility.

Jesus wants us to show this same humility for one another. It doesn't matter if we have a higher position, career, or place in society, we need Jesus' heart of compassion to serve one another in love.

Jesus, thank you for showing me humility. You have such great love for all people and I want to honor your words that tell me to do what you have done. As I go into the busyness of life today, I ask that your Holy Spirit gives me the grace to love as you do.

"Truly, truly, I say to you, a servant is not greater than his master, nor is a messenger greater than the one who sent him. If you know these things, blessed are you if you do them."

John 13:16-17 ESV

The workplace is one of great hierarchy. You probably have had a boss in the past that has acted with a superior attitude toward you, and perhaps you have been guilty of it yourself. Jesus wasn't suggesting that a servant is any less of a person than his master; rather, he was showing that he was gladly doing the will of his Father, even if it meant he had lower his status to do so.

Jesus says we are blessed if we also can humble ourselves for the sake of the higher calling.

God, I am sorry when I have not acted in humility toward others. Help me to acknowledge that you have sent us to do your will and that this requires serving others rather than serving myself.

What superior attitude do you need to let go of or forgive someone for?

Greater Works

"Truly, truly, I say to you, whoever believes in me will also do the works that I do; and greater works than these will he do, because I am going to the Father."

JOHN 14:12 ESV

The Bible is full of exciting accounts of power, healing, and resurrection. We find ourselves wishing that we had been there when the fire of God fell upon Elijah's sacrifice, or when Lazarus stepped out of the tomb.

God is clear that miracles didn't stop when the Bible ended. His power isn't limited by the ages, and he is just as omnipotent today as he was back then—so what is different? Why do we feel like there are fewer miracles today? God tells us that the works he will do through his believers will be greater than the works he did through his disciples. But these works will be done in those who believe.

God, give me faith again to believe in the miracles that you did in the Bible and to believe that you can do miracles today.

*"Whatever you ask in my name, this I will do,
that the Father may be glorified in the Son."*

JOHN 14:13 ESV

God does not lie. He tells us that by believing in him, we can and will perform miracles.

Believe God for something tonight. Don't buy into the lie that his power has been shelved; don't doubt his ability to work a miracle in your life. Believe him for something big, and ask him for it in faith, knowing that he can do it.

In this moment, powerful God, I ask that you remind me of your power and that your ways are higher than my ways. You are a supernatural God who does supernatural things, and I believe in your greatness and power on earth.

What miracle do you need to believe God for tonight?

Your Helper

"If you love me, you will keep my commandments. And I will ask the Father, and he will give you another Helper, to be with you forever, even the Spirit of truth, whom the world cannot receive, because it neither sees him nor knows him. You know him, for he dwells with you and will be in you."

JOHN 14:15-17 ESV

Jesus knew that the disciples couldn't keep his commandments without help. Israel hadn't been able to prove their faithfulness and neither can we. That's why part of the wonderful plan of salvation included the Holy Spirit who would teach us Jesus' ways until he returns.

The Holy Spirit is within you, to guide you in truth and to continue to teach you the ways of Christ.

Holy Spirit, thank you for helping me keep the commandments of our faith. Thank you for the grace to get through each day. Allow me to be aware of your presence in me today.

"I will not leave you as orphans; I will come to you. Yet a little while and the world will see me no more, but you will see me. Because I live, you also will live."

JOHN 14:18-19 ESV

The disciples were understandably afraid that their leader, friend, teacher, and Messiah was going to leave them. It was a confusing time for them to understand all that was about to take place.

Sometimes we are confused and afraid because we don't understand God's plan. Take comfort in the same words that he gave to his disciples, "I will not leave you." He placed the Holy Spirit within you and he will guide you through all of life's uncertainties.

Jesus, thank you for your Holy Spirit that lives in me and reminds me that you are always with me. I ask for your guidance each day and for your peace as I sleep tonight in the knowledge that you are in control.

What have you noticed about the Holy Spirit's presence in your life today?

Don't be Troubled

"The Advocate, the Holy Spirit, whom the Father will send in my name, will teach you all things and will remind you of everything I have said to you."

JOHN 14:26 NIV

After his resurrection, before Jesus ascended into heaven, he left his disciples with something they'd never had before: peace. More specifically, he gave them his Holy Spirit that would guide them in his peace—a gift not of this world.

Whatever the world can offer us can also be taken from us. Any security, happiness, or temporary reprieve from suffering is just that: temporary. Only the things of heaven are permanent and cannot be taken away. Let the Holy Spirit remind you of those words of truth today.

Holy Spirit, let your words of life bring peace to my heart today.

"Do not let your hearts be troubled and do not be afraid."

JOHN 14:27 NIV

"Do not let your heart be troubled," Jesus tells us. This means we have a choice. Share the things with him that threaten your peace, and then remember they have no hold on you. You are his, and his peace is yours.

Why is it so hard to find peace in this world? Because we're looking in this world. True peace is found in Jesus. There will be a lot of things that may have taken away your sense of peace today. Allow the Holy Spirit to speak to you and help settle your heart and mind.

Thank you, Jesus, that I do not have to be afraid. Watch over me as I sleep and let your peace wash over me.

What have you been troubled about lately? Will you allow his peace to replace your fear?

The Gardener

"I am the true vine, and my Father is the gardener. He cuts off every branch in me that bears no fruit, while every branch that does bear fruit he prunes so that it will be even more fruitful."

JOHN 15:1-2 NIV

Take a moment to reflect on a time when you felt you were giving the best of yourself. You may be thinking of times when you were utilizing your gifts and talents and could witness your positive influence in others around you. You may not have to reflect back that far, or you could be wondering where those times have gone.

Jesus describes himself as the vine. If we are being nourished from that source, we will produce fruit. In the times where we feel like we are not flourishing, it may be that the Father needs to do some necessary pruning—for the health of both the branch and the whole vine.

Heavenly Father, I ask you to show me areas of my life that you have chosen to prune and help me to be encouraged that you have done this so I can be fruitful in other areas of my life.

"You are already clean because of the word I have spoken to you. Remain in me, as I also remain in you. No branch can bear fruit by itself; it must remain in the vine. Neither can you bear fruit unless you remain in me."

JOHN 15:3-4 NIV

Rather than despair over his pruning, be encouraged that God has seen the fruit you have produced and is allowing a period of dormancy so you will flourish once again.

Take some time today to reflect on your gifts, submit them to Jesus, and wait expectantly for the great gardener to bring them back to life.

God, I have sensed that there are things in my life that you are asking me to cut back on. I pray as I reflect on these things tonight, that you will give me wisdom to know what is healthy for me to pursue right now, and what I need to give up. Thank you that you will restore to me every good thing if I continue to faithfully follow you.

What is the loving Father asking you to give up for now? What can you see flourishing in your life?

Relatives

Ruth replied, "Don't urge me to leave you or to turn back from you.
Where you go I will go, and where you stay I will stay. Your people
will be my people and your God my God. Where you die I will die,
and there I will be buried. May the LORD deal with me, be it ever so
severely, if even death separates you and me."

RUTH 1:16-17 NIV

Ruth was a diligent and faithful woman, yet this story also
gives testament to the bonds that can be shared between
people who are not of the same family. Naomi was Ruth's
mother-in-law and Ruth obviously had deep affection for her.

These days it can be harder to establish loving relationships
with our relatives and in-laws, but what testimony to others
it is when they see loyalty and deep connection between
families.

God, I pray for my relatives this morning. Help me to have a
gracious attitude toward them if I get a chance to see them or talk
to them today. Help me to forgive past hurts and to make the effort
to establish deeper relationships with my family.

When Naomi realized that Ruth was determined to go with her,
she stopped urging her.

RUTH 1:18 NIV

Naomi tried hard to convince Ruth to stay behind. Naomi
felt like the best thing for Ruth was to stay and re-marry
rather than make the long and hard journey with her back
to a people group that was not Ruth's own. Yet Ruth was
determined. She knew in her heart this is what she wanted to
do, and it turned out the best for her.

As you have thought about connections with family today,
perhaps you can recall times when you have felt convinced
that someone should do something a certain way. Learn, as
Naomi did, when it is best to end the conversation and move
on graciously.

God, thank you for your wisdom and discernment. As I reflect on
potential irritation or conflict with family members, give me the
understanding that I need to know when to end a conversation.
Bring peace to my family, in your name I ask.

Are you dealing with an issue right now where you need to
gently end the conversation?

Your Job

> Ruth went out to gather grain behind the harvesters. And as it
> happened, she found herself working in a field that belonged to
> Boaz, the relative of her father-in-law, Elimelech. While she was
> there, Boaz arrived from Bethlehem and greeted the harvesters.
> "The LORD be with you!" he said. "The LORD bless you!"
> the harvesters replied.
>
> RUTH 2:3-4 NLT

Let's face it, jobs are rarely glamorous. Ruth had to literally
find food in the fields from the leftovers of the harvesters that
had gone before. It can't have been easy out in the hot sun,
and there was no pay.

Hopefully this makes you grateful for whatever type of job you
are in. Whether you are looking after your children, working
part-time for some extra cash, or heading into a full-blown
career, it is all hard work. As you get started on your day job,
hear Jesus calling out with his assurance and blessing.

*Jesus, thank you for the job that I am in right now. Thank you for
the opportunity to earn money and provide for my household. Help
me to appreciate this job and to work hard, even when it doesn't
feel rewarding. Thank you that you are with me along the way.*

*Boaz asked his foreman, "Who is that young woman over there?
Who does she belong to?" And the foreman replied, "She is the
young woman from Moab who came back with Naomi. She asked
me this morning if she could gather grain behind the harvesters.
She has been hard at work ever since, except for a few minutes'
rest in the shelter."*

RUTH 2:5-7 NLT

When someone works hard, it gets noticed. The person in
charge of our workplace is usually very quick to see who is doing
well. Diligence paid off for Ruth, and it will pay off for you.

Did you see your place of work as an opportunity and blessing
today? It's easy to grumble about everything you have to do,
with little thanks, but be encouraged that God notices. He
cares that you have been hard at work, and he is ready to give
you rest and favor.

*God, I am thankful for the job that I have, as hard as it is. I can
get discouraged at times because it feels like I am not enjoying
every single moment. Give me perspective and remind me that your
loving eyes are on me the whole time, proud of the hard work that I
am putting in.*

What parts of your daily job do you love? What do you dislike?
Commit to being a diligent worker regardless of what you like
and do not like.

Kindness

"May the LORD reward you for your deeds, and may you have a full reward from the LORD, the God of Israel, under whose wings you have come for refuge!"

RUTH 2:12 NRSV

Ruth's kindness and loyalty to her mother-in-law was the talk of the town. Her strength of character must have been evident in the way she conducted herself, and because of this she found favor with Boaz, the owner of the land that she was collecting leftover food from.

As you begin to get ready for your day, remember that whether people notice your loving conduct or not, your reward is from God. He is the one in whom you will receive love and refuge.

Heavenly Father, as I stop for a moment to read a Scripture and reflect on your goodness, I ask for your Holy Spirit to fill me so I can be someone who does good deeds today with an encouraging heart. I don't seek a reward but thank you that I can receive shelter from the darkness of this world as I take refuge under your wings.

"May I continue to find favor in your sight, my Lord, for you have comforted me and spoken kindly to your servant, even though I am not one of your servants."

RUTH 2:13 NRSV

Boaz was a kind and generous man who did not need to show favor toward a foreign woman, gathering leftovers from his land. Boaz has often been described as a Christ figure, because this is what Christ did for us.

You can respond to Jesus in the same way that Ruth responded to Boaz. Thank him for comforting you and speaking kindly to you, even if you don't feel like you have deserved it today. He has a kind heart toward you.

Jesus, thank you that you find favor in what I say and do, even when I don't always act like a righteous person. I accept your kindness for me this evening, and rest in your unconditional love.

What have you been through today that you can submit to the kindness of Christ?

Special Treatment

At mealtime Boaz called to her, "Come over here, and help yourself to some food. You can dip your bread in the sour wine." So she sat with his harvesters, and Boaz gave her some roasted grain to eat. She ate all she wanted and still had some left over.

RUTH 2:14 NLT

It's a wonderful thing to make someone feel extra special. Can you remember the last time someone treated you to a fancy meal, or paid for treatment, or gave you a day off from your responsibilities?

Think of someone that you could spoil today, and be the person who gives because of the joy that it brings to others.

God, show me someone that needs some special treatment. Give me creative ideas of how I can help that person feel as special as they are. Use me to show them your love.

When Ruth went back to work again, Boaz ordered his young men,
"Let her gather grain right among the sheaves without stopping
her. And pull out some heads of barley from the bundles and drop
them on purpose for her. Let her pick them up, and don't give her a
hard time!" So Ruth gathered barley there all day, and when she
beat out the grain that evening, it filled an entire basket.

RUTH 2:15-17 NLT

Boaz's treatment of Ruth went to the next level. Not only
did he give her special treatment, but he got other people
involved and showed her favor without making himself
known. It's one thing to give generously, it's another thing to
give without receiving any recognition for it.

If you have had the opportunity to do something extra special
for someone, think about how you might make yourself
unknown. Let God be glorified in your generosity.

Father, thank you for showing me that generosity can take many
forms. Bless the people who have made me feel special over the
years, and give me an opportunity to bless others in return.

How can you show someone they are special, without
receiving the glory for yourself?

Integrity

He said, "Who are you?" And she answered, "I am Ruth, your servant; spread your cloak over your servant, for you are next-of-kin." He said, "May you be blessed by the Lord, my daughter; this last instance of your loyalty is better than the first; you have not gone after young men, whether poor or rich."

RUTH 3:9-10 NRSV

There are times in our lives when we are faced with a dilemma of integrity. We can choose to take the easy route and probably get away with it, or we can do what is right in the eyes of men and God.

Whether you are at home or in the workplace, people will notice when you are a person of your word. Without necessarily knowing it, your character is a model for those who you are leading, young or old. Ask for the discernment to do the most honorable thing in all circumstances.

God, I want to be someone who does the honorable thing. Fill my heart and mind with integrity so I am a shining example of your goodness.

"Now, my daughter, do not be afraid, I will do for you all that you ask, for all the assembly of my people know that you are a worthy woman. But now, though it is true that I am a near kinsman, there is another kinsman more closely related than I. Remain this night, and in the morning, if he will act as next-of-kin for you, good; let him do it. If he is not willing to act as next-of-kin for you, then, as the LORD lives, I will act as next-of-kin for you. Lie down until the morning."

RUTH 3:11–13 NRSV

Did you have the chance to show discernment and integrity today? At times you might have to stand in the gap for someone else. Boaz gave his relative the opportunity to take care of Ruth and Naomi, but he was willing to take his place if not.

Boaz was not obligated to esteem these woman; he did it out of generosity of spirit. Jesus showed this kind of favor toward us, and with his grace in our hearts, we can show this favor to others.

God, I want to be the kind of person that is willing to stand in the place of those who are struggling to do the right thing. I pray for those who come to mind right now, and ask that you give me a generous heart toward them.

Who might need you to stand in the gap for them?

Silver Linings

All the people who were at the gate and the elders said, "We are witnesses. May the LORD make the woman, who is coming into your house, like Rachel and Leah, who together built up the house of Israel. May you act worthily in Ephrathah and be renowned in Bethlehem."

RUTH 4:11 ESV

Ruth and Naomi were two suffering women, who began to be likened to Rachel and Leah, the women through whom the house of Israel was built up again. These two have become heroes of our faith.

People can experience times of great suffering and loss. During these times, we don't often see or expect the joy of what is around the corner. If you are feeling that sense of darkness, remember to look for those silver linings that bring the promise of the sun that is ready to appear.

God, help me see the positive things about my situation. In those times where I feel surrounded by discouragement and fear, I ask that I hear the gentle voice of the Holy Spirit, speaking a promise of a better day ahead.

> *"May your house be like the house of Perez, whom Tamar bore to Judah, because of the offspring that the LORD will give you by this young woman."*
>
> RUTH 4:12 ESV

Often other people are able to be more positive about our situations than we are. In times of discouragement, surround yourself with encouraging people. Let them speak words of life in the situation that you see as hopeless. Let them see a future in a time when you are unsure of what lies ahead.

Let the positivity of others influence your thoughts and behaviors. One day, it will be your turn to be the positive influence.

God, thank you that you give other people perspective in situations where I don't see anything good. I ask that you bring those people into my life this week so I can experience your encouragement.

Are you in need of others' positivity right now, or do you need to be an encouraging voice in someone's difficult situation?

Restored

Boaz took Ruth, and she became his wife. And he went in to her, and the LORD gave her conception, and she bore a son. Then the women said to Naomi, "Blessed be the LORD, who has not left you this day without a redeemer, and may his name be renowned in Israel!"

RUTH 4:13-14 ESV

Naomi and Ruth had lost everything, but God had a plan to restore their loss through the kindness of Boaz, and the birth of Ruth's firstborn, Obed. When Boaz married Ruth, he began a process of redemption that was eventually fulfilled in Jesus Christ—they were to become the great grandparents of King David.

You may have experienced loss and the feeling that you have been forgotten, but let your heart rest in the hope that God is your redeemer, and he will restore your life.

Father God, thank you for the example of Boaz and his loving-kindness. You have created good and kind people because you are good and kind. I ask for your restoration in those areas of my life that I have felt great loss. Renew my sense of purpose today.

"He shall be to you a restorer of life and a nourisher of your old age, for your daughter-in-law who loves you, who is more to you than seven sons, has given birth to him."

RUTH 4:15 ESV

Naomi had once changed her name because of bitterness from all that she had lost. God restored her hope through the son born to Boaz and Ruth; this son represented new life.

When you carry bitterness in your heart, it can destroy your joy. If there are things that you are harboring against another person, or even against God, it's time to start trusting in restoration. God doesn't want to see his children suffer and will always provide a way to restore new life to you. Accept this new life as you dwell in his presence tonight.

God, I want to be released from these feelings of hurt and bitterness. Restore to me the joy of a life lived in you, where there is hope for a good future, full of love.

What areas of hurt do you need to let go of tonight?

Promises

She said, "Oh, my Lord! As you live, my Lord, I am the woman
who was standing here in your presence, praying to the Lord.
For this child I prayed; and the Lord has granted me
the petition that I made to him."

1 Samuel 1:26-27 nrsv

We often pray without expecting much of a response, so it is
good to acknowledge those times when we see that God has
answered our prayers.

These stories in Scripture help to build our faith and so are
the stories of our answered prayers. They are there to be
shared. Be encouraged today, to continue to present your
requests to God, knowing that he is listening.

Father God, I have many prayers and petitions, some of them
answered, others not. I am encouraged that you do answer
prayers, understanding that sometimes it is not the answer I
want. Let me continue to remember and share those stories where I
have witnessed your answers and let these stories encourage those
who hear them.

"I have lent him to the LORD; as long as he lives, he is given to the LORD. She left him there for the LORD."

1 SAMUEL 1:28 NRSV

It's a nice change to see someone in the Bible keeping their promise to the Lord.

As good as it is to get the answer that you wanted from God, we need to remember that sometimes we have made promises to him. He won't hold us to these promises, as he is a gracious and merciful God, but how wonderful to be able to bless him by doing something to honor him.

God, I know that sometimes I have made promises that had the motivation behind it of getting what I want from you. I know that you are gracious enough to handle my bargaining, but I also want to continue to please you. Remind me of the things that I have said, out of the sincerity of my heart, that I can dedicate again to you this evening.

Have you made some promises to God that would be good to fulfil?

Lifted Up

"The Lord brings death and makes alive; he brings down to the grave and raises up. The Lord sends poverty and wealth; he humbles and he exalts."

1 Samuel 2:6-7 NIV

Hannah had her prayers answered and yet she acknowledged that sometimes things don't always turn out how we want.

God is the author of all and has power over everything, which makes us question his goodness when trouble comes. You may have a good day, you may have a bad day, but God is still in control. Honor him no matter what you go through today, always remembering that he cares for you.

God, I know you are the author of all things and that this day will be full of ups and downs. Remind me of your Word that is everlasting, and help me to put these things in perspective.

"He raises the poor from the dust and lifts the needy from the ash heap; he seats them with princes and has them inherit a throne of honor. For the foundations of the earth are the LORD's; on them he has set the world."

1 SAMUEL 2:8 NIV

While we don't often see life as fair, it's important to remember that God really cares about our troubles. He doesn't want to see people suffer, and he certainly wants to lift up those who need help.

If your day has been full of trouble, be encouraged that God wants you to look up at him and continue to be hopeful about the future. He is the God of the universe, and in him, you can do all things.

Father, you are compassionate and kind. Thank you that you can help me in my current troubles and that you give me the same heart of compassion to help others when they are in trouble. Give me hope tonight as I confess that this earth, and all that is in it, belongs to you.

What are your troubles and needs right now? Bring them to the God who cares for you.

I'm Listening

Samuel did not yet know the L{\sc ord}: The word of the L{\sc ord} had not yet been revealed to him. A third time the L{\sc ord} called, "Samuel!" And Samuel got up and went to Eli and said, "Here I am; you called me." Then Eli realized that the L{\sc ord} was calling the boy.

1 S{\sc amuel} 3:7-8 {\sc niv}

We can get confused about the voice of God when we are not used to him speaking. In Samuel's day, God spoke through the prophets, but since Christ came into our lives, he speaks through us.

It can be hard to be sure that God has spoken, but it is always good to respond, to question, and to seek wise counsel about what you think you have heard. God's voice is a blessing to all those who believe.

Lord God, thank you that you have chosen to speak to me and to speak through me. Help me to discern your voice today and to use wisdom when sharing your words.

Eli told Samuel, "Go and lie down, and if he calls you, say, 'Speak, LORD, for your servant is listening.' So Samuel went and lay down in his place. The LORD came and stood there, calling as at the other times, "Samuel! Samuel!" Then Samuel said, "Speak, for your servant is listening."

1 SAMUEL 3:9-10 NIV

A lot of things contribute to what we hear in our minds, and you would have heard a lot of those things today.

Our own thoughts, thoughts of others, programs, and social media are a few of those many things. When you think you hear the voice of God, ask him to speak again, make some time to be still and alone, and tell him you are listening. God wants to use you.

God, thank you for using me to speak truth and life in this world. Help me to be more confident when you are speaking to me, and give me the assurance that I am hearing your voice.

What is God saying to you right now?

Strength of Heart

*"Do not keep talking so proudly or let your mouth speak such
arrogance, for the LORD is a God who knows,
and by him deeds are weighed."*

1 SAMUEL 2:3 NIV

It's a competitive world and we are prone to falling into the
trap of making ourselves appear better than others or make
our stories seem bigger than they really are. We talk about our
strengths, skills, jobs, and victories a lot more than we talk of
our failures. We post our glory moments to social media and
often leave out the junk.

God wants us to celebrate the good things in our life, but
measure your motivation for sharing your wins. Make sure
that you are not speaking from a heart of arrogance. God
cares not about what you say but from the heart in which you
conduct yourself.

*God, help me not to compare myself to others. Forgive me when
I have boasted in order to look better than others. Help me to lift
others up and be a positive influence in the lives of those people
who I encounter today.*

*"The bows of the warriors are broken,
but those who stumbled are armed with strength."*

1 SAMUEL 2:4 NIV

Were you able to influence people in a positive way today? Perhaps you have had some encounters that have been discouraging or irritating. When our pride is challenged, it can be hard to let go and hand it over to God.

Take encouragement from this verse, that those who appear as warriors can actually be broken, but those who seem weak, God arms with strength. It is a strong thing to humble yourself before God and men. Remember that he loves you, no matter what has happened in your day.

God, I feel a bit like the person who stumbled today. Thank you for reminding me that you will give me strength in times like this. Help me to get over my feelings of insignificance or wounded pride, and help me to pick myself up again so I can face tomorrow with renewed positivity.

How have you felt broken today? Let God arm you with renewed strength tonight.

Obedient Hearts

Samuel replied, "What is more pleasing to the LORD: your burnt offerings and sacrifices or your obedience to his voice? Listen! Obedience is better than sacrifice, and submission is better than offering the fat of rams."

1 SAMUEL 15:22-23 NLT

When you have been wronged and somebody offers up a simply, "Sorry," it doesn't feel like a true apology if they continue to wrong you. Sometimes saying the right thing, or doing the right formalities isn't enough to show love.

God didn't want Israel's sacrifice's just for the sake of ritual; he wanted their obedience because that would mean that they understood why he wanted them to keep his commandments. Love God and love others. This is what God is calling you to do today.

Father, I am sorry when I have paid lip service to Christian morality. I know that you desire my heart and not just my religious actions. Teach me to respond in my heart to your call to love you and love others.

"Rebellion is as sinful as witchcraft, and stubbornness as bad as worshiping idols. So because you have rejected the command of the LORD, he has rejected you as king." Then Saul admitted to Samuel, "Yes, I have sinned. I have disobeyed your instructions and the LORD's command, for I was afraid of the people and did what they demanded. But now, please forgive my sin and come back with me so that I may worship the LORD."

1 SAMUEL 15:24-25 NLT

Saul had to hear some harsh words about the way that he had been leading the people of Israel. It wasn't the outward religious wrongs, but it was his heart that was rebellious and stubborn. He wasn't willing to listen to God's voice because he was more concerned about what the people were demanding.

You might not have done anything immoral today, but it is important to take a look at your heart and see if you have any stubbornness toward God's ways. Acknowledge any sin and ask for forgiveness.

God, I am reminded this evening that even though I may appear to be walking in righteousness, sometimes my heart is far from your ways. Forgive me if I have been avoiding your voice and help me to worship you again in spirit and in truth.

Is there any rebellion or stubbornness in your heart as you reflect on your actions and thoughts today?

Extraordinary

*When they arrived, Samuel took one look at Eliab and thought,
"Surely this is the LORD's anointed!" But the LORD said to Samuel,
"Don't judge by his appearance or height, for I have rejected him.
The LORD doesn't see things the way you see them. People judge by
outward appearance, but the LORD looks at the heart."*

1 SAMUEL 16:6-7 NLT

It is uplifting to read that God doesn't judge by outward
appearances, but it can be a challenge to imitate God in this
respect. Jesse thought his eldest looked the part of a king, yet it
was David, the youngest with a good heart, whom God chose.

While we don't always know someone's heart, we ought to
give people the benefit of not judging them by what we first
see or hear from them. We cross a lot of new people in one
day. Perhaps you can see people from a different perspective
today.

*God, thank you that you care more about the heart of a person
than what is displayed on the outside. Help me to approach people
with this same consideration today, and to see beyond the surface.*

Samuel asked, "Are these all the sons you have?" "There is still the youngest," Jesse replied. "But he's out in the fields watching the sheep and goats." "Send for him at once," Samuel said. "We will not sit down to eat until he arrives." So Jesse sent for him. He was dark and handsome, with beautiful eyes. And the LORD said, "This is the one; anoint him."

1 SAMUEL 16:11-12 NLT

David wasn't even considered as an option to be anointed as Israel's next king, he was out doing his usual duties of shepherding. God will choose extraordinary things out of the most ordinary circumstances.

You might feel like today has just been another of those ordinary days, but God sees your faithfulness and your strength of character, and he wants you to be ready to do great things. You are the one; you are anointed.

God, help me to see the extraordinary things in my everyday life. Thank you that you are giving me opportunities to be faithful in the small things so I am prepared for even better things.

What extraordinary things has God placed in your heart to be a part of?

Wear Your Own Shoes

*Then Saul gave David his own armor—a bronze helmet and a coat
of mail. David put it on, strapped the sword over it, and took a step
or two to see what it was like, for he had never worn such things
before. "I can't go in these," he protested to Saul. "I'm not used to
them." So David took them off again.*

1 SAMUEL 17:38-39 NLT

God wants to use you in so many different ways, be it in your
daily life or in a specific mission that he sets out for you. God
doesn't, however, want you to try and be like somebody else
in the way that you approach things. You don't have to talk like
a famous preacher, or lead a Bible study like your friend. You
don't have to sing in the band to be influential.

God needs you to be you. He wants you to wear the things that
make you who you are in order to do his work. David couldn't
wear Saul's armor; he just needed his everyday attire to get
the job done. Wear your own shoes as you walk into today's
tasks, and be proud of them.

*God, thank you for giving me a specific personality, set of
experiences, style, and opportunities that are uniquely mine. Help
me to be comfortable with the person I have become and to use my
unique self to accomplish your will.*

He picked up five smooth stones from a stream and put them into his shepherd's bag. Then, armed only with his shepherd's staff and sling, he started across the valley to fight the Philistine.

1 SAMUEL 17:40 NLT

Have you been confident today in your own skin? Have you realized that God wants to use the skills and tools that are uniquely yours?

You might not have read the latest theology book or written a famous worship song, but you can be sure that God wants whatever you have, just your five smooth stones, to go out and conquer your Goliath. Be brave, be strong, and be you.

Lord Jesus, thank you for your encouragement in wanting to use the things that make me, me. Thank you that whether I have little or much, you can always use me. Give me ideas and dreams as I go to bed this evening that I can put into action this week.

What are your five smooth stones?

Looking Ahead

When they had come together, they asked Him, saying, "Lord, will You at this time restore the kingdom to Israel?" And He said to them, "It is not for you to know times or seasons which the Father has put in His own authority. But you shall receive power when the Holy Spirit has come upon you; and you shall be witnesses to Me in Jerusalem, and in all Judea and Samaria, and to the end of the earth."

ACTS 1:6-8 NKJV

We can be impatient at times, especially when we have held onto hope for a long time. The Israelites were desperate to be released from their oppression; they wanted to experience victory in their nation.

You might have hopes for a relationship to be restored, for a family member to receive salvation, to have a child, or to get a promotion. It isn't God's nature to tell us exactly how things are going to turn out, but he does assure you that you will have the power of the Holy Spirit and you can trust that God will still work in your circumstances.

Holy Spirit, thank you that you are with me. Let me become more aware of your presence so I will be assured that you are still working powerfully in my circumstances. I hold onto the hope that you will bring my hopes to fulfilment.

When He had spoken these things, while they watched, He was taken up, and a cloud received Him out of their sight. And while they looked steadfastly toward heaven as He went up, behold, two men stood by them in white apparel, who also said, "Men of Galilee, why do you stand gazing up into heaven? This same Jesus, who was taken up from you into heaven, will so come in like manner as you saw Him go into heaven."

ACTS 1:9-11 NKJV

How often do we find that we are looking so far into the future that we forget about our present? Jesus didn't want everyone to keep staring up into the clouds until he returned; he wanted them to continue to play their part in furthering the kingdom.

Jesus will return, but until then, be encouraged that he has so many things for you to do. Be aware of the present circumstances where he gives you the opportunity to enjoy and take part in spreading the good news. Don't worry about the future because he has that under control.

Jesus, thank you that you will return one day. Thank you for allowing me to be a part of your kingdom coming, here on earth. Help me not be so consumed with the future that I forget to live in the moment.

What future things are you so focused on that you are forgetting what is right before you?

Power Together

When the Day of Pentecost had fully come, they were all with one accord in one place. And suddenly there came a sound from heaven, as of a rushing mighty wind, and it filled the whole house where they were sitting.

ACTS 2:1-2 NKJV

It's interesting to note that the power of the Holy Spirit came when all the believers were in one place. The Holy Spirit is with us individually, but it's important to spend time with other believers because it builds our faith, encourages us in difficult times, and brings life where we may not find hope on our own.

The Holy Spirit can be gentle or powerful and it is good to expect that he can fill a room with his presence.

Holy Spirit, thank you for your power and movement in my life. There are circumstances in my life where I need you to work powerfully, and I ask that I would see that power today.

*There appeared to them divided tongues, as of fire,
and one sat upon each of them. And they were all filled with
the Holy Spirit and began to speak with other tongues,
as the Spirit gave them utterance.*

ACTS 2:3-4 NKJV

The Holy Spirit was so evident to the early church. People could feel, see, and hear the presence of God. The languages that they were speaking could be understood by other people and this got everyone talking.

When we ask for God's presence, we need to expect that it will be obvious. The Holy Spirit wants to be made known in your life so others can witness Christ's power within you.

Holy Spirit, thank you for being a tangible presence in my day-to-day life. Thank you for making your presence obvious, even tonight as I dwell on how near you are to me. Help me to sleep with the knowledge that you are near, and give me peace in knowing that you will be with me for another day.

Did you feel God's presence today? Are others seeing God's Spirit at work in you?

Goodwill

*They worshiped together at the Temple each day, met in homes
for the Lord's Supper, and shared their meals with great joy and
generosity - all the while praising God and enjoying the goodwill
of all the people.*

ACTS 2:46-47 NLT

It would be great if all our church experiences matched the
description of this one, but we can be left disappointed by the
lack of community and genuine engagement in generosity
and goodwill toward one another.

These days we can go to church and leave without any sense
of being together. Why not be an instigator of change if this is
the case in your faith community? It doesn't have to be big—
invite someone over for lunch, give a little extra to someone
who is struggling, or offer a prayer or word of encouragement
to someone you are sitting behind. A little kindness goes a
long way.

*God, give me an opportunity to contribute a spirit of goodwill
toward others that share this faith. Help me to be a witness to
those outside of the faith, that they would see the love between
Christians as a light to Christ's love for them.*

*Each day the Lord added to their fellowship those
who were being saved.*

ACTS 2:47 NLT

God wants us to enjoy being together as a family of believers.
We are united in Christ and there are times when we need to
behave more in unison than we do.

It may take a bit of effort on your part, but being generous in
word and deed toward your brother or sister in Christ will
be one of the biggest witnesses to those around you. How
wonderful it would be to experience leading people to Christ
because of the love they have seen between people in the
church.

*Jesus, thank you for the other believers in my life who continue
to encourage me in my faith. Help me to be an encouragement to
these people and to show them grace and generosity. If there is
someone out there tonight who is seeking you, may they find you.*

What are some ways you could show some goodwill toward
another believer tomorrow?

No Other Name

"Let me clearly state to all of you and to all the people of Israel that he was healed by the powerful name of Jesus Christ the Nazarene, the man you crucified but whom God raised from the dead. For Jesus is the one referred to in the Scriptures, where it says, 'The stone that you builders rejected has now become the cornerstone.'"

ACTS 4:10-11 NLT

It's hard to imagine that after all Jesus' miracles and teaching, people still wanted to crucify him. He didn't come in violence or arrogance, yet he was still despised by many. Despite all the rejection, Jesus was victorious.

Be encouraged if you are facing challenges today, that while people may reject you for no good reason, you can be victorious. Stand tall and be proud of who you are in Christ.

Jesus, thank you for reminding me that you understand rejection. Help me during my low points to take courage that my confidence comes from you and not others.

There is salvation in no one else! God has given no other name under heaven by which we must be saved.

ACTS 4:12 NLT

The one thing that the people in Jesus' day needed was salvation, yet they crucified the only person who could offer it. They didn't believe that Jesus was the Messiah.

We live in a society where people typically don't believe that Jesus is the only way to salvation. We have to struggle against a concept that all truths can be accepted. Remember this Scripture and hold firm to your faith. It is Jesus, and only Jesus, who saves.

God, sometimes I can be complacent about my faith and take on the world's view that there are many truths. Thank you for reminding me that you are the only way. Help me to be secure in this knowledge and to share it with others when I get the chance.

What are your greatest challenges to sharing Jesus with others?

Guided Steps

As for Philip, an angel of the Lord said to him, "Go south down the desert road that runs from Jerusalem to Gaza." So he started out, and he met the treasurer of Ethiopia, a eunuch of great authority under the Kandake, the queen of Ethiopia. The eunuch had gone to Jerusalem to worship, and he was now returning. Seated in his carriage, he was reading aloud from the book of the prophet Isaiah. The Holy Spirit said to Philip, "Go over and walk along beside the carriage."

ACTS 8:26-29 NKJV

We rarely know God's plan when he speaks to us, but Philip is a great example of the reward in paying attention to God's directions. God didn't tell Philip the whole plan, but he guided him each step of the way.

As you take some time this morning to acknowledge your dependence on God, remember that the Holy Spirit is there to guide you in each step that you take. All you need to do is be willing to pay attention.

Holy Spirit, speak to me today. Thank you that you are always guiding me and that you want to work in and through my life. I choose to pay attention to your Word today.

Philip ran over and heard the man reading from the prophet Isaiah. Philip asked, "Do you understand what you are reading?" The man replied, "How can I, unless someone instructs me?" And he urged Philip to come up into the carriage and sit with him.

ACTS 8:30-31 NKJV

God was able to use Philip to not only help this man to understand Scripture, but he also led him to salvation and Philip was able to baptize him. Philip was ready to hear and obey God and to respond to his call for that day.

Your day is always better when you choose to listen and respond to the Holy Spirit's leading. It may not be a conversion, but it could be a simple act of showing Christ-like kindness to someone who needs it. If you missed that chance today, there is always tomorrow.

Holy Spirit, thank you for your gentle guidance during my day. Please give me eyes to see and ears to hear the needs around me. Give me peace as I sleep, knowing that you are ever present.

In what ways have you been able to respond to the promptings of the Holy Spirit?

Dramatic Conversions

*Ananias went and entered the house. He laid his hands on
Saul and said, "Brother Saul, the Lord Jesus, who appeared to you
on your way here, has sent me so that you may regain your sight
and be filled with the Holy Spirit." And immediately something
like scales fell from his eyes, and his sight was restored. Then he
got up and was baptized, and after taking some food,
he regained his strength.*

ACTS 9:17-19 NRSV

The conversion of Saul was pretty dramatic. This was the man
who had been persecuting the Christians for their belief, and
God chose him to become one of the biggest advocates for
Christ.

If you think back to your conversion it was perhaps less
dramatic; yet at some point it must have seemed liked
your eyes were opened to the truth. Our God is amazing.
Remember this conversion as you go about your day and
let the knowledge of the truth that you have inside you be
expressed in some way to others.

*God, thank you for revealing yourself to me so I would believe. I
am so grateful for the opportunity to be a part of your kingdom on
earth and I ask I would be bold enough to begin to declare your
truth to the world.*

*For several days he was with the disciples in Damascus,
and immediately he began to proclaim Jesus in the synagogues,
saying, "He is the Son of God."*

ACTS 9:19-20 NRSV

Saul's conversion was more than just experiencing a miracle
of blindness and then sight. This miracle was more than
physical; it represented the state of Saul's heart in being
blinded to Jesus as the Son of God and then receiving the
truth with that stark realization. His belief system turned
around almost instantly.

Be encouraged that even if you didn't get the chance today
to share the good news, God can work miracles in people's
hearts. Continue to be faithful in being like Christ, and pray
that he works wonders in the people who you are around.

*Jesus, thank you that you used someone that seemed so hard-
hearted toward you to convert huge amounts of people to faith.
Help me to never stop believing that you can do miracles in the
hearts of people around me.*

Who are the people in your life that need Christ but
seem opposed to the Christian faith? Pray for a dramatic
conversion.

Work of Faith

*Now I commend you to God and to the message of his grace,
a message that is able to build you up and to give you the
inheritance among all who are sanctified.*

ACTS 20:32 NRSV

Paul did incredible works for Christ. He preached, performed miracles, was put in prison, and was beaten for his faith. Paul held firm to his calling despite all the obstacles, and he learned to be content and joyful throughout the hardest times. His words to carry on this faith are encouraging.

You might feel like you have gone through a lot for your faith, whether it is people who don't believe you, or living a hard life where you still proclaim that God is good. Remember that today this message from hundreds of years ago is for you—it is a message of grace, a message able to build you up when you remember the inheritance you have in Christ.

God, I have felt discouraged about my faith at times, especially when I feel that people around me belittle me for my belief. Help me to remember the inheritance I have in you and to be strengthened by your message of grace.

I coveted no one's silver or gold or clothing. You know for yourselves
that I worked with my own hands to support myself
and my companions.

ACTS 20:33-34 NRSV

Paul had a lot of support from believers, but he also had to continue to work for himself. Sometimes we think that all Paul did was go from mission to mission; yet at times he had to stay and earn his own money in his profession—as a tent maker.

Whatever you were busy doing today, remember that God not only wants you to be a great missionary for him, but that he values the work that you already do because it is part of his plan for you.

Father God, thank you for giving me work to do. Thank you that not only do you want me to speak your truth, but to live your truth. Give me peace as I rest from a hard day today, knowing that you think I have done a good job.

In what ways are you able to support yourself and those in the faith? Be encouraged that God is pleased with your work.

Grief

"How the mighty have fallen in the midst of the battle!
Jonathan lies slain on your high places. I am distressed for you,
my brother Jonathan; very pleasant have you been to me;
your love to me was extraordinary."

2 Samuel 1:25-26 esv

The relationship of David and Jonathan is known for being a
deep friendship, closer than brothers. It is fitting that when
Jonathan dies in battle, David writes and mourns for him. It
is often said that the greater the love, the greater the grief.

You may have experienced the loss of a loved one or know
of someone who has, and it is important that we are able
to express this grief, remembering that God is our great
comforter.

God, today I remember those whom I have loved and lost. I pray
that you would help me to express my grief in a way that is healing
and recognizes your comfort. Thank you that you care for my
heart.

"How the mighty have fallen, and the weapons of war perished!"

2 SAMUEL 1:27 NKJV

A whole lot of things can change in one day. In this particular battle, Israel lost their king. The whole nation would have been mourning.

When significant events happen in our lives or in our nation, remember that God is always in control. Nothing has surprised him, and he is able to comfort and restore.

God, thank you that you are always in control. Thank you that no matter what has happened in my day, I can find comfort and peace in you.

How have you seen God restore life in times of great distress?

Intervention

Abner called to Joab, "Shall the sword devour forever? Do you not know that the end will be bitter? How long will it be before you tell your people to turn from the pursuit of their brothers?"

2 SAMUEL 2:26 ESV

If you have spent enough time around children you will know that sometimes the fighting between siblings seems endless, and often pointless. We all recognize that fighting rarely gets us what we want and yet we still enter into arguments and disputes, rarely considering the consequence.

As Abner concluded to Jacob, fighting will often end in bitterness. As you prepare to talk, plan, and work with people today, remember that peace is better than the sword.

God, thank you for giving me opportunities to work and discuss things with people. Help me to conduct these discussions today with peace and grace in all circumstances.

Joab said, "As God lives, if you had not spoken, surely the men
would not have given up the pursuit of their brothers until the
morning." So Joab blew the trumpet, and all the men stopped and
pursued Israel no more, nor did they fight anymore.

2 SAMUEL 2:27-28 ESV

Sometimes our fighting gets out of control and we need
intervention. Perhaps we are the ones who are called to
intervene when things get out of hand.

Speaking up for justice can be a hard job, but the
consequences of not suggesting an alternative can be dire.
Joab recognized that the courage of Abner to speak up would
actually save lives.

God, I pray for those difficult circumstances that are surrounding
me right now. Thank you that you have called me to be a
peacemaker. I recognize that sometimes this means having to speak
in boldness for justice. Give me the strength to allow intervention in
my life or to be the person who intervenes for your cause.

Are you in the middle of a dispute that needs intervention?
Are you being called to intervene in a situation that has
gotten out of control?

Celebrations

David danced before the Lord with all his might,
wearing a priestly garment.

2 Samuel 6:14 NLT

David was a keen worshipper, but he also had a great reason to dance. The Ark of the Covenant was back in his possession, and having the Lord's presence with him meant that God's favor was with David and his kingdom.

David had a huge reason to celebrate. You have a reason to celebrate too. The presence of God is with you, he is in your heart and that means his favor is with you. Dance before the Lord like no one is watching today.

God, thank you for sending your Son, Jesus, who made a way for your presence to be living inside of me. Bring me the joy of knowing that I have your strength, power, and grace within me, and give me an extra spring in my step as I go about my day.

David and all the people of Israel brought up the Ark of the LORD with shouts of joy and the blowing of rams' horns.

2 SAMUEL 6:15 NLT

Celebrations are so much better with others; we need to be able to share our joy and thanksgiving.

When the Ark of the Lord was brought back to the Israelites, there was a party with music, dancing, shouting, and singing. Celebrations are part of our faith and remind us of the goodness of God.

Jesus, thank you that I have been reminded of your presence in me today. Even though I am weary tonight, I pray that you would continue to give me energy that comes with the joy of following you. Let my heart attitude be an encouragement to other Christians in my life this week.

What can you celebrate about God this week, and with whom can you celebrate?

Sovereign Lord

"You are God, O Sovereign LORD. Your words are truth, and you have promised these good things to your servant."

2 SAMUEL 7:28 NLT

It is good to remember and acknowledge that God is sovereign. This world has kings, rulers, presidents, and many leaders, but none are as great as our God. He is the everlasting king and he is the one that makes promises that are enduring and true.

Remind yourself today, as you go into a world full of different systems and beliefs, that God is truth and that he will continue to be good toward you, his faithful servant.

God, you are sovereign, and you are my Lord. Thank you for showing me favor despite a world that has shown me hardship. Thank you that I can lift my eyes above the things of the world to see your ways as the truth. I honor you today and ask that your truth would shine through me.

> *"May it please you to bless the house of your servant, so that it may continue forever before you. For you have spoken, and when you grant a blessing to your servant, O Sovereign LORD, it is an eternal blessing!"*
>
> 2 SAMUEL 7:29 NLT

As you take this time to sit down and read a Scripture, let yourself reflect on God's blessings. It may have been a hard or frustrating day; you would have had moments of feeling successful and moments of feeling failure.

Remember, as a servant of the sovereign Lord, that you and your household are blessed. You may not feel as though you have been blessed with much talent or wealth, but God has blessed you with eternal life and one day all things will be restored.

God, thank you for blessing me with the promise of eternity. Encourage my heart this evening as I rest in knowing that many blessings are yet to come.

What blessings have you received from God throughout your life?

On Behalf Of

David asked, "Is there anyone still left of the house of Saul to whom I can show kindness for Jonathan's sake?"

2 SAMUEL 9:1 NIV

Love and hate can be emotions that carry through generations. David's love for Jonathan gave him the desire to show kindness toward Jonathan's relatives.

We live in world where people readily hold onto bitterness from the past. Take a page out of David's book today, and think of who you could show love to on behalf of someone you have really cared about.

God, I take the time this morning to pray for all those families that are holding on to hate and bitterness in their heart because of past wrongdoings. Soften those hearts toward the grace that is found in you. If there is anyone that I can show kindness to on behalf of others that I love, please bring them to mind today.

When Mephibosheth son of Jonathan, the son of Saul, came to David, he bowed down to pay him honor. David said, "Mephibosheth!" "At your service," he replied. "Don't be afraid," David said to him, "for I will surely show you kindness for the sake of your father Jonathan. I will restore to you all the land that belonged to your grandfather Saul, and you will always eat at my table."

2 Samuel 9:6-7 NIV

Mephibosheth had every reason to be afraid of what the king could do to him. His grandfather, Saul, had often hated David and sought to kill him a number of times.

Instead of revenge, David chose to overlook Saul's hatred because of the greater good—his love for Jonathan. Mephibosheth received the blessing of a man who chose love over evil.

Jesus, thank you for reminding me of the soft heart that David had toward his great friend Jonathan. Thank you for the gift of compassion and kindness. Give me insight in how to pay this kindness forward to others around me.

In what ways can you show extreme kindness to someone on behalf of someone you love?

Battle Plans

Joab saw that there were battle lines in front of him and behind him; so he selected some of the best troops in Israel and deployed them against the Arameans. He put the rest of the men under the command of Abishai his brother and deployed them against the Ammonites. Joab said, "If the Arameans are too strong for me, then you are to come to my rescue; but if the Ammonites are too strong for you, then I will come to rescue you."

2 SAMUEL 10:9-11 NIV

Christians speak of peace, love, and grace, but there are times when we have to fight for our faith. This isn't usually a physical battle, but can be a battle of the mind, heart, emotions, or will.

We need other Christians in this life to help us in our battles. Sometimes the battle is too strong for a friend and we have to come to the rescue. At times, the battle will be too hard for us and we will need to call on our friends for help. As you prepare for the day ahead, be ready with God's armor for whatever may come your way.

God, thank you for friends that will be willing to come to my rescue in times of need. I pray you would help me be attentive to the troubles that others may be having and to stand alongside them and help them fight.

"Be strong, and let us fight bravely for our people and the cities of our God. The LORD will do what is good in his sight."

2 SAMUEL 10:12 NIV

The world is full of so many things that are not God's way. Your day may have been surrounded by all kinds of worldly images, habits, and behaviors. Rather than be discouraged by the lack of morality in the world, be a brave warrior for what is good.

Our battle isn't a physical battle, but we are called to stand up for truth. God's goodness will always prevail; we are on the winning side. Let this truth be what allows you to be brave in the face of opposition.

Heavenly Father, give me strength and cause me to be brave for your cause. I know that your goodness has always prevailed, and yet sometimes I am discouraged by the evil in the world around me. As I sleep tonight, let the words of this Scripture be real to my heart; you will do what is good in your sight.

What opposition have you been facing lately that needs to be bravely met with God's truth?

Confrontation

"I gave your master's house to you, and your master's wives into your arms. I gave you all Israel and Judah. And if all this had been too little, I would have given you even more. Why did you despise the word of the Lord by doing what is evil in his eyes? You struck down Uriah the Hittite with the sword and took his wife to be your own. You killed him with the sword of the Ammonites."

2 Samuel 12:8-9 NIV

God had shown David great favor. The temptation with this favor was that David eventually took liberty with his status and power. God wants to give us good things and humanity has shown time and time again that we are not trustworthy. David tried to cover up his sin a few times, but none of that worked. He was confronted by the prophet, Nathan, and forced to acknowledge his sin before men, and before God.

It is in our nature to cover up our sin, but don't wait to be confronted when you have wrong to admit. Be brave and own up to your wrongdoing, knowing that the grace of Jesus has been provided to you through the power of the cross.

Jesus, I am thankful that I am not the only one to have sinned greatly. I know that my sinful condition is no different than others, but I ask that I always turn to you and ask for forgiveness instead of waiting for my sin to be exposed. Thank you for your ever-abounding grace.

"The sword will never depart from your house, because you despised me and took the wife of Uriah the Hittite to be your own."

2 SAMUEL 12:8-9 NIV

You are forgiven for any of the sins you have committed; they are in the past. Don't dwell on these things, but instead acknowledge any of the consequences that may have come from living apart from God's ways.

David's sin was forgiven, but there was still a fallout from his actions. Consider the consequences before you make decisions, and use the wisdom that Christ has placed within you.

God, I confess my wrongdoing, as I dwell in your presence here tonight. I thank you for your sacrifice on the cross that allows me to sit closely with you because you have taken away the guilt and shame. I acknowledge my wrongs before you now, and thank you that I can live in the cleansing power of your love.

What sin do you need to confess right now to avoid confrontation and consequence?

Evidence

Since the creation of the world God's invisible qualities—
his eternal power and divine nature—have been clearly seen,
being understood from what has been made,
so that people are without excuse.

ROMANS 2:20 NIV

You only need to view the vastness of the ocean or the glory of the night stars to wonder about the world and its beginnings. While modern science has come a long way toward explaining how things within our natural world work, there is nothing that will ever adequately explain supernatural wonders or the true beginning of the universe.

Any deep thinking and observation of the world should lead to faith in a Creator. Allow yourself to marvel in the glory of creation today.

Lord God, Creator of the universe, I am in awe of your creation and the wonders that are all around me. Help me to acknowledge your glory today as I see your handiwork in the small and big things of this world.

Although they knew God, they neither glorified him as God nor gave thanks to him, but their thinking became futile and their foolish hearts were darkened.

ROMANS 2:21 NIV

Our days are surrounded by people who don't know God or acknowledge him for anything in their lives. In fact, it seems that people are quick to attribute good things to themselves and then blame all the bad things on God. This is the futile thinking of the world, either that God isn't fair or good or simply that he doesn't exist at all. This is why it is good to notice creation as you go about your day.

When you have seen the beauty of creation, either in nature, an adorable animal, or in the goodness of humans, you can be encouraged that you are living in the light.

God, thank you for the things that I have seen and heard today that have reminded me of your light and life in this world. Thank you that my heart and mind can dwell on eternal things.

What things have you noticed today that reflect God's glory?

Judgment

You, therefore, have no excuse, you who pass judgment on someone else, for at whatever point you judge another, you are condemning yourself, because you who pass judgment do the same things. Now we know that God's judgment against those who do such things is based on truth.

ROMANS 2:1-2 NIV

Simply put, it's not right to judge other people. We live in a society where we feel free to express our thoughts, opinions, and even judgments on what others are doing, wearing, or saying.

While we are entitled to our feelings and opinions, we should be standing up for mercy and letting God be the one who ascribes worth and ultimate judgment because he is the only one who knows the true heart. Remember to be merciful and gracious in your thoughts and speech toward others today.

Father God, you are the one and only true and righteous judge. Thank you that I don't need to be the one to decide what is wrong because I know that I do wrong things as well. Thank you for your grace that shows me that I should also be gracious to those around me.

*When you, a mere human being, pass judgment on them and
yet do the same things, do you think you will escape God's
judgment? Or do you show contempt for the riches of his
kindness, forbearance and patience, not realizing that God's
kindness is intended to lead you to repentance?*

ROMANS 2:3-4 NIV

It is not pointing the finger at someone that leads them to
want to repent. When we allow our own judgments on the
matter to be expressed, people can become defensive and
upset.

Your own repentance shouldn't be because you feel guilt, but
rather because you feel loved. Show this same love toward
one another, and let this love and kindness lead people back
to restoration with God and with others.

*God, I am so blessed that your love, kindness, and patience has
led me toward you. Thank you for forgiving my sin. This evening,
as I think about your love for me, help me to have love for others so
they may be led toward your forgiveness and grace.*

How have you seen God's kindness lead you to repentance?
Who can you show this same kindness and patience to?

His Standards

God has shown us a way to be made right with him without keeping the requirements of the law, as was promised in the writings of Moses and the prophets long ago. We are made right with God by placing our faith in Jesus Christ. And this is true for everyone who believes, no matter who we are.

ROMANS 3:21-22 NLT

There was nothing wrong with the law that God's people had been following since the days of Moses, except that nobody could live exactly to its standard. Paul was pointing out that this was something that the law showed us; that we were incapable of doing the right thing without help.

That's why it's important to believe that Jesus did the right thing for us, and it is our belief in him that makes us righteous. It doesn't matter who you are today, it is your faith that saves you.

Jesus, I believe that you have covered all my shortcomings. Thank you that it is not how closely I stick to a set of rules that makes me righteous, but it is my relationship with you and my belief in your grace that saves me. Encourage my heart as I head into this day.

Everyone has sinned; we all fall short of God's glorious standard. Yet God, in his grace, freely makes us right in his sight. He did this through Christ Jesus when he freed us from the penalty for our sins.

ROMANS 3:23-24 NLT

You may have come back from a day full of things that didn't go right. You might be frustrated at yourself, your kids, or your co-workers. Life is full of disappointments, especially when we are hoping for better outcomes.

God had a standard too, and we all fall desperately short until we realize that it's not our shortcomings that God measures us on; he sees us through our renewed life in Christ. Let go of today's disappointments and be encouraged that Christ is in the business of making all things right again.

Christ Jesus, thank you for setting me free from my own expectations. I am sorry when I judge myself and others based on a set of rules. You have given me freedom through your death on the cross, and I choose to rest and celebrate that freedom tonight.

What standards are you holding yourself to that you need to let go of?

Endurance by Hope

We can rejoice, too, when we run into problems and trials, for we know that they help us develop endurance. And endurance develops strength of character, and character strengthens our confident hope of salvation.

ROMANS 5:3-4 NLT

As a Christian, you have the joy and peace of knowing that this life, or this world as we know it, is not the end. While we may experience struggles and disappointment, or see a world full of pain and suffering, we know that we are part of God's great restoration plan.

When you can see the end of the race, you can continue to run it, knowing that the goal is in sight. Whatever you face today, face it with endurance with the end goal in sight.

Lord God, I am encouraged in remembering that all my problems, and all the difficulties around me, will one day be made right and restored. Help me to endure the difficult times with strength of character and with hope so others can witness the steadfast joy that keeps me going.

This hope will not lead to disappointment. For we know how dearly God loves us, because he has given us the Holy Spirit to fill our hearts with his love.

ROMANS 5:5 NLT

Have you been able to get through the day with the hope of Jesus in your heart? At times it takes determination and strength of will to remember to push through the discouragement and know that your hope is not futile.

The Scriptures promise that you will not be disappointed in the end. Christ will return, and the troubles of this life will cease to exist. God has also given us the Holy Spirit to help us in our times of weakness. Let him minister to your heart tonight and ask for restoration of a deep hope within your soul.

Holy Spirit, help me to see beyond my troubles today. I know I cannot escape difficult times, so I ask for your strength and endurance. I know that can only come because I recognize your love and the truth that one day this world will be restored to goodness.

What difficulties are you facing at this time? Ask the Holy Spirit to remind you of the hope you have through Christ.

Adoption

All who are led by the Spirit of God are children of God. For you did not receive a spirit of slavery to fall back into fear, but you have received a spirit of adoption. When we cry, "Abba! Father!" it is that very Spirit bearing witness]with our spirit that we are children of God.

ROMANS 8:14-16 NRSV

We don't always feel like we are any different to others in the world around us. In a way we are not because we are all human. However, when you chose to believe in redemption through Jesus Christ, you became a child that is led by God's Spirit, not the spirit of the world.

You belong to the family of God and you have nothing to fear. God is your Father and he loves you so much that when you call out to him, he hears and responds.

Father God, I accept that I am part of your family now and that you care for me as a loving Father would care for his children. Help me to be led by your Spirit today, not a spirit of fear. Let me be someone who shares your acceptance with others so they might become of this family too.

If children, then heirs, heirs of God and joint heirs with Christ—if, in fact, we suffer with him so that we may also be glorified with him.

ROMANS 8:17 NRSV

We know that while Jesus was on earth, he had a very special relationship with the Father. In fact, he says that he and the Father are one. Jesus listened to his Father's instruction and obeyed the will of the Father and it was promised that he would be glorified after his suffering to sit at the right hand of God.

Isn't it amazing that we get to share in this same gift? It might mean suffering for a time, but we are also destined to be glorified and be with God, our Father.

God, I sometimes fear the suffering that this world brings. I pray that you would give me perspective tonight, as I remember that while Jesus suffered, he also was raised to life to be glorified with you. Encourage my spirit so I can face tomorrow with wonderful expectation that your goodness toward me will prevail.

What things have you gone through today that have reminded you that you are a child of God?

On Your Side

What then are we to say about these things? If God is for us, who is against us? He who did not withhold his own Son, but gave him up for all of us, will he not with him also give us everything else?

ROMANS 8:31-32 NRSV

There is a lot of conflict in this world, from nation against nation, to family member against family member. Conflict, whether big or small, is not a part of God's intention for humanity. Christ wants unity in our lives.

Whatever you face today, whether a disagreement with your spouse, disobedience from a child, or a dispute with your neighbor, remember that God's justice will prevail. Whether you are right or wrong, God is for you, and although you may be trying to defend yourself from others, you never have to defend yourself from God because he accepts you exactly as you are.

God, sometimes I feel like the whole world is against me. Please help me to settle those areas of conflict with grace and humility. Give me a gentle spirit as I speak to others today. Thank you that I can rest assured that you are on my side and that you care about my heart.

*Who will bring any charge against God's elect? It is God who
justifies. Who is to condemn? It is Christ Jesus, who died, yes,
who was raised, who is at the right hand of God,
who indeed intercedes for us.*

ROMANS 8:33-34 NRSV

We may not feel overt persecution in our day-to-day lives, but
sometimes we feel the subtle disapproval from those who do
not know or accept Christ. The world is pretty hostile toward
the Christian faith and can condemn us for our morality or
beliefs.

If you have experienced this today, pray for those who have
condemned you. Remember that God accepts you for who you
are, and he will justify his children.

*Jesus, thank you that you understand what it is like to be wrongly
accused. You went through the worst of human hatred and
misunderstanding and yet you still loved us all enough to die for
us. Please intercede for me as I experience rejection for my faith,
and continue to remind me that I am justified through you.*

In what ways have you felt condemned or accused lately?
Bring these hurts to the foot of the cross.

Harmony of Believers

May the God of endurance and encouragement grant you to live in such harmony with one another, in accord with Christ Jesus, that together you may with one voice glorify the God and Father of our Lord Jesus Christ.

ROMANS 15:5-6 ESV

The church has been, unfortunately, too well-known for its many divisions and factions. We argue with one another over too many points of difference.

Instead of looking at where you differ from others, why not focus on what you agree on? It is not in our disagreements where we will find truth; it is in our unity. This is what God uses as a witness to his love. Make an effort today to humbly acknowledge that your thoughts and opinions are not better than others. Strive for a unified voice instead.

God, I am sorry when I have focused on the differences in faith. I know that at the end of it all, a lot of these things will not matter. Help me to remember, in my discussion with other Christians today, to glorify you by focusing on what makes us unified—your grace.

*Welcome one another as Christ has welcomed you,
for the glory of God.*

ROMANS 15:7 ESV

When we humbly recognize that none of us can truly know all things, we allow ourselves to level out the playing field with one another. It is much easier to have genuine community with our brothers and sisters in Christ when we all think of each other as equals.

This creates a welcoming spirit that the world needs to see in order to recognize the grace and power of Christ in the body of believers.

God, I am sorry when I have allowed my differing opinions to get in the way of welcoming other believers into conversations and spaces. Help me to be a voice of acceptance and grace so you are glorified.

Have you had a welcoming heart toward other believers for the sake of God's glory?

Succession

The king's servants came to congratulate our LORD King David, saying, "May your God make the name of Solomon more famous than yours, and make his throne greater than your throne." And the king bowed himself on the bed.

1 KINGS 1:47 ESV

It is part of our humanness to want our legacy to live on long after we are gone. David had at least two sons vying for the throne, and David wanted that son to be Solomon. Rather than wanting to be the best king that ever lived, David longed for a king to rule the people even better than he had.

As you make plans for the future, remember to think of the people who will come after you. Are you making a path for them to follow in your footsteps? Are you longing for their positive impact to be even greater than yours?

Lord God, thank you for the life that you have called me to live. I want to do great things for your kingdom, but I also want to pave a way for those who come after me. Help me to encourage and equip them to do even better.

The king also said, "Blessed be the LORD, the God of Israel,
who has granted someone to sit on my throne this day,
my own eyes seeing it."

1 KINGS 1:48 ESV

We don't always get the chance to see promises fulfilled in our lifetime. God has his own timing and sometimes we won't see it this side of eternity.

David felt blessed because he was able to see his son, Solomon, become the king of Israel. His heart had yearned for another good king and now the promise was being fulfilled.

God of all creation, thank you for your greater plan that I know you will fulfil. Help me to trust that the promises you have made either to me or to this generation will be fulfilled. Let me be blessed by seeing some promises with my own eyes.

What promises from God do you hope to see with your own eyes?

His Ways

When David's time to die drew near, he commanded Solomon
his son, saying, "I am about to go the way of all the earth. Be
strong, and show yourself a man, and keep the charge of
the LORD your God, walking in his ways and keeping his statutes,
his commandments, his rules, and his testimonies, as it is written
in the Law of Moses, that you may prosper in all that you do and
wherever you turn."

1 KINGS 2:1-3 ESV

We don't need books or inspirational speakers to tell us how
to be successful: we just need to heed the advice of David to
his son, Solomon. Be strong and walk in God's ways, and then
you will prosper in all that you do.

As you get ready for today's activities, think about what it
means to be strong and walk in God's ways. Strength doesn't
have to mean that you can withstand anything that comes
your way, it simply means that you continue to trust God
despite everything you face.

Father, I choose to stay strong and unwavering when it comes
to what I know your Word says. Thank you that I have the holy
Scriptures to dwell on. Give me greater understanding of your Word
so I can discern your direction for my life.

If your sons pay close attention to their way, to walk before me in faithfulness with all their heart and with all their soul, you shall not lack a man on the throne of Israel.

1 KINGS 2:4 ESV

There were a lot of successors to David's throne that did not walk before God with faithfulness of heart. Leaders seem to face particular challenges when it comes to pride, greed, wealth, and fame.

Having a great position of power can often be a temptation to stray from God's ways of humility and justice. If you are a leader in any area, remember these temptations and choose to follow God's ways above your own ideas and motivation.

Holy Spirit, be my guide as I try to walk in your ways. I don't always know which way is right and I am confounded by my own motivations. Give me strength of character to hold fast to the path of righteousness that you have set before me.

What area do you recognize as a weakness in your own life? How can you submit these areas to God's ways?

Discernment

"Your servant is in the midst of Your people which You have chosen, a great people who are too many to be numbered or counted. So give Your servant an understanding heart to judge Your people to discern between good and evil. For who is able to judge this great people of Yours?"

1 KINGS 3:8-9 NASB

Whether you are still studying, at home with children, or working in a full-time career, the decisions that you have to make get more complicated as your responsibilities increase.

It may have seemed like a simple thing for Solomon to have asked for discernment, but in reality a whole nation relied on him for his answers. You need discernment in your decision-making even as you go about your day-to-day business. Let God show you wisdom every step of the way.

God, give me an understanding heart today, to make decisions and discern between good and evil. I cannot do this on my own and need your wisdom. Thank you for the presence of your Holy Spirit to guide me.

*It was pleasing in the sight of the L*ORD *that Solomon had asked this thing. God said to him, "Because you have asked this thing and have not asked for yourself long life, nor have asked riches for yourself, nor have you asked for the life of your enemies, but have asked for yourself discernment to understand justice, behold, I have done according to your words. Behold, I have given you a wise and discerning heart, so that there has been no one like you before you, nor shall one like you arise after you."*

1 KINGS 3:10-12 NASB

God wants us to acknowledge him in everything we do. He is ready and willing to provide us with wisdom and direction in our decisions, but we need to be ready to ask. Sometimes we are consumed with asking God for things like health and provision.

As you spend some time with your heavenly Father this evening, remember that a wise and discerning heart will lead to greater blessing than money or fame.

God, I am humbled that I am a child in your kingdom. Thank you for the privilege of being an heir to all that you have. Help me to focus tonight on what you require of me in the area of justice, that I would have a wise a discerning heart to display your love to the world.

What do you truly desire from God?

The Answer Is No

> "The LORD said to my father David, 'Because it was in your heart
> to build a house for My name, you did well that it was in your
> heart. Nevertheless you shall not build the house, but your son
> who will be born to you, he will build the house for My name.'"

1 KINGS 8:18-19 NASB

We might ask things of God with all the right intentions, yet
sometimes God just needs to say no. It is hard to accept no
as an answer, but we need to trust that God has the bigger
picture in mind. He is the one that is ultimately in control of
his plan and although he is pleased with us, it doesn't always
mean we get what we want.

Today, as you go about your tasks, be encouraged that God is
pleased with you, and trust that he will figure out the rest.

*God, give me humility and grace to accept that even some of my
best intentions will not be answered in the way that I want them
to be. Help me to recognize when your greater plan is at work and
give me a thankful heart that I can trust you.*

"The LORD has fulfilled His word which He spoke; for I have risen in place of my father David and sit on the throne of Israel, as the LORD promised, and have built the house for the name of the LORD, the God of Israel."

1 KINGS 8:20 NASB

Even when God says no to a good intention, he still works out his plan for good. David didn't see the temple that he had in his heart to build, yet it was still built. Solomon likely built the temple even better than his father would have because of his great wisdom. The new temple was built out of the best material with the best workmanship known to man.

You might have to accept that your good intentions are the start of something incredible, but someone else may get the chance to do the thing you had been wanting to do. God is always on the throne, and he will prevail.

God, I pray for the people who may finish the work or the plan I have started. Thank you that you have used me and that you can use others. Help some of these dreams that I have that are a part of your will to be even bigger and more beautiful than I could have imagined.

What dream could God be saying no to you about? Can you accept that he might make this happen through someone else?

Dwelling Within

"Will God indeed dwell on the earth? Behold, heaven and the highest heaven cannot contain You, how much less this house which I have built!"

1 KINGS 8:27 NASB

It seems a little absurd that the Israelites carried around the Ark of the Covenant, said to house the presence of God. God wasn't limited to a special box, yet the ark was symbolic of God's presence with us.

Even the magnificence of Solomon's temple doesn't seem adequate to house the presence of the Creator of the universe. It may seem just as absurd that God would dwell in a human body, but he did that as well—in Jesus Christ and now in us.

Lord God, you are the Lord over everything, yet you continue to show your love toward me by allowing your presence to dwell in me. Let your presence spill out of my life and into the lives of others today.

"Have regard to the prayer of Your servant and to his supplication, O LORD my God, to listen to the cry and to the prayer which Your servant prays before You today; that Your eyes may be open toward this house night and day, toward the place of which You have said, 'My name shall be there,' to listen to the prayer which Your servant shall pray toward this place."

1 KINGS 8:28-29 NASB

Solomon had spent such a long time, devoting the best for a temple in which to worship God. He knew that heaven itself couldn't contain the greatness of God, yet he believed that God would still allow his presence to be near those who truly came to worship him.

When you take the time to think of yourself as this temple, it can be humbling to know that God dwells within you despite your lack of effort to make it a great place to worship. Praise Jesus that he makes this temple a beautiful place.

God, I am sorry that I have paid little attention to myself your temple. It seems such a sacred thought to ponder, yet I know that Jesus is what makes me worthy to be able to be in your presence. As I set aside time right now to read your Word and worship you, encourage me with the knowledge that your eyes are on me.

How can you prepare yourself better to receive God's presence in your life?

Turning Back

At the time of sacrifice, the prophet Elijah stepped forward and prayed: "Lord, the God of Abraham, Isaac and Israel, let it be known today that you are God in Israel and that I am your servant and have done all these things at your command. Answer me, Lord, answer me, so these people will know that you, Lord, are God, and that you are turning their hearts back again."

1 Kings 18:36-37 NIV

How many times have you prayed for that one friend or family member to turn back to God? Elijah challenged Ahab with a miracle in order to prove God's power, and as a result, he was confident that God would reveal himself as alive.

This act turned many Israelites back to God. You probably won't save that friend with physical fire from heaven, but you can always ask God to reveal himself in a tangible way to your loved ones.

God, I pray again for my friend or family member who needs to turn back to you. Help them to recognize that you are the one true and living God who cares for them. Answer me, so these people will know that you are God and that you are turning their hearts back.

*The fire of the LORD fell and burned up the sacrifice, the wood, the
stones and the soil, and also licked up the water in the trench.
When all the people saw this, they fell prostrate and cried,
"The LORD —he is God! The LORD —he is God!"*

1 KINGS 18:38-39 NIV

There are times when God chooses to demonstrate his power.
Throughout Scripture, we see a God who loves his people so
much that he does what it takes to turn them back to him.

Don't become discouraged thinking that God is silent in this
day and age. Our God is alive and powerful and willing to
move in the hearts of those who have hearts that are open to
him. Look around you and be willing to be a vessel through
whom God can move.

*God, as I prayed this morning, turn people back to you. I give you
my hands, heart, and feet to be someone to work through so your
living power can be recognized.*

Be encouraged that the Lord is God.

Power in the Quiet

*A great and powerful wind tore the mountains apart and
shattered the rocks before the LORD, but the LORD was not in the
wind. After the wind there was an earthquake,
but the LORD was not in the earthquake.*

1 KINGS 19:11 NIV

God doesn't always meet our expectations. Elijah may have
expected the God who brought fire from heaven to be in the
powerful wind and the almighty earthquake, but this is not
where he was.

As you make preparations for your day, remember that God
wants you to meet with him and he wants to speak with you
but not always in the ways you might expect. Listen for him
everywhere not just where you expect him to be.

*God, I open my heart to hear your voice. Help me to discern when
you are speaking today, in spite of all the noise around me. Give
me moments of quiet and calm where I can find you.*

After the earthquake came a fire, but the LORD was not in the fire.
And after the fire came a gentle whisper. When Elijah heard it,
he pulled his cloak over his face and went out and
stood at the mouth of the cave.

1 KINGS 19:12-13 NIV

Sometimes we have to wait for the storms of life to pass before we are ready to hear what God really has to say. God gives us time and space to hear his voice.

As you take a moment to quiet yourself from a busy day, listen for God's small whispers to you. Allow yourself to step away from the mess and just rest. Wait at the mouth of the cave and discern what is going on in your mind and heart. God is here and waiting.

Holy Spirit, today has been another busy day. Quiet my mind and heart so I can hear your gentle whisper. Help me to discern your voice from the other ideas and emotions. Bring me peace as I lay my head down to rest.

What is God whispering to you in this moment?

Fools for Him

*The message of the cross is foolishness to those who are perishing,
but to us who are being saved it is the power of God.*

1 CORINTHIANS 1:18 NKJV

Have you ever watched a television program with the sound
turned off? When we don't hear what is going on and don't
recognize the context, people's actions look strange and
might be hard to figure out. Unfortunately, many people
won't hear the message of the cross as good news because
their eyes have not yet seen the truth.

Be encouraged today that although some will fail to accept
the good news of Jesus Christ, others' eyes can be opened to
the truth within you. Rely on the wisdom of God and not the
wisdom of men.

*God, as I think of the people I will come across today, many of
whom do not know you and seem to not want to know about you,
I pray that my life would be a wonderful witness to the reality of
your hope and love.*

It is written: "I will destroy the wisdom of the wise,
and bring to nothing the understanding of the prudent."

1 CORINTHIANS 1:19 NKJV

At the end of the day we may feel like we have not made a significant impact on anything or anyone.

Be encouraged that today you were an example of the living God and that your life shares good news whether you feel like you have or not. Each day that you continue to have faith in Jesus Christ, you are carrying the good news.

God, thank you that I carry you with me each day. I pray that you would give me opportunities tomorrow to share the good news. Give me the right words at the right time.

What will you be able to share about the good news with someone tomorrow?

Unity of Believers

When one says, "I belong to Paul," and another, "I belong to Apollos," are you not merely human? What then is Apollos? What is Paul? Servants through whom you came to believe, as the Lord assigned to each.

1 CORINTHIANS 3:4-5 NRSV

Division in the church is a heartbreaking thing to see unfold. You may have been part of a church split or may have heard of one happening and felt disappointed or discouraged by it.

In Paul's day people valued the speaker and how persuasively they spoke. They developed preferences and groups based on speakers. This very thing can happen in our churches today. Remember it is not about the person, it is about the one who unifies us—Jesus. He is the one we should follow.

Lord God, I thank you for the body of Christ: the gathering place of believers. I pray for my church and the wider community of faith that we would experience unity and grace in all the decisions being made there. Help me to contribute positively toward my church.

I planted, Apollos watered, but God gave the growth.
So neither the one who plants nor the one who waters is anything,
but only God who gives the growth.

1 CORINTHIANS 3:6-7 NRSV

A key part of being united is being able to recognize each other's differences and accept people for who they are. If we continue to be negative toward certain individuals, we create barriers and the potential to create "us and them" sides.

In reality, nobody can claim the success because it is God who gives the growth. Paul knew that it was important for the church to stand united because unity is the biggest witness of the message of love that Jesus came to convey.

God, I asked for forgiveness for a heart that is willing to approve of people who I disagree with. Give me your heart for all people so we can stand united and together accomplish your will on earth.

What people do you need to be more tolerant with, despite your disagreements?

Train to Win

Don't you realize that in a race everyone runs, but only one person gets the prize? So run to win! All athletes are disciplined in their training. They do it to win a prize that will fade away, but we do it for an eternal prize. So I run with purpose in every step. I am not just shadowboxing.

1 CORINTHIANS 9:24-26 NLT

Apathy is a very real struggle. It can be hard to get motivated for work, cleaning up the house, or getting your assignments done. God doesn't want us to be apathetic in our faith. We can easily become distracted by things in life that don't matter as much as eternity.

Paul is suggesting here that we run to win, not just to endure life but to do the very best that we can. It's not about competition; it is about enthusiasm.

God, thank you for the day that you've given me. I pray that I would see the value of eternity in the little things that I do for you. Give me energy each day to run this race of faith.

*I discipline my body like an athlete, training it to do what it
should. Otherwise, I fear that after preaching to others
I myself might be disqualified.*

1 Corinthians 9:27 NLT

It can be exhausting even thinking about the amount of
training a professional athlete puts into their particular
sport. It feels almost impossible that we could get ourselves
into that kind of shape.

Paul was using this analogy to describe the hard work it takes
to maintain our faith in this life. This world needs us to be an
example of a life lived with purpose.

*God, thank you that I do have purpose in life. I pray where I am
dragging my feet that you would help me to lift my eyes toward
you and find inspiration to continue running with purpose toward
the goal of eternity. Let my life be an inspiration to others.*

Where are you struggling to see purpose in your life? Ask God
to breathe new inspiration into this area.

Power to Resist

No temptation has overtaken you but such as is common to man; and God is faithful, who will not allow you to be tempted beyond what you are able, but with the temptation will provide the way of escape also, so that you will be able to endure it.

1 Corinthians 10:13 NASB

We often think of temptation as being seductive or sensual, but there are many forms of temptation that we face every day. We might be tempted to gossip, or be negative about a situation, or not have control of our temper. God doesn't put these things in front of us to see whether we will pass the test; rather, he wants us to recognize that we can overcome temptation through his strength and by his grace.

He has given us a way out by giving us access to the Spirit of Christ. Be encouraged today when you are tempted to sin, whether small or big, and know that God has provided a way out for you.

Father, I thank you for the power of Christ that you have placed within my heart; please let me draw on that power today as I resist all forms of temptation.

Flee from idolatry. I speak as to wise men; you judge what I say.

1 Corinthians 10:14 NASB

The Holy Spirit has been with you today whether you feel like it or not. Temptations would have come to you in small or big forms, and your ability to resist those temptations is only about your ability to except the power of the Holy Spirit to help you in those situations.

If you've given into temptation today, ask the Lord for forgiveness. If you have succeeded in avoiding temptation, be thankful for the power of the cross in your life.

God, I thank you that you have given me a way out in every single situation. I ask for your forgiveness and peace tonight as I sleep. Help me to know that I can do all things through you.

What temptations are you facing right now that need to be met with the power of Christ?

Embracing Difference

There are different kinds of spiritual gifts, but the same Spirit is the source of them all. There are different kinds of service, but we serve the same Lord.

1 Corinthians 12:4-5 nlt

We live in a world that still values certain things over others. This makes us believe that some things we do have more importance than others. We often apply this way of thinking to the way that we see ourselves within the context of our Christian family.

At church, we make certain gifts seem more important than our own. It's critical to understand that there are differences in the way people think, act, and feel. These differences all are used by the Spirit to do something great. We serve God in different ways but the point is that we serve the same God.

Jesus, I am sorry where I have placed certain gifts and talents in some kind of hierarchy. Help me to recognize my own worth in the body of believers that I'm part of, and help me to see the worth of every single person who contributes toward your church.

*God works in different ways, but it is the same God
who does the work in all of us.*

1 CORINTHIANS 12:6 NLT

We are all guilty of expecting God to work in a certain way and
then feeling disappointed when he doesn't. Sometimes we
are quick to judge whether God is or isn't working in other
people. It's not our place to judge what God is doing, we are
each accountable for our own thoughts, actions, and feelings.

Be encouraged that God has given you something unique, and
that he wants you to be a part of his greater work. Be aware
that he may work in a way that is different from your own
opinions and thoughts.

*God, thank you for today and for giving me the opportunity to be
myself. Help me to recognize the gifts that you've given me and to
know that you value them and want me to use them to further
your kingdom.*

What are the different kinds of spiritual gifts that God has
given you? How are you using these within the church?

Heart Motivation

If I speak with the tongues of men and of angels, but do not have love, I have become a noisy gong or a clanging cymbal. If I have the gift of prophecy, and know all mysteries and all knowledge; and if I have all faith, so as to remove mountains, but do not have love, I am nothing.

1 CORINTHIANS 13:1-2 NASB

Love is such a universal word and concept that we often try to pin it down to certain concepts. We think that if we talk about love, or have a lot of faith, or give to the poor and sacrifice everything, we are demonstrating love.

Doing these things are right but they're only as good as the motivation that starts them.

Jesus, thank you for showing me what love really is. I cannot begin to comprehend the fullness of this love, but I thank you that it exists in my life and in this world. Help my heart motivation to always be that of love first and deeds second.

If I give all my possessions to feed the poor, and if I surrender my body to be burned, but do not have love, it profits me nothing.

1 CORINTHIANS 13:3 NASB

If your heart is full of love and compassion for the poor and you give, that is amazing. If your heart is to contribute and edify the church and you do that through prophecy, that is amazing.

If you are motivated by love to sacrifice all that you have, that is amazing. This is real love. This is the excellence of love.

Heavenly Father, as I think back on my day I am grateful for the love that I have received and the love that I have been able to share. I thank you that this comes from a motivation of knowing that I am wholly loved by you. Give me a heart full of joy because of this love as I take time to be in your presence this evening.

How have you received love today? How have you shared love?

Heavenly Bodies

Let me reveal to you a wonderful secret. We will not all die, but we will all be transformed! It will happen in a moment, in the blink of an eye, when the last trumpet is blown. For when the trumpet sounds, those who have died will be raised to live forever. And we who are living will also be transformed.

1 CORINTHIANS 15:51-52 NLT

The concept of eternal life in Paul's day was a hard one for people to get their heads around. Now we are excited by the hope of eternity because we know with certainty that Jesus died and rose again. This means that we share in the same experience as Jesus: we will one day rise again and have our eternal life still to live.

This isn't the end and that should give you wonderful hope as you go about your day. Know that you are being transformed into his glory day by day.

Jesus, thank you that you died for me. Thank you for showing me death was defeated for good. Help me to live today in the knowledge that this is not the end and one day all things will be made new.

Our dying bodies must be transformed into bodies that will never die; our mortal bodies must be transformed into immortal bodies.

1 CORINTHIANS 15:53 NLT

When we get home from a day we often want to sit down and relax. This is because our bodies having been active and can become weary.

Won't it be wonderful when we realize that our new bodies are not perishing and we will not feel the weariness of the day? In the meantime, look after your body and allow yourself to rest and trust in the hope of the future glorious body.

God, I thank you for creating my whole person and that this body matters as well as my soul. Help me to be kind to my body. Thank you that one day I will be transformed with an eternal human form.

In what ways can you honor the body that God has given you? How can you give yourself the rest that you need?

Determine the Problem

The people of the city said to Elisha, "Look, our Lord, this town is well situated, as you can see, but the water is bad and the land is unproductive." "Bring me a new bowl," he said, "and put salt in it." So they brought it to him. Then he went out to the spring and threw the salt into it, saying, "This is what the LORD says: 'I have healed this water. Never again will it cause death or make the land unproductive.'"

2 KINGS 2:19-21 NIV

It is in our human nature to be able to discern the positive and negatives of different situations. When you are making important decisions, you will often think about the pros and cons of that decision. The people of this city knew that they had a good thing with their location, but something needed to change about their water supply or it would be the end of them.

Perhaps you can apply this principle to a project you are working on, a relationship that needs working out, or simply something going on in your heart and mind. Figure out what needs healing and ask God to help right the wrong.

God, I need your wisdom to figure out some of the situations I am facing at the moment. Please help me to clarify what the problem is and then help me to trust you to heal and restore the things that are broken. I surrender to your work in my life today.

The water has remained pure to this day,
according to the word Elisha had spoken.

2 KINGS 2:22 NIV

Have you been able to gain insight into some of the difficult situations you are facing? Remember that the people brought their problems to Elisha, who asked and believed God to sort it all out.

You might have a trusted family member, friend, or leader who you can talk through your problems with. Perhaps you just need to go straight to Jesus and lean on his advice. Remember that having faith is just as important as knowing what is wrong. Be encouraged to hand over the problem to God and trust that he can make things whole.

God, thank you that you can bring healing into all kinds of situations. I need your help tonight. I ask for your peace as I leave my burdens and frustrations in your hands.

What problems have you been able to identify in your circumstances? Communicate these to God and let him provide the solution.

Filled Up

"Now bring me a harpist. While the harpist was playing, the hand of the LORD came on Elisha and he said, 'This is what the LORD says: I will fill this valley with pools of water. For this is what the LORD says: You will see neither wind nor rain, yet this valley will be filled with water, and you, your cattle and your other animals will drink.'"

2 KINGS 3:15-17 NIV

When three kings of Israel were preparing for battle, they needed to know that God was going to go with them. Instead of simply destroying the enemy, God gave them what they needed for strength—water, and plenty of it.

If you expect today to be filled with challenges, remember that God doesn't necessarily remove the challenge, but he will provide you with the strength to get through it.

God, thank you for giving me what I need to get through this day. Fill all my pools with your living water so I can draw from this source to refresh me and give me strength.

The next morning, about the time for offering the sacrifice,
there it was—water flowing from the direction of Edom!
And the land was filled with water.

2 KINGS 3:20 NIV

The Lord's provision is always generous. He didn't provide just a little bit of water, he provided so much that the land was filled with water.

God has provided in abundance for you, even if you haven't felt that way. As you allow God to fill you up, let his love and presence spill over into the places you go and the people you meet.

God, thank you so much for providing me with the strength to not only get through this day with endurance, but to get through the day victorious. Thank you for your living water that flows through me. Please continue to fill my heart and mind with your goodness.

As you reflect on your day, where have you seen God refresh and strengthen you?

Start Pouring

*Elisha said to her, "What shall I do for you? Tell me, what do you
have in the house?" She answered, "Your servant has nothing in
the house, except a jar of oil." He said, "Go outside, borrow vessels
from all your neighbors, empty vessels and not just a few. Then
go in, and shut the door behind you and your children, and start
pouring into all these vessels; when each is full, set it aside."*

2 KINGS 4:2-4 NRSV

When Elisha asked this woman to make him some bread she
would've had to make the decision between herself, her son,
and this stranger. This woman showed generosity by putting
the stranger first, just as Christ put the sinner before himself.
She didn't know that God would provide her with enough
food for the rest of her life, but she still offered.

Remember today, as you put others before yourself that God
makes sure he provides for those who are generous.

*God, thank you that I already have so much to give. There are
times when I feel like I have nothing left and I am still being asked
to give. Help me to continue to be generous, trusting that you will
continue to provide for me.*

*She left him and shut the door behind her and her children; they
kept bringing vessels to her, and she kept pouring. When the vessels
were full, she said to her son, "Bring me another vessel." But he
said to her, "There are no more." Then the oil stopped flowing. She
came and told the man of God, and he said, "Go sell the oil and
pay your debts, and you and your children can live on the rest."*

2 KINGS 4:5-7 NRSV

At the end of the day it's very easy to relate to this woman
who felt like she had nothing left in her jar. You may feel
empty right now of the ability to give anything in the way of
emotional or physical energy. This is the time for you to allow
God to replenish your resources.

As you rest in his presence right now, let him refresh those
areas of your life that need filling so you are ready for another
day of generosity.

*God, I do feel weary, not only physically but emotionally and
sometimes even spiritually. I ask that you fill those areas where I
have given of myself and feel drained. Allow the presence of your
Holy Spirit to renew my energy so I may continue to be a blessing to
others in my life.*

What areas do you feel empty and in need of God's presence
to fill you up?

Weird and Wonderful

*Naaman became angry and went away, saying, "I thought that
for me he would surely come out, and stand and call on the name
of the LORD his God, and would wave his hand over the spot,
and cure the leprosy! Are not Abana and Pharpar, the rivers of
Damascus, better than all the waters of Israel? Could I not wash
in them, and be clean?" He turned and went away in a rage.*

2 KINGS 5:11-12 NRSV

It is almost humorous when we consider how much like
Naaman we can be when God wants to work in our lives.
Naaman couldn't see how washing in a dirty river was going to
do anything; he trusted his own intellect over the word of God.

We are usually praying for a quick and sensible fix to all our
problems. We want instant healing, the exact job that we want
to become available, or our anxiety issues to go away. God
wants to help you, but he has different, and better, ways than
you can come up with. Don't be angry at God's plan, just obey.

*God, I am sorry for getting angry at you when I have asked you for
help. I know that your ways are better, but sometimes I can't figure
out what you are doing, so I revert to trusting my own intellect.
Forgive me and help me to obey, even when I don't understand.*

*His servants approached and said to him, "Father, if the prophet
had commanded you to do something difficult, would you not have
done it? How much more, when all he said to you was, 'Wash, and
be clean'?" So he went down and immersed himself seven times in
the Jordan, according to the word of the man of God; his flesh was
restored like the flesh of a young boy, and he was clean.*

2 KINGS 5:12-14 NRSV

God's invitation isn't usually very complicated. Even the
servants could see the simplicity of what was being asked and
they convinced Naaman that there was no harm in trying. God
is willing to work with the emotions of anger, confusion, and
frustration.

If you have those feelings this evening, express them to God,
but remember the words of the servants in this Scripture and
ask yourself, "Is it really that hard to obey what God is asking
of me?" Remember that God fulfils his promises.

*Holy Spirit, I give you this part of my evening to speak to me about
what you want me to do to experience the healing and restoration
that I need in my situations. You know that I want to be made
clean and whole, and I want this for all my relationships.*

What is God asking you to do in order for your situation to
experience healing?

Surrounded by Glory

When an attendant of the man of God rose early in the morning and went out, an army with horses and chariots was all around the city. His servant said, "Alas, master! What shall we do?" He replied, "Do not be afraid, for there are more with us than there are with them."

2 KINGS 6:15-16 NRSV

At times we wake up in the morning and feel dread or anxiety about the day ahead. We might feel as though there is a great army of trouble surrounding us as we look out.

If this is how you are feeling, ask God what to do. Give yourself time to still yourself before your Creator, the one who knows all things. He knows you better than anyone else. Hear him say back to you, "Do not be afraid, there are more on your side than against you."

Lord God, thank you that when I feel overwhelmed, you stand beside me and cause me to see that with you, I can conquer everything that I am facing today. Give me courage as I face battles, knowing that good is far greater than evil.

Elisha prayed: "O LORD, please open his eyes that he may see." So the LORD opened the eyes of the servant, and he saw; the mountain was full of horses and chariots of fire all around Elisha.

2 KINGS 6:17 NRSV

If you have faced a lot of challenging issues today, remember to ask God, as Elisha did, to open your eyes so you can see what is really going on.

Be encouraged that while you may feel alone or with little strength, you actually have a whole army of angels from God standing with you in battle. God's spiritual forces are much more than the enemies you come up against.

Father God, open my eyes so I can see how strong the army is that is fighting with me. Thank you that you always give me strength to get through the challenging times. Let this time that I have set aside now, be a time where I receive strength and renewal from your ministering angels.

What particular emotional, physical, or spiritual battle feels too overwhelming for you right now? Allow God to open your eyes to see all the help that you have in him.

One and Only

"The statutes and the rules and the law and the commandment that he wrote for you, you shall always be careful to do. You shall not fear other gods, and you shall not forget the covenant that I have made with you. You shall not fear other gods, but you shall fear the LORD your God, and he will deliver you out of the hand of all your enemies."

2 KINGS 17:37-39 ESV

Unfortunately, the fall of ancient Israel was because of their idolatry; worshipping other idols was a big part of the culture of those times. We don't carve out idols these days, and yet our culture still pursues all kinds of other things that draw our attention entirely away from our Creator.

Your day doesn't have to be full of these others things; determine today to honor God in your actions and words, and resist the things of the world that would try to draw you away from him.

God, it can be hard to know how to follow you without getting distracted by the various idols of this world. Give me wisdom today to be careful to obey your voice.

They would not listen, but they did according to their former manner. So these nations feared the LORD and also served their carved images. Their children did likewise, and their children's children—as their fathers did, so they do to this day.

2 KINGS 17:40-41 ESV

We have a very mixed bag of spirituality. Our western culture tolerates all forms of religion and worship, yet it also pursues wealth, beauty, and fame. It's easy to be caught between putting God first and thinking a lot about how to make ourselves looks and feel better.

This kind of half-dedication to God continues to plague generation after generation. Be encouraged that Jesus came to set us free from this pattern. We can serve God in purity and holiness through the power of Christ.

Jesus, thank you that your death on the cross gave me the enabling power that I need to serve you and not this world.

What areas of your life are not submitted to Christ? Hand them over to him and experience the freedom of living wholly for the one true God.

Restore Righteousness

The king went up to the house of the LORD, and with him all the men of Judah and all the inhabitants of Jerusalem and the priests and the prophets, all the people, both small and great. And he read in their hearing all the words of the Book of the Covenant that had been found in the house of the LORD.

2 KINGS 23:2 ESV

King Josiah was truly grieved when they found the covenant that God had made with Israel and he realized that, as a nation, they had been entirely unfaithful to this covenant.

You may be called to restore righteousness to a place or a group of people. It may not even be your fault that things have gone wrong, but you can be God's spokesperson, stand up for justice, and do what is right in God's eyes.

God, thank you that I can be reminded of your promises as I read Scripture. Thank you for the challenge today of standing up for your Word and what is right. I want to be a vessel for you to use.

The king stood by the pillar and made a covenant before the LORD, to walk after the LORD and to keep his commandments and his testimonies and his statutes with all his heart and all his soul, to perform the words of this covenant that were written in this book. And all the people joined in the covenant.

2 KINGS 23:3 ESV

You may have witnessed a renewal ceremony where people renew their vows after many years. Vows are often made in public because it holds a lot of weight to speak things out, knowing that others can hold you accountable.

It's important to remember the things that you have promised and to be bold enough to share these promises with others.

God, I want to continue to keep your commandments and walk in your ways with all my heart and soul. Forgive me when I have broken a promise and help me to boldly tell others about my commitment to you.

What promise have you made to God and to others that you might need to renew?

God of All Comfort

Blessed be the God and Father of our LORD Jesus Christ, the Father of mercies and God of all comfort, who comforts us in all our affliction, so that we may be able to comfort those who are in any affliction, with the comfort with which we ourselves are comforted by God.

2 CORINTHIANS 1:3-4 ESV

Comfort is a universal need. It is present through community with one another and with God. When we are going through trials, we rely on God and others to help us through our grief and pain.

When you have received comfort, you are much better equipped to help others in their times of need. It also helps to know that Christ faced the worst kind of affliction and can understand your emotions. Look to comfort someone who needs it today.

God, thank you that you understand what it is like to be uncomfortable, exposed, and hurt. I am comforted knowing that you understand and that you care. Help me to show this same comfort toward others today.

As we share abundantly in Christ's sufferings,
so through Christ we share abundantly in comfort too.

2 CORINTHIANS 1:5 ESV

We usually don't feel as though we have suffered anything as severe as Christ suffered, yet the longer we live, the harder things seem to get. Over the years we learn that following Christ means hanging onto him in the good and the terrible times.

Remember tonight, that although you may be facing a great amount of pain, Christ is there to comfort you. Ask him to be near to you now.

God, thank you for suffering on the cross so I could be free. I know that at times I complain about things that are not a big deal. I ask that you would provide me with all the comfort I need.

Where do you need to experience God's comfort tonight?

Unveiled

*Whenever anyone turns to the Lord, the veil is taken away.
Now the Lord is the Spirit, and where the Spirit of the Lord is,
there is freedom.*

2 CORINTHIANS 3:16-17 NIV

It can be helpful to understand that those who haven't
accepted Jesus are not seeing life clearly. What a difference
it makes when that veil is taken away and life becomes full of
meaning and possibility.

You experience freedom because you know the truth. Today,
you will see many people who still have that veil over their
face. Be gracious toward them and pray that they would turn
to God so they can also experience freedom.

*God, I pray for those people in my life who still have not turned
toward you. Holy Spirit, reveal your truth so they may also walk in
freedom.*

We all, who with unveiled faces contemplate the Lord's glory, are being transformed into his image with ever-increasing glory, which comes from the Lord, who is the Spirit.

2 CORINTHIANS 3:18 NIV

Transformation in the natural world doesn't happen instantly in the way that a superhero goes from normal to amazing. Seeds become flowers slowly, babies become adults slowly.

This is like the transformation taking place in your heart. Your veil was taken off to see what Christ has done for you, and now you are in the process of being transformed to be like him.

God, thank you that a future glory awaits me. I am blessed to have a wonderful future of life in you. Help me to approach tomorrow with the perspective that I am heading toward glory.

What transformation have you seen in your own life that has glorified God?

Look at Eternity

*We do not lose heart. Though outwardly we are wasting away,
yet inwardly we are being renewed day by day. For our light and
momentary troubles are achieving for us an eternal glory
that far outweighs them all.*

2 CORINTHIANS 4:16-17 NIV

When our bodies start to fail us, either with sickness or just
getting older, we can begin to feel down. It's hard to see that
we are being transformed to greatness when we seem to be
confronted with more trouble as life goes on.

Discouragement starts with fixating on the problem rather
than the truth of the future. If you are feeling down on life
right now, remember that one day all will be made right. Let
yourself look toward Jesus instead of your daily troubles.

*God, keep my eyes above any trouble that may come into my day.
Help me to set aside worry, anxiety, and other stresses, knowing
that they are only temporary.*

We fix our eyes not on what is seen, but on what is unseen, since what is seen is temporary, but what is unseen is eternal.

2 CORINTHIANS 4:18 NIV

It's in our nature to review and replay things of the day in our minds. Sometimes we remember the things someone said to make us laugh, or we replay an argument or some advice we gave.

It may take a bit of effort, but try looking at your day with the thoughts of the things that went on that were unseen. Think of the joy you experienced when laughing, think of the life you brought to someone else's day with your kind words. These are the things of eternity, and they are worth fixing your eyes on.

Father, I am grateful for the life that you have given me. Open my eyes to see the things of this world that do not matter, and allow me to dwell on things that are part of your lasting goodness.

In what ways can you see God's eternal goodness in your day-to-day life?

New Life

He died for everyone so that those who receive his new life will no longer live for themselves. Instead, they will live for Christ, who died and was raised for them. So we have stopped evaluating others from a human point of view. At one time we thought of Christ merely from a human point of view. How differently we know him now!

2 Corinthians 5:15-16 NLT

The morning is a good time to remind yourself that you have a new life. When we are weary from the day it is nice to go to bed and allow your body and mind to rest so you can re-set for the day ahead.

Remember your new life before you do all your usual things. You have Christ inside of you, so let yourself walk in this new life. Jesus showed us that this life didn't end in death, so we can live in a manner that shows we have the hope of eternity.

Jesus, you have shown me the way from death to life. Restore this hope of eternity in my heart so my words and actions are affected with joy and peace. Let your hope inside of me be a witness to those who don't yet know you.

Anyone who belongs to Christ has become a new person.
The old life is gone; a new life has begun!

2 Corinthians 5:17 nlt

We can look back over a day and dwell on the things that went wrong. You might be ashamed of an argument you had, or you may have regrets that you didn't speak up with an opinion. Perhaps you just don't feel like you were very productive.

Don't dwell on today; look forward to tomorrow. The new life that you have in Christ gives you grace for your mistakes and enables you to develop character as a new creation in him.

Jesus, forgive me for those things I have done wrong today. Thank you that your forgiveness means I can now look ahead without being dragged down by the past. Thank you for this new life that gives me hope, each and every day.

What things are you dwelling on that are part of the old life? Recognize your new life and live in that grace.

Today Is the Day

As God's partners, we beg you not to accept this marvelous gift of God's kindness and then ignore it.

2 CORINTHIANS 6:1 NLT

When you give someone a gift you hope that they cherish and use what they have been given. God's gift of grace to us is the best gift that we could hope for, yet we can ignore it by continuing to trudge around in guilt.

Let God's kindness toward you motivate you to do right, rather than doing things out of feeling guilty. God is kind because he loves you. Remind yourself of this all throughout the day.

God, I accept your kindness toward me as a wonderful gift that changes the way I live. Give me moments today to remember your kindness so I am not ignorant toward your grace.

God says, "At just the right time, I heard you. On the day
of salvation, I helped you." Indeed, the "right time" is now.
Today is the day of salvation.

2 CORINTHIANS 6:2 NLT

The law of the Old Testament was an attempt to guide people
toward doing right. God made covenants with his people
to encourage doing right. None of these things, however,
were able to keep people from turning away from God. Sin
remained prevalent.

This is why we need to accept that there is nothing that we
can do to achieve our own salvation; this is the very thing
Christ did for you. He helped you achieve righteousness when
you couldn't do it yourself. Accept Christ again today, and
celebrate your salvation.

Jesus, thank you so much for helping me to have a right
relationship with the Father. I'm sorry for sometimes forgetting
that I can't earn my salvation but that it is a precious gift from
you. Thank you for this day, and that I am walking in the light.

When did you first accept salvation from Jesus Christ?
Celebrate that day, and the days ahead of living in his new life.

Equal Pay

Whatever you give is acceptable if you give it eagerly. And give according to what you have, not what you don't have. Of course, I don't mean your giving should make life easy for others and hard for yourselves. I only mean that there should be some equality.

2 CORINTHIANS 8:12-13 NLT

Most of us hold on to our hard-earned money because we live at the edge of our means. When you look at your spending, you may be able to identify a few things that could be given up for the sake of being able to save a little more for times when you and others are in need.

God doesn't ask you to give so you make yourself poor, but he does want you to be part of helping those who do not have as much as you do. Is there something that you can hold back from spending your money on today so you can give to a greater cause?

God, thank you for providing me with all that I need. Give me wisdom to know how to spend well so I can have a little extra to give when you show me someone in need. Help me to be a good steward of your money.

Right now you have plenty and can help those who are in need. Later, they will have plenty and can share with you when you need it. In this way, things will be equal.

2 CORINTHIANS 8:14 NLT

God's system of equality is always the best system. When you have plenty, make sure to give, so when you are in need, others will be generous to you. It's a bit of a "pay it forward" situation and it makes sense that our generosity will someday come back to us.

God doesn't want us to have divisions because some are poor and others are rich. Instead, he longs for us all to have what we need.

God, help me to be generous even when I am the one in need. I know you want a heart that is motivated by love and equality for all people. I pray you would use me to be a part of this wonderful proficiency of giving and receiving.

Do you need to be more generous, or do you need to pray for some generosity to be extended your way?

Thorns

Concerning this thing I pleaded with the Lord three times that it might depart from me. And He said to me, "My grace is sufficient for you, for My strength is made perfect in weakness." Therefore most gladly I will rather boast in my infirmities, that the power of Christ may rest upon me.

2 CORINTHIANS 12:8-9 NKJV

We are quick to plead for God to take away the things we are struggling with like ill health, weak will power, or faltering relationships.

God can move powerfully in these situations because, instead of relying on your own strengths, you realize your dependency on him. This speaks volumes to people around you who see that you have made the most out of your struggles.

Father God, thank you that you care enough about me to make sure that I have everything that I really need. Help me to stop complaining about the struggles in my life and to see them as blessings because they prove your strength and power in my life.

*I take pleasure in infirmities, in reproaches, in needs,
in persecutions, in distresses, for Christ's sake.
For when I am weak, then I am strong.*

2 CORINTHIANS 12:10 NKJV

Has your day had reproach, need, persecution, or distress?
Rejoice! It may not feel like a time to be happy, yet you can
be encouraged that God is at work in you, perhaps even more
powerfully than if you had a victorious day.

God takes over when you are weak, so you can boast in his
greatness and glorify his name. Consider it a privilege to go
through hard times for the sake of the good news of Jesus.

*God, thank you for my weakness. I know that nobody is perfect so
I choose to acknowledge that I need your help. As you guide me, let
your power of change be evident to those around me.*

What are your weaknesses? How can you see God working
through your imperfections?

Give Thanks

Oh, give thanks to the Lord! Call upon His name;
Make known His deeds among the peoples!

1 CHRONICLES 16:8 NKJV

There are so many things that we can be grateful for even in times of distress. As you go about your morning routines and preparations for the day ahead, make a point to think about all those things you are thankful for: a cup of coffee, a nice shirt to wear, a simple but loving goodbye to those you live with.

When your heart is full of thankfulness, you will naturally display your love in all that you say and do. This is how we can make known God's deeds to all people.

Thank you so much, God, for all the beautiful things that you have brought into my life. Let my heart and mind fill up with the great things that you have done for me and let this spill over into how I conduct myself today.

Sing to Him, sing psalms to Him; Talk of all His wondrous works!
1 Chronicles 16:9 nkjv

Singing songs is something that we are used to doing with other believers, usually in church or some other group setting. It's a beautiful thing to all sing words that affirm our faith and identity in Christ.

This Scripture reminds us that we are singing the songs to God, not just about him. At times we can get caught up in the instrumentation or someone next to us who sings beautifully and forget that our words and songs are intended for him. Let's remember to sing to him and then to tell others about all that he has done.

God, you have done wondrous works. I praise you as the amazing Creator of this world, who is above all and yet so near to all. Help me to continue to praise you in the quiet of my home, but also outside of my home, so others will hear of your faithfulness to me.

What song or poem can you sing to God, right now, in the quietness of your own home?

The Lord Reigns

Tremble before Him, all the earth. The world also is firmly established, It shall not be moved. Let the heavens rejoice, and let the earth be glad; and let them say among the nations, "The LORD reigns."

1 CHRONICLES 16:30-31 NKJV

The world is part of God's creation and his strength is reflected in nature. Look at the roaring ocean, the grandeur of mountains, and the swift movement of a cheetah. His strength is everywhere.

If the things that God created are this powerful, how much greater is his power? This is why you can rejoice and be glad—because you know in your heart that your God reigns above everything. Carry that confidence with you into your day today.

Creator God, you are full of strength and creativity. Let me see your power in creation today, and let it remind me of your strength that you make available to me.

Let the sea roar, and all its fullness; let the field rejoice, and all that is in it. Then the trees of the woods shall rejoice before the Lord, For He is coming to judge the earth.

1 CHRONICLES 16:32-33 NKJV

It might seem strange to rejoice that God is coming to judge the earth, but for God's creation, it will be a wonderful thing when God restores his creation to its intended glory.

When we see all the destruction around us, both within humanity and creation, we ought to long for the day when God brings justice. When you are covered by God's grace, justice is not something to be feared, it is a glorious future to rejoice and hope for.

God, thank you for the future restoration of all your creation. Thank you that there is already beauty in the ocean, the field, and the trees. I also recognize the beauty in people were made by your voice. Help me to rejoice in the face of your return.

What do you look forward to in God's restored creation?

The Eternal Throne

"It shall be, when your days are fulfilled, when you must go to be with your fathers, that I will set up your seed after you, who will be of your sons; and I will establish his kingdom. He shall build Me a house, and I will establish his throne forever."

1 CHRONICLES 17:11-12 NKJV

David wanted to build another house for the Lord to dwell in, just as Israel had done time and time again with the ark, tents, and other tabernacles. God, however, had his plan through Jesus. The houses or temples that the people built for the Almighty were always pointing toward the house that God would dwell in once and for all, that is, Jesus Christ.

This was a kingdom that would never again be defeated or need to move; this is an eternal kingdom with the eternal king. Today, remember that you are a part of that new kingdom.

God, thank you that you always made a way for your presence to be with your people. Thank you that through Jesus Christ, I have you with me all the time. Let me draw near to you in all circumstances today.

"I will be his Father, and he shall be My son; and I will not take My mercy away from him, as I took it from him who was before you. And I will establish him in My house and in My kingdom forever; and his throne shall be established forever."

1 CHRONICLES 17:13-14 NKJV

David would probably not have known that God was talking about sending his Son from heaven into the world to save all humanity. We have the benefit of looking at Scripture after Jesus and realizing the master plan that God was setting up through his people.

David had a big part to play in the master plan. We are a bit like David now, waiting for Jesus to return and set up his kingdom forever. We don't know exactly what this is going to look like, but be assured that God is using you to achieve this wonderful restoration of the world.

God, I don't understand what the future holds, but I know that it will be great. Help me to approach life with hope and not fear. I choose tonight, to be confident that your kingdom will one day be fully present.

How do you think God is using you to help bring his kingdom on earth?

Wise Intentions

"Is not the LORD your God with you? And has He not given you rest on every side? For He has given the inhabitants of the land into my hand, and the land is subdued before the Lord and before His people."

1 CHRONICLES 22:19 NKJV

When David spoke these words to Solomon, he was affirming that Solomon's wisdom had brought peace to the people and the land. It was from this time of great peace that Solomon was able to build the temple for the LORD.

Applying wisdom to your day-to-day life has a wonderful consequence; it is one of peace for you and your household. Remember today, that while it may seem insignificant, each small wise choice that you make will turn into a life that can significantly honor God.

God, please give me wisdom when I lack it today. Help me to honor you in my conversations and decisions so I can bring peace to all my circumstances.

"Set your heart and your soul to seek the LORD your God. Therefore arise and build the sanctuary of the LORD God, to bring the ark of the covenant of the LORD and the holy articles of God into the house that is to be built for the name of the LORD."

1 CHRONICLES 22:19 NIV

How good it is that you have chosen this evening to sit down and reflect on God. When you make dedicated time with God, conversing with him becomes a part of your every day—a necessity to find your day complete.

How it delights God when we spend time in his presence.

God, it's not easy to develop healthy habits of spending time with you. Thank you that you are with me in this time. Help me to make this a more habitual part of my life.

What could a different routine look like for you? How might you make it more intentional in meeting the Lord?

All the Way

Be strong and courageous, and act; do not fear nor be dismayed, for the LORD God, my God, is with you. He will not fail you nor forsake you until all the work for the service of the house of the LORD is finished.

1 CHRONICLES 28:20 NASB

What are you not doing right now because of fear? Are there things you are keeping quiet about simply because you're afraid? Are there steps forward that you aren't taking because you're frightened about what may happen if you do? Are there stirrings in your heart that you're neglecting because you're afraid of how you may be criticized?

God has great things in store for you, and he has promised to be with you because he wants to see those things come to fulfilment. Don't let fear get in the way.

God, let me put my faith into action in small ways today, so I can get used to stepping out in faith and be ready for it when you ask me for the big thing.

There are the divisions of the priests and the Levites for all the service of the house of God, and every willing man of any skill will be with you in all the work for all kinds of service. The officials also and all the people will be entirely at your command.

1 CHRONICLES 28:21 NASB

God provided skilled workers and authoritative officials to make sure that Solomon had every resource available to him in order to complete the temple according to the plans that he had for God's house to be built.

God doesn't just ask you to step out in faith for him without providing you with the right resources. As you think about the people and skills that are in your life, remember that God has put them there to help you in your God given mission.

Father, I feel blessed when I think of who and what you have placed strategically around me so I can accomplish your will for my life. Thank you that I have people to encourage me; thank you for giving me strengths and weaknesses. Help me to continue to use these blessings for your glory.

What people have you been blessed to have in your life right now? What skills are you grateful that God has given you?

Gifted Blessings

"Who am I and who are my people that we should be able to offer as generously as this? For all things come from You, and from Your hand we have given You. For we are sojourners before You, and tenants, as all our fathers were; our days on the earth are like a shadow, and there is no hope."

1 CHRONICLES 29:14-15 NASB

As you start this day with an intentional heart toward God's Word, allow yourself to dwell on the blessings that you have in this life. It could be a skill or talent that you have been able to use, your wonderful kids, or your nice home. You are bound to have a few things that you feel blessed with. Remember to acknowledge that all these things are from God.

We didn't choose where we would be born, or who we would be born to. We didn't choose the natural talents we were gifted with. These were all from the Creator. Our generous God gave us so much. Without him we would have nothing.

Lord God, thank you so much for the talents, skills, and all my other earthly blessings. I choose to approach this day with gratitude, knowing that you are the giver of all good things. Father, you are the giver of life and the many blessings within it. Give me perspective tonight as I reflect on my life as a blessing and give me opportunities this week to give back to you in some way.

"O Lord our God, all this abundance that we have provided to build You a house for Your holy name, it is from Your hand, and all is Yours".

1 Chronicles 29:16 NASB

If God indeed gave you all the good things in your life, then he truly is the rightful owner of it all. It's from his goodness and grace that he gives you ownership of these skills and blessings.

Hopefully you have been able to recognize these blessings in your life today, and to acknowledge God as the source. Make a commitment this evening to give something back to God, even if all you have to give is your gratitude and praise.

Father, you are the giver of life and the many blessings within it. Give me perspective tonight as I reflect on my life as a blessing, and give me opportunities this week to give back to you in some way.

What skills and blessings are you thankful God has provided you with?

Good Motives

"I know, my God, that you examine our hearts and rejoice when you find integrity there. You know I have done all this with good motives, and I have watched your people offer their gifts willingly and joyously."

1 CHRONICLES 29:17 NLT

The thought of being examined can bring out a lot of insecurities. We usually don't want people to look too closely at us physically or emotionally for fear of what they might see.

God knows you better than anyone else because he created you and has been walking alongside you all your life. You shouldn't be afraid of God examining your heart because there is nothing there that will surprise him. In fact, be prepared for God to be pleased with you because what he sees is your good motives and integrity. God sees you with eyes of love.

God, examine my heart and find the integrity and good motives that I have there. Help me to offer my gifts willingly and joyously today.

*"O Lord, the God of our ancestors Abraham, Isaac, and Israel,
make your people always want to obey you.
See to it that their love for you never changes."*

1 Chronicles 29:18 nlt

When we see good things happening with God's children, we
don't want it to end. So many great things can happen when
people's hearts are motivated toward God's kingdom.

Think about this prayer from so long ago and dwell on the
thought that you are one of those people who this prayer was
intended for. How wonderful it is to know that obedience
and love for God has carried through from generation to
generation.

*Heavenly Father, I am so encouraged that your Word has carried
through all these generations to the very one that I am a part of
now. I pray that from here on, people would always want to obey
you and that their love for you never changes.*

How have you seen others display obedience and love for God?

No Other Gospel

I am astonished that you are so quickly deserting the one who called you to live in the grace of Christ and are turning to a different gospel—which is really no gospel at all. Evidently some people are throwing you into confusion and are trying to pervert the gospel of Christ.

GALATIANS 1:6-7 NIV

In Paul's time, it was vitally important that people believed and shared the pure truth of the gospel. They did not have the fortune of the written gospel and therefore had to rely on the testimony of the apostles. It was imperative that this gospel was preserved by the church.

These days we have so many different versions of truth and plenty of people who want to change the message of Christ. Don't forget to reference the wonderful Word of God when you need to be reminded of the truth.

God, please protect me from the confusion that others may try to throw at me about your good news. Help me to have faith in your Word and to diligently remind myself of Scripture so the truth of the gospel can remain pure in my heart.

Even if we or an angel from heaven should preach a gospel other than the one we preached to you, let them be under God's curse!

GALATIANS 1:6-7 NIV

Paul is very good at reminding us about the severity of trying to change the gospel. It is good to be reminded that the only true gospel is the first one that Christ preached.

We may have our different interpretations and understanding of Scripture, but we cannot contend or change what Jesus taught about the cross and his kingdom. There is no other way to the Father than through Jesus Christ.

Jesus, thank you so much for saving me from my sin and making a way to redeem all your creation through your sacrifice on the cross. Help me to defend the truth of the gospel by learning your words and following your ways.

Are there doubts that you have about Jesus or the gospel that you need to confront right now? Read the words of Jesus and remind yourself again of the truth.

Law and Faith

We ourselves are Jews by birth and not Gentile sinners; yet we know that a person is not justified by works of the law but through faith in Jesus Christ, so we also have believed in Christ Jesus, in order to be justified by faith in Christ and not by works of the law, because by works of the law no one will be justified.

GALATIANS 2:15-16 ESV

The Jews had to change their mindset of thinking that keeping the law brought salvation, to understanding that somehow just believing in Jesus was their justification. Sometimes we have to change our paradigm of thinking and behaving because of what Christ has done.

You might be someone who checks all the boxes in your moral code book, which is a wonderful thing, and yet there's a point where you have to realize that this isn't where your salvation or faith merits come from. It's all about faith in the grace of Christ.

Jesus, I know that you are pleased with my conduct and doing good things. Give me a new perspective on the fact that I am justified because I believe in you. Help me to reserve my judgments about people today, because I know it is their belief, not actions, that save them too.

I do not nullify the grace of God, for if righteousness were through the law, then Christ died for no purpose.

GALATIANS 2:21 ESV

We can get too comfortable with the knowledge that Christ died for us; sometimes it is worth reminding ourselves why. If we were able to save ourselves through any other means, either works, good deeds, rituals, or reaching some sort of selfless state, then Christ would have not needed to die.

In fact, Jesus questioned God in the garden the night before the crucifixion with the very same sentiment—if only there were another way. Christ died to claim our righteousness because there was no other way. As you reflect on your salvation this evening, remind yourself that you are saved because of Jesus.

God, I don't want to nullify your grace by trying to do things that will earn your favor, or my salvation. Let me rest in the peace of knowing that there is no other way than to believe in you. Tonight I affirm again, I believe in you.

In what ways might you be trying to earn God's favor?

One Under Christ

In Christ Jesus you are all children of God through faith, for all of you who were baptized into Christ have clothed yourselves with Christ. There is neither Jew nor Gentile, neither slave nor free, nor is there male and female, for you are all one in Christ Jesus.

GALATIANS 3:26-28 NIV

Thankfully, the gospel is not limited to how we look, act, or feel. It is not our gender, our social status, or how we behave that is going to determine our eternity. We should be the people who are standing up for equality within our society because this is the message of our faith.

Race, status, gender, or any other difference should not affect how we treat others. Everyone deserves love, respect, and kindness. Be someone who extends this grace to others throughout your day.

Jesus, I am reminded of your inclusiveness today. Help me to deal with any prejudices I have, whether big or small, and give me a heart full of grace and compassion toward all people.

*If you belong to Christ, then you are Abraham's seed,
and heirs according to the promise.*

GALATIANS 3:29 NIV

For Jewish people of Paul's time, being a descendant of
Abraham was as important as being a descendant of royalty.
God had given an eternal promise through Abraham, and
everyone wanted to be a part of this promise.

The only qualification that any of us need to be part of this
great family is to belong to Christ. It was good news back
then, and it is good news for you now. Be encouraged to share
this good news to all kinds of people who you meet because
the kingdom of heaven is for all.

*God, I am so glad that you have included me in your family. I
want others to feel included as part of this promise. Give me the
words and the wisdom to know how and when to share my hope
with others.*

Who can you share the gospel with this week?

Abba Father

*Because you are his sons, God sent the Spirit of his Son into our
hearts, the Spirit who calls out, "Abba, Father."*

GALATIANS 4:6 NIV

Abba was an affectionate term for father in Paul's day. The
word describes a deep and loving relationship like that
between children and parents. You may have a wonderful
childhood experience, but you may also have had a difficult
and strained relationship with your parents.

Let God bring healing into your heart with the understanding
that he is the parent that never failed you. He has welcomed
you as his child and loves you unconditionally.

*Abba Father, thank you for your immense love for me. Heal the
hurts that have come from the past and let me be an example of
how that healing can positively affect the ways I think and act
today.*

You are no longer a slave, but God's child; and since you are his child, God has made you also an heir.

GALATIANS 4:7 NIV

Our culture prides itself on being free to express ourselves how we want to, and to live in whatever way makes us happy. In reality, the world doesn't offer freedom because it doesn't offer us the truth.

Now that you are saved through your belief in Jesus, you are a child simply because you know the truth. You are going to be part of a redeemed life and restored creation. This new life is your inheritance.

Jesus, you have set me free from the darkness of living in unbelief. Thank you that knowing the truth has given me freedom in all areas of my life. Let my freedom be expressed in ways that declare your truth to the people I meet each day.

What were you a slave to in your former life that you have been set free from in Christ?

Hold onto Truth

Where is that joyful and grateful spirit you felt then? I am sure you would have taken out your own eyes and given them to me if it had been possible. Have I now become your enemy because I am telling you the truth?

GALATIANS 4:15-16 NLT

At times we can feel despondent and unsure about our faith. When we think back to some of our better experiences with God, we can remember the joy and gratefulness, yet life can get the better of us and rob us of that joy. Some days we love our church, our Bible, and our worship songs, and other days we are full of negative thoughts.

Guard yourself from this negativity and allow yourself to hang on to the joy and gratefulness that comes from understanding that you are loved wholly by your heavenly Father.

Father, I am sorry for being skeptical of this faith and the people in my life who stand up for Christ. I am grateful for the work that people put into the church, I am grateful for having your Word, the holy Bible, so readily available to me. Keep my heart thankful as I head into my day today.

Those false teachers are so eager to win your favor, but their intentions are not good. They are trying to shut you off from me so that you will pay attention only to them.

GALATIANS 4:17 NLT

It is still important to be vigilant and sure of the Christian faith. There are so many faith alternatives out there, and while we all express the Christian faith differently, there are some core beliefs that we need to stand firm on.

When you hear others speak about Christianity in a way that is different to what you believe, make sure to question their motives. If they seem like they have selfish intentions, go back to the simple truth of the message that you read in the Bible; this is our true assurance of faith in Christ.

God, give me wisdom and discernment to know what is your truth, and what is merely human pride that gives false teaching. Thank you for the simplicity of your message which is really that you created a way for my salvation and that my belief, and only my belief, is what saves me and gives me eternal life.

Have you felt persuaded by other teachings that are not part of the gospel of Christ?

In Step

*The fruit of the Spirit is love, joy, peace, patience, kindness,
goodness, faithfulness, gentleness, self-control;
against such things there is no law.*

GALATIANS 5:22-23 ESV

The evidence of the Spirit at work in your life, and in the life
of others, is shown in this list of qualities that no one can
argue with. If you are confused as to whether something is of
God, put it through the fruit test. See if what that person is
saying or doing results in love, joy, and peace.

If you are wondering if you have made the right decision, ask
yourself if there has been patience, kindness, and goodness
in the process. If you are attempting to achieve something,
have you been faithful, gentle, and able to control yourself?

*God, let your work in my life be obvious to others. Holy Spirit, I
need your grace so I can be all these things. As I make decisions
and have conversations today, let me walk in the Spirit and do all
things out of a good heart motivation.*

*Those who belong to Christ Jesus have crucified the flesh
with its passions and desires. If we live by the Spirit,
let us also keep in step with the Spirit.*

GALATIANS 5:24-25 ESV

We have a former life that we can't quite get rid of until all of creation is fully restored. Yes, we have been redeemed, but we are still involved in the struggle of leaving behind those things that are not a part of the new kingdom.

This is why we are urged to keep in step with the Spirit so our hearts are fixed on the kingdom and not on the old passions and desires.

Holy Spirit, I know that you are right beside me each day, helping me to become more and more like Christ. Let me always be receptive to your guidance so I can keep in step with you and show the world the wonderful fruit of a life in Christ.

How have you seen the Spirit at work in your life today?

Good Sowing

Do not be deceived: God is not mocked, for whatever one sows, that will he also reap. For the one who sows to his own flesh will from the flesh reap corruption, but the one who sows to the Spirit will from the Spirit reap eternal life.

GALATIANS 6:7–8 ESV

If you planted a rose seed, you wouldn't expect to get a weed. When we do things out of a heart of love for Christ and others, we will reap good things from what we have put in.

Walking with the Holy Spirit will teach us how to live a Christ-centered life and anything we do in Jesus' name will produce something good. As you head into a day full of unknowns, remember that what you say and do reflects Christ within.

Holy Spirit, be my guide today. Help me to recognize when I am sowing into the wrong things or with the wrong heart motivation. I want to reap things for you, so help me to sow from a heart led by you.

*Let us not grow weary of doing good, for in due season we will
reap, if we do not give up. So then, as we have opportunity,
let us do good to everyone, and especially to those who are
of the household of faith.*

GALATIANS 6:9-10 ESV

A flower is a good reminder of the lengthy process it took
to get it there. The seed plants, germinates, and sprouts,
and then has to grow strong, and perhaps even go through a
couple of seasons before it begins to flower.

We can become impatient to see all our good efforts come to
something beautiful. The Scripture says not to become weary
because it will happen in God's good time.

*God, give me opportunities to plant seeds of faith, love, and joy
into my relationships and situations. Remind me that there is
always something good that I can be doing to make a difference in
the lives of people. Help me to endure the harder seasons, knowing
that the beauty is still to come.*

Did you get the chance to sow something good today?

Nothing Greater

*"Give me now wisdom and knowledge to go out and come in
before this people, for who can govern this people of yours,
which is so great?"*

2 CHRONICLES 1:10 ESV

Solomon knew that there was no greater commission than to
lead the people of Israel with justice. Because of his request
for wisdom, he led a kingdom that was peaceful for forty
years. That was not small feat in his day.

What is it that you need from God right now in order to lead
your family, a team, or project with fairness, love, and peace?
Today is a new day and God is able to give you enough wisdom
to make good decisions in all that you do.

*God, I need your wisdom today. Help me to see my responsibilities
as an opportunity to serve you and to serve others with grace and
justice. I want people to know that good decisions are part of being
instructed by the king of all.*

God answered Solomon, "Because this was in your heart, and
you have not asked for possessions, wealth, honor, or the life of
those who hate you, and have not even asked for long life, but
have asked for wisdom and knowledge for yourself that you may
govern my people over whom I have made you king, wisdom and
knowledge are granted to you."

2 CHRONICLES 1:11-12 ESV

King Solomon understood the value of wisdom better than
any other. When God offered him anything he desired, King
Solomon responded with a request for wisdom. He could
have asked for fame, or riches, or success in warfare; instead,
he asked for understanding.

King Solomon sought knowledge and instruction first, and
ended up being the most wise, wealthy, famous, successful
king that ever lived.

Father, you have provided wisdom to guide me and lead me into
a blessed life. Help me to ask for your wisdom in all my situations
and to desire godliness above the other precious things in this life.

What situations have you come across today that you need to
seek God's wisdom for?

Expressions of Praise

The trumpeters and musicians joined in unison to give praise and thanks to the LORD. Accompanied by trumpets, cymbals and other instruments, the singers raised their voices in praise to the LORD and sang: "He is good; his love endures forever."

2 CHRONICLES 5:13 NIV

There is rarely a Christian church where a service is not accompanied with some form of music and singing. It is a part of our humanity to express ourselves through music, and it is part of our faith to express our praise in song.

It doesn't matter if you can play an instrument or sing along to the tune, God delights in you raising your voice as an expression of your love for him. What a beautiful sound it must be to him when his children sing together and acknowledge his goodness.

God, thank you for music and songs. Please bless those musicians and singers who gather the church to worship in song, so we can corporately express our praise to you. Help me to contribute to this collective praise with enthusiasm.

The temple of the LORD was filled with the cloud, and the priests could not perform their service because of the cloud, for the glory of the LORD filled the temple of God.

2 CHRONICLES 5:13-14 NIV

God's presence is always with us, but sometimes there are some significant moments when his presence fills a whole room and everybody feels it. Have you had the chance today, or this week, to worship with other believers?

Find some time to add this into your week so you can experience God in a new and refreshing way. Let go of some of the distractions and barriers that prevent you from really expressing your gratitude and joy for the God of creation who loves you so much.

God, I need to be with other people to worship this week. I ask for some opportunities to get together with others, even if it isn't in the form of a traditional church service. Thank you for your presence that dwells amongst a few that are gathered in your name.

Where can you go to worship with others this week?

Temple for His Presence

"In the future, foreigners who do not belong to your people Israel will hear of you. They will come from distant lands when they hear of your great name and your strong hand and your powerful arm. And when they pray toward this Temple, then hear from heaven where you live, and grant what they ask of you."

2 CHRONICLES 6:31-32 NLT

Isn't it marvelous that the God of Israel has always been seen as a God for all people? God never intended that people were excluded from his great redemptive plan; the future has always been that all people would hear about the power and love of the God of Israel and draw near to him.

You have come to Christ because of this realization, whether you are the first in your family to receive him or whether it has been passed down to you through the generations. Be encouraged today that his salvation has always been for you, and it needs to extend to others.

God, it is amazing to read these ancient words and realize that we are part of these foreign people who have heard of your great name. Thank you so much for your salvation. May I always be ready to share the power of your name with others.

"All the people of the earth will come to know and fear you, just as your own people Israel do. They, too, will know that this Temple I have built honors your name."

2 CHRONICLES 6:32 NLT

The great temple of Solomon must have been extraordinary and was a prominent symbol of God's presence with the people of Israel. It's sometimes mind blowing to know that Jesus said this temple wasn't needed anymore, but that God now dwells within us.

You might not feel as though you are that impressive of a place to dwell, but don't let those thoughts stop you from experiencing God. Remember that it is Christ within that makes us beautiful. Let yourself soak in his presence tonight.

Lord God, your power and greatness sometimes overwhelms me and makes me feel unworthy. Help me to realize the truth of what Christ has done; that I am now worthy to receive your presence. Fill me with your deep sense of peace as I lay my head down to rest this evening.

Why do you feel unworthy this evening? Let go of those thoughts and let the truth of your worthiness sink deep into your heart and mind.

If Only

*"If My people who are called by My name will humble themselves,
and pray and seek My face, and turn from their wicked ways,
then I will hear from heaven, and will forgive their sin
and heal their land."*

2 Chronicles 7:14 NKJV

Jesus Christ came to redeem our world, but it still seems
very broken. It can be hard to reconcile what Christ has done
when you see pain and suffering around you every day. If
only people would humble themselves, seek his face and turn
from their ways, they could be made whole.

Praise God that you have turned toward him. Go into your day
and be a part of the rescue mission to see people forgiven of
their sin and receive healing from their brokenness.

*God, thank you for making me whole. I want to spread your
healing to a broken world around me. I pray for people in my life
right now who are experiencing brokenness and ask that you
would intervene in their circumstance. Help them to see your light
and your face.*

"My eyes will be open and My ears attentive to prayer made in this place. For now I have chosen and sanctified this house, that My name may be there forever; and My eyes and My heart will be there perpetually."

2 CHRONICLES 7:15-17 NKJV

God was so pleased that Israel had sought his presence because this is how he would be able to speak to them. When you have turned yourself toward the Lord, he is willing to see your circumstance and listen to your prayers.

It is not about you being a good person that gives you bargaining power, it is simply that you have turned to him and asked to be with him. His promise to you this evening is that when you stay close to him, his eyes and heart will be with you forever.

Father, I turn my face toward you now, asking for your presence to fill me with assurance that you are forever with me, listening and responding, as an attentive parent. I love you and need more of you in my life.

What do need to ask of your heavenly Father tonight?

Friendly Advice

Then King Rehoboam consulted the elders who stood before his father Solomon while he still lived, saying, "How do you advise me to answer these people?" And they spoke to him, saying, "If you are kind to these people, and please them, and speak good words to them, they will be your servants forever."

2 CHRONICLES 10:6-7 NKJV

How do you deal with complaining people? Perhaps it's the children in your life, your co-workers, or maybe even your friends who have complaints against you. Even if their complaints are unjustified, there is a principle that speaking a kind word will soften a heart toward you.

Instead of becoming self-righteous, be kind and you will find yourself in a much more favorable situation. Listen to the advice of the wise.

God, I need your patience when people are grumbling about me or to me. Give me the grace to be kind instead of angry and to treat these people with respect. Thank you that kindness will result in loyalty.

He rejected the advice which the elders had given him,
and consulted the young men who had grown up with him,
who stood before him.

2 CHRONICLES 10:8 NKJV

Your friends have the power to lead you closer to God or push you away from him. Surround yourself with people who will echo God's words to you rather than lead you off course with their advice.

Evaluate yourself to make sure you are being the kind of friend who will lead others closer to Christ by your influence and your advice.

As I reflect on my day, God, I can see those people who have been very encouraging to me. I want to be with people who are wise and able to lift me up in my faith. I also ask for the love and grace to be a good and wise friend to others.

Who have you spent time with today? Are they people who are wise and encouraging?

His Battle, Not Yours

"Listen, all you people of Judah and Jerusalem! Listen, King Jehoshaphat! This is what the LORD says: Do not be afraid! Don't be discouraged by this mighty army, for the battle is not yours, but God's. Tomorrow, march out against them. You will find them coming up through the ascent of Ziz at the end of the valley that opens into the wilderness of Jeruel."

2 CHRONICLES 20:15–16 NLT

Being defeated in battle would have been very frightening in the times of the kings of Israel. It meant bloodshed and great loss, including loss of territory. Fear of having those battles would have been great.

We don't face the same physical intensity of those battles, but we have our own battles to face in life. We may feel attacked by unbelievers, or in the middle of some unfair rumors, or struggling with our health. We are afraid of loss in an emotional and physical sense. Let this Scripture speak to you today: "Do not be afraid, for the battle is not yours, but mine." Let God take your fears away and give you courage to face whatever is coming your way.

God, I am so glad that I do not have to face this battle in my own strength. Give me the courage to stand up even though I feel weak. Give me the strategy and discernment to know what to do next.

"You will not even need to fight. Take your positions; then stand still and watch the Lord's victory. He is with you, O people of Judah and Jerusalem. Do not be afraid or discouraged. Go out against them tomorrow, for the Lord is with you!"

2 Chronicles 20:17 nlt

Isn't it good to know that God doesn't always make us go through the battle. God wants to defeat the darkness in your life without the need to fight. All he is asking of you is to take your position and trust that he will take care of the rest.

You can stand back and watch God take the victory, because he is with you. Don't be afraid or discouraged; allow peace to settle on your heart, right now, in this moment, as you hand over the control to him.

God, thank you that you are a God of peace and that you do not expect me to do all the fighting. I give you my thoughts and plans and actions toward these difficult situations and pray that you would be victorious. Give me peace as I sleep.

What are you trying to control in the battle that God is calling you to hand over to him?

Taking It Too Far

A prophet of the LORD named Oded was there in Samaria when the army of Israel returned home. He went out to meet them and said, "The LORD, the God of your ancestors, was angry with Judah and let you defeat them. But you have gone too far, killing them without mercy, and all heaven is disturbed."

2 CHRONICLES 28:9 NLT

We can read the Old Testament and get a bit concerned about how it appears God dealt with people. God has always been merciful. He was angered by King Ahaz because the Israelite army showed no mercy to the tribe of Judah. He even went as far as to say that all of heaven is upset.

It's good to be reminded of God's love and justice in a world where we see such a lack of it. Remember to show mercy to people who come across your path today.

God, you are a just and merciful God. Help me to imitate this to others so I can be a good representation of who you really are. Thank you that righteousness comes through your death on the cross and that all have received your grace.

"Now you are planning to make slaves of these people from Judah and Jerusalem. What about your own sins against the LORD your God? Listen to me and return these prisoners you have taken, for they are your own relatives. Watch out, because now the LORD's fierce anger has been turned against you!"

2 CHRONICLES 28:10-11 NLT

God is a God of justice. Humans get the idea of justice wrong and this is why God says that no one can judge the hearts of men except himself. We have to trust that God's ways are really the best ways.

When we condemn others, or seek justice ourselves, we are not doing things God's way. God is concerned with our own sin, not the sins of others. Show your trust in God and leave the judgment and consequences of other's actions up to him.

God, you reserve the right to judge the hearts of men. Forgive me when I have overstepped my calling to show mercy. Help me to concentrate on doing right before you because only you know my heart.

When have you tried to take matters into your own hands? Give these matters back to God.

Eyes of Your Heart

I pray that the eyes of your heart may be enlightened in order that you may know the hope to which he has called you, the riches of his glorious inheritance in his holy people, and his incomparably great power for us who believe.

EPHESIANS 1:18-19 NIV

Believing in Jesus isn't just about being given all the right information, nor is it about being convinced with the most persuasive argument. Believing involves the heart and the transformation that takes place when someone is illuminated with the truth of the gospel.

As you go into the world today and meet various people, pray this same prayer for them—that the eyes of their heart would be opened to the good news of Jesus Christ.

God, my eyes have been opened to your truth and my heart wholly accepts that you are the Savior of the world. I pray for those people I come into contact with today and ask for your grace to be extended to them. Holy Spirit, open the eyes of their hearts.

That power is the same as the mighty strength he exerted when he raised Christ from the dead and seated him at his right hand in the heavenly realms, far above all rule and authority, power and dominion, and every name that is invoked, not only in the present age but also in the one to come.

EPHESIANS 19-21 NIV

Jesus has called you to a life of strength and power from above. You may have felt discouraged today, perceiving the empathy of people toward the Christian faith or even a lack of any kind of belief in a power greater than themselves. The world's thinking is futile.

There is no hope for those who do not believe in the eternal life that Jesus Christ has promised and shared with us. You have been called and blessed with inheritance of the age to come. Let that joy overwhelm your heart this evening.

Thank you, God, that you have saved me from the futile thinking of this world. There is so much hope to be found in your Word and I pray that I would be someone who shares this bright future with others.

Are your thoughts dwelling on the difficulties of today or on the hope of eternity?

Fully Alive

You were dead in your transgressions and sins, in which you used to live when you followed the ways of this world and of the ruler of the kingdom of the air, the spirit who is now at work in those who are disobedient. All of us also lived among them at one time, gratifying the cravings of our flesh and following its desires and thoughts. Like the rest, we were by nature deserving of wrath.

EPHESIANS 2:1-3 NIV

It is possible to live our lives without being fully alive. Jesus made the differentiation between living without him and living with him. Without Jesus we don't have hope; we are stuck in our sins which can only lead to death.

Once we accept the freedom that Jesus won for us, we have an eternal perspective and the awareness of how trapped we were in sin. You can choose to approach this day with the joy of knowing that your new life has already begun.

God, I thank you that all my sins and wrong doings have been dealt with on the cross and that I can rise again this morning as a new person. I enter this day with the knowledge that I am fully alive.

*Because of his great love for us, God, who is rich in mercy, made us
alive with Christ even when we were dead in transgressions—
it is by grace you have been saved.*

EPHESIANS 2:4-5 NIV

Sometimes we make mistakes and wish that we could go back
and re-live the moment so we can do it better. Life in Christ
gives us this second opportunity to right the wrong and to live
in the fullness of forgiveness.

If you regret something that you said or did today, bring it to
the Lord confidently knowing that you are forgiven and that
you can begin again right now.

*Jesus, help me to reclaim the truth that I am living a new life that
is being restored by you. Forgive me of all my sins, and cleanse me
through the power of your holy name.*

What area of your life do you need to die to tonight and rise
again victorious?

His Handiwork

It is by grace you have been saved, through faith—and this is not
from yourselves, it is the gift of God— not by works,
so that no one can boast.

EPHESIANS 2:8-9 NIV

Think of the last sunrise you saw and remember the
breathtaking beauty of seeing the light dawn on a new day.
There are so many beautiful displays of God's creation and we
don't have to look far to appreciate it.

Consider now that you are a part of this handiwork and you
are as beautiful as the sunrise, the majestic cliffs, or the
wondrous display of stars in the night sky. God planned all of
creation; he planned the creation of humanity—the creation of
you. Go into your day knowing that God has a purpose for you.

God, thank you for reminding me that I am a beautiful part of
your handiwork. Thank you that you made me for a purpose.
I am blessed to be a part of the redemptive work that you started
on earth, so help me to continue that work today.

We are God's handiwork, created in Christ Jesus to do good works, which God prepared in advance for us to do.

EPHESIANS 2:10 NIV

You may not feel majestic or grand about the things you do for God, but know that every little thing you do for him is good. He created you with the gifts that would work together with others' gifts to contribute toward building his kingdom.

His master plan and design is beyond our comprehension, but recognize that his plans include and build on all the effort you put in to your work, family, and the community you are part of.

God thank you that even though I don't always see that I am doing anything good, you are still at work through me and in all the small and diligent things that I do. Thank you that you have a calling on my life.

In what small, good ways are you contributing to building his kingdom?

On the Horizon

You have been united with Christ Jesus. Once you were far away from God, but now you have been brought near to him through the blood of Christ.

EPHESIANS 2:13 NLT

Have you ever seen a black speck on the horizon of the ocean, realizing it is a vessel but not sure exactly what type or how large it is? It seems like it is something spectacular, but you can't make out any of the features or understand what its purpose is until it gets nearer.

Jesus Christ brought God's plan for humanity close to us so now when we look at him we understand the detail and beauty of what God has done for us. We were far away from the truth, but now it has been brought close.

Jesus, thank you for helping me to see things clearly when I didn't understand or know quite what salvation meant. Help me to bring that vessel closer to others today so they may experience your nearness as well.

Christ himself has brought peace to us. He united Jews and Gentiles into one people when, in his own body on the cross, he broke down the wall of hostility that separated us.

EPHESIANS 2:14 NLT

In the same way that God provided us a way to be close to him, he also provided a way for us to be close to others. There don't need to be barriers between people groups; God didn't intend for there to be divisions because of race, gender, or status.

If you have confronted forms of hostility for any reason today, ask for God's peace to unite you with those who have created a barrier. Christ came to break down those walls.

God, as I think about those situations in my life, and even in the world, that need healing from division and hostility, I pray that you would give me the courage to stand up for unity and peace. Thank you that you pursue equality. Help me to be like you in this.

Who can you pray for tonight that needs to experience unity and peace?

Grounded in Love

I pray that, according to the riches of his glory, he may grant that you may be strengthened in your inner being with power through his Spirit, and that Christ may dwell in your hearts through faith, as you are being rooted and grounded in love.

EPHESIANS 3:16-17 NRSV

When storms come, most trees are exposed to the elements of the wind and rain. Strong winds can bend certain trees almost to the ground, yet when the storm moves on, the tree is still standing strong.

Your strength is something that God is working in you from the inside out. Each day that you ground yourself in the truth of his Word and his love for you, you are growing in understanding and in strength. When the storms come, you are like a tree that might get thrown around a little, but you will remain with your roots firmly in the soil of God's goodness.

God, I trust in your love and I believe in your Word. I pray that as I grow in you, you would help me to bravely face the storms of life that come, knowing that you will keep me standing at the end of it all.

*I pray that you may have the power to comprehend, with all the
saints, what is the breadth and length and height and depth,
and to know the love of Christ that surpasses knowledge,
so you may be filled with all the fullness of God.*

EPHESIANS 3:18-19 NRSV

Knowing the love of Christ for you doesn't just make you feel
good, it actually helps you to grow in your understanding and
knowledge of him. We can't fully comprehend the enormity of
his love, but when we see a glimpse of it, we begin to see why
he humbled himself and came to earth, and why he submitted
himself to the wretchedness of the cross.

Fill yourself with this wonder in this moment.

*Lord Jesus, I know that I cannot begin to comprehend how
wonderful your love is for all mankind. Help me to experience
some of that love right now as I dwell on the enormity of what you
have done for me, and for all your creation. Allow my mind and
body to rest easily tonight so I am refreshed for a new day.*

How have you experienced God's amazing love lately?

United in Spirit

*Always be humble and gentle. Be patient with each other, making
allowance for each other's faults because of your love.*

EPHESIANS 4:2 NLT

This life doesn't lend itself to being humble and gentle. We
are pressed for time, pressured with deadlines, and worried
about money. There is a lot of stress to deal with, and often
the ones we love the most end up having those feelings of
stress directed toward them.

Gentleness doesn't typically come to the top of the list in the
ways that we treat others. If you are feeling stressed about
your day or week ahead, give God the burden. He can handle
your emotions. As he takes the burden from you, remember
to be gracious in how you deal with others and be empathic
toward their stresses too.

*God, I feel like it is impossible to always be humble and gentle, but
I want to be. Relieve me of the stresses that I am facing right now
and give me a patient and gentle spirit, so I can be uplifted by my
loved ones and be a positive influence in their lives when they need
it the most.*

Make every effort to keep yourselves united in the Spirit, binding yourselves together with peace. For there is one body and one Spirit, just as you have been called to one glorious hope for the future.

EPHESIANS 4:3-4 NLT

There is no better support than those people in your life who fully understand you and who are on your side one hundred percent. We can support each other despite our difference of opinions, temperaments, or ways of doing things. Unity is not about being the same, but about working together toward the same goal.

Think of those believers in your life who all are working to see God move in this world. Let peace settle in your relationships so you are not fighting against this goal, but working toward it.

God, today I have been reminded of the goal of unity within my relationships, and particularly with other believers. Thank you that we all share the glorious hope of an eternal future. Holy Spirit, continue to remind me to make every effort to keep a spirit of unity in my relationships.

Who do you need to make peace with tonight?

Fully Armed

Put on all of God's armor so that you will be able to stand firm against all strategies of the devil. For we are not fighting against flesh-and-blood enemies, but against evil rulers and authorities of the unseen world, against mighty powers in this dark world, and against evil spirits in the heavenly places.

EPHESIANS 6:11-12 NLT

When you leave your house for the day, you usually make sure everything is turned off, windows are shut, doors are locked, and the alarm is on. We do a lot to protect our homes from destruction and theft. It makes sense, then, that we protect ourselves from the strategies of evil.

As you head out the door today, remind yourself of God's truth, be ready to do right, bring peace wherever you go, and dwell on the good news of your salvation. We need all this spiritual preparation so we are fully armed for the day.

God, I know that you have equipped me with everything that I need to fend off the attempt of the enemy to discourage or disrupt me today. I thank you for saving me, I state my belief in your Word, I choose peace over chaos, and I stand firm in your love. Thank you for your strength within me today.

Put on every piece of God's armor so you will be able to resist the enemy in the time of evil. Then after the battle you will still be standing firm.

EPHESIANS 6:13 NLT

Whether you feel victorious about your day or not, God has been with you the entire time. Even if you come home feeling emotionally or spiritually battered and bruised, know that you have fought well because you were wearing your spiritual armor.

Resisting temptation and defeating discouragement can leave you tired. Ask God to refresh you tonight so you will continue to stand firm in your faith and in all circumstances.

God, today has been hard and I feel weary. I know that battles are part of this life, but I am worn out from fending off the darkness that threatens to steal my joy. Thank you for the strength of your Word and the knowledge of your truth. Restore my joy and strength to me tonight.

What battles have you encountered today? Let God tend to your pain and heal any wounds.

Foundations

All the people gave a great shout, praising the L ORD because the foundation of the L ORD's Temple had been laid. But many of the older priests, Levites, and other leaders who had seen the first Temple wept aloud when they saw the new Temple's foundation. The others, however, were shouting for joy.

E ZRA 3:11-12 NLT

The foundations of any building are a sign of new beginnings. It is little wonder that this was a momentous day for the Israelites; the temple was finally being rebuilt. For some, the new beginnings were a joyous occasion, but for those who had seen the first temple there was the kind of weeping that mourns and rejoices at the same time, perhaps like a new birth after a death.

You might be waiting for something great to happen in your life, so why not take some time to recognize the foundations that are being laid and to celebrate, with laugher or tears, at the new beginnings that God is going to bring.

God, help me to recognize the construction that is happening in my heart. Thank you for the foundations of truth, provision, and trust that you have put in my life. Help me to reconcile the past laments with the future hope.

The joyful shouting and weeping mingled together in a loud noise that could be heard far in the distance.

EZRA 3:13 NLT

What a noise it must have been for a whole nation's weeping and joyful shouting to be heard from far off. It would be like hearing a stadium erupt when a team scores. It's amazing the kind of impact people can have when they are gathered together to celebrate.

God receives all expressions of praise. You might be someone who likes to shout at the top of your lungs when you are full of joy, or perhaps you are more moved to happy tears. God loves it all.

God, I love you and I want to express my love in a way that is consistent with the way that you made me. Help me to shout, sing, whisper, and weep without worrying about what anyone else will think. Thank you that you love all my expressions.

In what ways to do you feel like expressing yourself to God now? Give yourself some time to do this.

Discouragement

Zerubbabel, Joshua and the rest of the heads of the families of Israel answered, "You have no part with us in building a temple to our God. We alone will build it for the LORD, the God of Israel, as King Cyrus, the king of Persia, commanded us." Then the peoples around them set out to discourage the people of Judah and make them afraid to go on building.

EZRA 4:3-4 NIV

These tribes of Israel had a particular calling from God to rebuild the temple, but the people who surrounded them did not agree with that calling. There are days when you feel like everyone is against you and sometimes there really are people who attempt to stop you from doing what you feel called to do.

The enemy will do anything he can to discourage you from serving God and carrying out his calling on your life. Don't stop building just because the locals are taunting you. Hold onto the promises that God has given you and go for it.

God, I want to approach this day with vigor in carrying out your work. I feel challenged when I read that these people had to stop building because of the attempts of the enemy. I draw on your power today, and choose to stand up to those who oppose me.

They bribed officials to work against them and frustrate their
plans during the entire reign of Cyrus king of Persia and down to
the reign of Darius king of Persia.

EZRA 4:5 NIV

People can go over and above to try and stop something that
they don't believe in. You might not have felt any persecution
for your faith, but it is always good to be praying for the
advancement of the kingdom.

We don't want to see God's restoration plan be stalled on
account of the world's neglect of the truth. Rather than
allowing the enemy to get a foothold, defend the gospel and
make sure that God's Word, and his church, prevails.

Thank you, heavenly Father, that you are more powerful and
more knowing than anything on this earth. Thank you that you
already know those plans in place to try and stop your kingdom
from advancing. Give me discernment to know when to pray for a
breakthrough.

What plans from God have been frustrated by others lately?

A Little Relief

"For a brief moment, the LORD our God has been gracious in leaving us a remnant and giving us a firm place in his sanctuary, and so our God gives light to our eyes and a little relief in our bondage."

EZRA 9:8 NIV

At times we can feel trapped in our jobs, our home life, or just the ordinary routine of life. It is part of our human nature to seek freedom; therefore, any form of restriction seems to plague us.

If you are feeling particularly stuck in a situation or place, ask for brief moments from God where you feel his freedom and grace. When you begin to see God in the small things, you remember God's faithfulness and this becomes like a light that gives you relief and hope at the end of the tunnel.

God, you have always been gracious to your people. Thank you for giving me a glimmer of hope this morning. Remind me to bring this glimmer into the lives of the people I come across today.

"Though we are slaves, our God has not forsaken us in our bondage. He has shown us kindness in the sight of the kings of Persia: He has granted us new life to rebuild the house of our God and repair its ruins, and he has given us a wall of protection in Judah and Jerusalem."

EZRA 9:9 NIV

God still has his way of getting his work done, despite the human obstacles that we throw in the way. Even though the Israelites had been held captive because they had not kept God's commands, God did not forsake them.

His grace gave them a chance to rebuild the things that were once torn down. Not only did he provide them with the resources, but also with protection. God is looking out for you.

Father, you know my heart and the weight that I sometimes feel because of all the tasks and responsibilities that I have on my plate. Thank you that you can give me rest from those things as I read your Word and find life in Scripture. Help me to be someone who willingly helps to build your house.

Where is God giving you a little relief from responsibilities and burdens?

Hear Me

"The survivors there in the province who escaped captivity are in great trouble and shame; the wall of Jerusalem is broken down, and its gates have been destroyed by fire." When I heard these words I sat down and wept, and mourned for days, fasting and praying before the God of heaven.

NEHEMIAH 1:3-4 NRSV

God hears you. Whether you are shouting praises of thanksgiving, crying tears of mourning, or singing phrases of glory, God hears. He listens. He does not abandon or ignore. He hears your voice. He hears your heart. He hears your shouts, your whispers, and your thoughts.

God takes us as we are, where we are. We don't have to filter, pretend, or please. He meets us, loves us, and accepts us right in this moment.

God, turn your ear toward me this morning. I have a lot of questions, a lot of decisions to make, and I need your help. Some days I feel like I am drowning and I need saving. I know that you understand my needs, so I will continue to call on your name from morning to night.

"O L ORD God of heaven, the great and awesome God who keeps
covenant and steadfast love with those who love him and keep his
commandments; let your ear be attentive and your eyes open to
hear the prayer of your servant that I now pray before you day and
night for your servants, the people of Israel, confessing the sins of
the people of Israel, which we have sinned against you. Both I and
my family have sinned."

NEHEMIAH 1:5-6 NRSV

Some days we don't feel worthy of sitting in God's presence.
But you are here now. He is a beautiful, caring God who
takes us as sinners and holds our hand as we walk the path to
salvation.

He protects us, encourages us, and fully loves us. Remember
this truth today so your soul can rest in his goodness.

*God, at the end of the day I don't seem to be thinking about
your goodness. I need you, Holy Spirit, to gently whisper that
into my ear. You are gracious, you are righteous, you are full of
compassion. You protect me, save me, and give me rest.*

Do you believe God hears you? What do you want to tell him
right now?

Rebuilding

"You see the trouble we are in: Jerusalem lies in ruins, and its gates have been burned with fire. Come, let us rebuild the wall of Jerusalem, and we will no longer be in disgrace."

NEHEMIAH 2:17 NIV

It is natural to mourn for the good things that once were. Jerusalem had been a beautiful thriving city in Nehemiah's day and the ruins he saw represented the destruction of his past. The desire to rebuild was a noble and heartfelt yearning.

As you reflect on the past you may grieve things that have been seemingly destroyed. God could be drawing you and calling you to rebuild those walls and make that area of your life great again.

God, I desire to see some of my dreams that have been lost over time restored. Thank you that you don't forget what you have placed in my heart and that the things that are meant to be rebuilt will happen in your time.

> *"I also told them about the gracious hand of my God on me and what the king had said to me. They replied, 'Let us start rebuilding.' So they began this good work."*
>
> Nehemiah 2:18-19 NIV

We usually can't reach those glorious dreams like a city wall without other people. If God is calling you to rebuild some of those walls from your past as part of your future, then bring people along for the journey.

You will know if the plan really is from God when people begin to eagerly join you and say, as they did to Nehemiah, "let us start rebuilding."

God, give me discernment to know what you want me to leave in my past and what you want me to rebuild for my future. Thank you that this isn't about me but about your kingdom. Please bring the people into my life who will help me to restore what has been lost.

What does God want you to rebuild, and who can you ask to help you?

Don't Give Up

"We built the wall and the whole wall was joined together to half its height, for the people had a mind to work. Now when Sanballat, Tobiah, the Arabs, the Ammonites and the Ashdodites heard that the repair of the walls of Jerusalem went on, and that the breaches began to be closed, they were very angry. All of them conspired together to come and fight against Jerusalem and to cause a disturbance in it. But we prayed to our God, and because of them we set up a guard against them day and night."

NEHEMIAH 4:6-9 NASB

There were so many reasons for Nehemiah to give up on rebuilding the wall. They were insulted from every angle, they were threatened with attacks, and there was so much rubble that the workers were getting exhausted and their strength was giving out. Nehemiah continued to pray and figured out how to cover each of these problems.

You will have dreams for your future; God doesn't want to give up on your heart's desires. Figure out the things that are going come against you and discover a strategy for how to work through those.

Father, thank you for the promises that you made to me. There are still dreams and hopes that I have for the future, but I don't really know how they're going to happen. Give me the strategy and strength of character to never give up.

*"Half of my servants carried on the work while half of them held
the spears, the shields, the bows and the breastplates; and the
captains were behind the whole house of Judah. Those who were
rebuilding the wall and those who carried burdens took their load
with one hand doing the work and the other holding a weapon."*

NEHEMIAH 4:16-17 NASB

Nehemiah had to be prepared for everything, so he had his
people multi-task. They would build with one hand and hold
weapons and shields in the other.

We don't always get to the final dream without all the other
necessary parts of life. We have other jobs to do while we are
working toward the bigger things.

*God, help me to see the value in the day-to-day tasks of life.
I know that you want me to be prepared for everything as I work
toward my dreams and aspirations. Thank you for equipping me
to be someone who can do a lot of things at the same time.*

What is the spear or shield that you are holding in your
hand that you need to give more value to? Recognize the
significance in multi-tasking.

Defend the Oppressed

"What you are doing is not right! Should you not walk in the fear of our God in order to avoid being mocked by enemy nations? I myself, as well as my brothers and my workers, have been lending the people money and grain, but now let us stop this business of charging interest. You must restore their fields, vineyards, olive groves, and homes to them this very day. And repay the interest you charged when you lent them money, grain, new wine, and olive oil."

NEHEMIAH 5:9-11 NLT

The system of our world hasn't changed much from Nehemiah's time. The rich lend to the poor and they charge interest so they eventually get more. It is a heavy burden for those who have borrowed.

We rarely blink an eye at the idea of a mortgage these days, but the truth is that we are a society that is in debt. Nehemiah saw the strain that this placed on those who were already struggling and encouraged grace and mercy toward those who were being oppressed. This is God's heart, that we all work toward restoring that which is broken and lost.

God, I pray you would give me a new perspective on debt. Help me to be wise with what I borrow, but also help me to be a generous giver that does not expect anything in return. Give me the will today to stand up for the oppressed.

"We will give back everything and demand nothing more from the people. We will do as you say." Then I called the priests and made the nobles and officials swear to do what they had promised.

NEHEMIAH 5:12 NLT

Are there things that you are expecting back from people who have borrowed from you? It can be hard to let go of the feeling of injustice, but remember that you gave out of the fact that you had more than the other.

True generosity is letting go of the idea of fairness and being confident that God will continue to provide for you. It might be something as small as owing money for a dinner, but give someone a break from their concern of debt today.

God, thank you for your abundant generosity toward me. You have provided me with more than enough and I want to show mercy toward others, so you will be glorified through my actions.

Who can you extend grace to and relieve them of a debt?

Time to Feast

Nehemiah continued, "Go and celebrate with a feast of rich foods and sweet drinks, and share gifts of food with people who have nothing prepared. This is a sacred day before our Lord. Don't be dejected and sad, for the joy of the Lord is your strength!"

NEHEMIAH 8:10 NLT

When the words of the law were read out to the people of Israel they began to weep. It can be a sobering thing to realize your sin before the Lord. It is right to feel a sense of mourning for the things that we have done wrong and for the consequences of wrong, yet God does not want you to dwell on guilt. He wants you to celebrate because he is a God that gives mercy and restoration.

As you get up and get ready for your day, don't be dejected and sad, let God's joy in your heart be your strength.

God, there have been many times when I have turned away from you. At times I have pursued my own ways and I have regrets. Allow me to receive your mercy and to live in the joy of knowing that I am forgiven today and forever.

The Levites, too, quieted the people, telling them, "Hush! Don't weep! For this is a sacred day." So the people went away to eat and drink at a festive meal, to share gifts of food, and to celebrate with great joy because they had heard God's words and understood them.

NEHEMIAH 8:11-12 NLT

Understanding God's Word is a thing to be celebrated. When God's words confuse you, ask for discernment and clarity. Seek out wisdom about what the Scriptures say.

Your heart will rejoice when you understand the Word because you are beginning to understand the father heart of God. Let his love fill you tonight, and remember to celebrate his love with others.

God, thank you for giving me wisdom and discernment to understand your Word. Holy Spirit, thank you for helping me to understand and get life from what I read in Scripture. Guide me each day to know more of you and help me to celebrate those times when I see the truth of your Word.

How can you celebrate the joy of understanding the goodness of God?

Reminded of Miracles

"You performed signs and wonders against Pharaoh and all his servants and all the people of his land, for you knew that they acted insolently against our ancestors. You made a name for yourself, which remains to this day. And you divided the sea before them, so that they passed through the sea on dry land, but you threw their pursuers into the depths, like a stone into mighty waters. Moreover, you led them by day with a pillar of cloud, and by night with a pillar of fire, to give them light on the way in which they should go."

NEHEMIAH 9:10-12 NRSV

God has always been with his people, providing them with miracles to show his power and reality and giving them mercy when they failed.

It is good to be reminded of God's goodness to those who have chosen to follow him. Be encouraged today about the stories of old and the new stories that God is creating for you now.

Almighty God, you have shown goodness to your people from the beginning of time, and you are still with us today. Remind me of the ways that you have worked in my life, and encourage me to continue to follow you.

"You came down also upon Mount Sinai, and spoke with them from heaven, and gave them right ordinances and true laws, good statutes and commandments, and you made known your holy Sabbath to them and gave them commandments and statutes and a law through your servant Moses. For their hunger you gave them bread from heaven, and for their thirst you brought water for them out of the rock, and you told them to go in to possess the land that you swore to give them."

NEHEMIAH 9:13-15 NRSV

As you read about all the amazing things that God did for the Israelites, remember that this same God is with you now.

He is just as powerful, just as miraculous, and just as merciful. God always delivers on his promise, and you are a part of that promise.

Father God, you have done wonderful things in my life and are continuing to do amazing things. Fill my mind and heart with the stories of the ways that you have worked in my life, and give me the courage to tell people about your works tomorrow.

What stories can you tell about God's amazing work in your life?

Love on the Increase

I pray that your love will overflow more and more, and that you will keep on growing in knowledge and understanding. For I want you to understand what really matters, so that you may live pure and blameless lives until the day of Christ's return.

PHILIPPIANS 1:9-10 NLT

The beauty of love is that it keeps growing. If we feed love with the right motivation, it will increase. As we understand more about love, we know the deep importance of sharing this love with all people.

Love gives us the purest lens in which to view other people. With it, we gain better insight and more grace into situations. If you come across a difficult situation with somebody today, remember the lens of love and let it guide you to do the right thing.

God, I thank you for the path that love leads me on. I pray that I would follow that path because I know that this is the way to have right relationships with people. Help my love for others to grow more today.

May you always be filled with the fruit of your salvation—
the righteous character produced in your life by Jesus Christ—
for this will bring much glory and praise to God.

PHILIPPIANS 1:11 NLT

Were you able to view people through the lens of Christ's love today? People can be hard to love sometimes, but the more we put it into practice, the easier it becomes.

When we practice love, we honor Jesus because we display exactly the kind of life that he showed on earth. You will begin to see the fruit of your love toward people as you allow it to increase.

God, I'm sorry I have failed to show love in situations where I needed to. Thank you that your love for me allows me to love others.

Who needs to experience your increasing love this week?

Who First?

Do nothing from selfish ambition or conceit, but in humility regard others as better than yourselves. Let each of you look not to your own interests, but to the interests of others.

PHILIPPIANS 2:3-4 NRSV

Can we ever truly grasp what Jesus had to give up in order to become human and walk this earth with us? Scripture tells us that although Jesus had equality with God, he gave up his supreme entitlement to become human.

We may never quite understand this act, but we can accept that Jesus' birth and death on the cross was our ultimate example of sacrifice. Are you willing to sacrifice, as in the example of Jesus, regarding others before yourself?

God, today I choose to look out for the interest of others. Thank you that I can be confident in your love for me, and that this confidence can lead me to make others feel important and special.

Let the same mind be in you that was in Christ Jesus.

PHILIPPIANS 2:5 NRSV

Do you recognize selfish ambition in your life? Reflect on Jesus' sacrifice, and in your thankfulness, make a commitment to imitate him by seeing the good in others and pursuing their interests above your own.

This is not to attribute a higher worth based on superior authority or qualities, but to understand people's value in light of Christ.

God, sometimes I don't feel I have the energy to expend on others. Help me to relax tonight and be encouraged to look outside myself. I know you will present me with an opportunity to love outrageously and I ask for the strength to be up to that challenge.

What can you do to imitate Christ in his humility and sacrifice this week?

Against the Dark Sky

Do everything without complaining and arguing, so that no one can criticize you. Live clean, innocent lives as children of God, shining like bright lights in a world full of crooked and perverse people.

PHILIPPIANS 2:14-15 NLT

The temptation to complain or bicker can be overwhelming at times. Any discussion involving opinions and decision will have a certain amount of tension because we all want to be heard, and we all value our own opinions.

Our complaints are often valid and true, but we miss the joy that the Lord desires for us when we seek out only the negative. Choose to be positive and truthful today.

God, I often get pulled into the negativity of this world, so I ask that I would be sensitive to the prompting of the Holy Spirit when I start to head down that path. Keep my words full of life and love.

Hold firmly to the word of life; then, on the day of Christ's return, I will be proud that I did not run the race in vain and that my work was not useless.

PHILIPPIANS 2:14-15 NLT

Choosing to be positive and to speak positively is something that will make you stand out like the stars against a black sky—did you get a good sense of that today? If not tomorrow is another day.

This letter from Paul to the Philippians was written thousands of years ago, but it could just have easily been written today. We still live in a warped and crooked generation. Let's shine like stars against the dark sky. Let us hold firmly to his Word as we speak life to those around us.

God, as I reflect on my day and my words, I pray you would show me the times when my words were uplifting and helpful. Forgive me when I have had unkind words or a grumbling heart. Teach me to speak words of wisdom and to have a positive attitude toward life.

Are there people in your life who are causing you to be negative? What can you do to avoid negative conversations?

Garbage

I once thought these things were valuable, but now I consider them worthless because of what Christ has done. Yes, everything else is worthless when compared with the infinite value of knowing Christ Jesus my Lord. For his sake I have discarded everything else, counting it all as garbage, so that I could gain Christ and become one with him. I no longer count on my own righteousness through obeying the law; rather, I become righteous through faith in Christ. For God's way of making us right with himself depends on faith.

PHILIPPIANS 3:7-9 NLT

Once you've experienced the true beauty of a relationship with Christ, everything else becomes somehow insignificant. What you once held dear no longer seems important.

Compared to knowing Christ as your Savior, everything else the world values just pales in comparison.

God, as I get ready for a new day, I pray that I would be able to see the insignificance of some of the things that I pursue, and that I would see the significance of others. I ask that you give me discernment of what is garbage and what is treasure.

I want to know Christ and experience the mighty power that raised him from the dead. I want to suffer with him, sharing in his death, so that one way or another I will experience the resurrection from the dead!

PHILIPPIANS 3:10-11 NLT

Have you fully embraced the ways of God? Would you be willing to lose everything for him?

Grasp a hold of the beauty he's offering. Pray for a heart that's glad to be rid of earthly treasures and eager for what's in store for a true believer.

Jesus, I believe that not only did you die to restore humanity, but that you rose again to show us we have eternal life in you. This is an amazing truth about humanity that I want to share with the world. Give me the boldness to be a witness of what you have done for us.

What does the resurrection mean to you? How can you translate this meaning to an unbeliever?

Citizens of Heaven

Join together in following my example, brothers and sisters, and just as you have us as a model, keep your eyes on those who live as we do. For, as I have often told you before and now tell you again even with tears, many live as enemies of the cross of Christ. Their destiny is destruction, their god is their stomach, and their glory is in their shame. Their mind is set on earthly things.

PHILIPPIANS 3:17-19 NIV

When we spend a great deal of time with people, we begin to act as they do. We start to emulate their actions and copy their behavior. When we choose our friends, we need to choose wisely. Are we surrounding ourselves with those who follow the example Christ set for us? Or is our crowd one that does whatever the flesh desires?

Seek friends who are determined to live as Christians are called to do. Together, you can set your eyes on the prize of an eternal life in heaven.

God, remind me of the people in my life who are pursuing the same goal as me. Help me to prioritize my time with them.

*Our citizenship is in heaven. And we eagerly await
a Savior from there, the Lord Jesus Christ.*

PHILIPPIANS 3:20 NIV

Often our day can be so full of the world that we take our eyes
off the prize of eternity with Jesus.

You may have been earning money, or spending money, or at
home looking after the kids. None of these things are wrong;
in fact, they are wonderful. But God wants us to remember
where we really belong. As you are doing things in the world,
remember to keep your eyes on Christ.

*God, thank you for small reminders of your kingdom on earth.
Remind me of your presence while I am doing these earthly things,
so I can always hold on to your joy in this life.*

What does it look like to consider yourself a citizen of heaven?

Thoughts

Whatever is true, whatever is honorable, whatever is right,
whatever is pure, whatever is lovely, whatever is of good repute,
if there is any excellence and if anything worthy of praise,
dwell on these things.

PHILIPPIANS 4:8 NASB

Do you ever catch yourself dwelling on the negative aspects
of life? We can be nonchalant when someone tells us
good news, but talk for hours about conflict, worries, and
disappointment.

It is good to communicate things that aren't going so well
in our lives, but we can also fall into the trap of setting our
minds on the wrong things. Give your mind over to truth,
honor, purity, and other lovely things today. You are sure to
find goodness in unexpected places.

God, thank you for creating me with your goodness in my heart.
If I am tempted today with negative talk or harmful gossip, I pray
you would give me the wisdom and grace to resist the bad and
choose good.

The things you have learned and received and heard and seen in me, practice these things, and the God of peace will be with you.

PHILIPPIANS 4:9 NASB

Paul saw the need to address negativity within the church of Philippi. It seems there were people in the church that thought too highly of themselves and allowed discord to reside in their midst.

Think of what dwelling on the negative actually does: it creates feelings of hopelessness, discouragement, and a lack of trust in our God who is good, true, and just. Choose to dwell on the true, noble, just, pure, and lovely things, and experience the refreshing nature of a positive outlook.

God, as I go to bed tonight, I repent of dwelling on the wrong things and I pray you would surround me with the light of your truth, honor, righteousness, purity, love, and excellence.

Can you find anything in your life and the lives of others that have virtue or are worthy of praise?

Yes You Can

*I have learned to be content whatever the circumstances. I know
what it is to be in need, and I know what it is to have plenty. I have
learned the secret of being content in any and every situation,
whether well fed or hungry, whether living in plenty or in want.*

PHILIPPIANS 4:11-12 NIV

When life is good, it is easy to praise God. My life is full of
blessings, we think to ourselves. He is so good to me. But
what happens when life is hard? Do we continue to give him
the glory when we're thrown curveball after curveball?

Pray for contentment today whatever your circumstance.
There is no crisis that God is not willing to walk you through.
You can do anything with him at your side.

*God, I don't often know what I am walking into at the beginning
of the day, but I trust that no matter what the circumstances are,
I can do all things with you.*

I can do all this through him who gives me strength.

PHILIPPIANS 4:11-13 NIV

Regardless of our circumstance, whatever our situation, we need to continue to give God the praises he so richly deserves.

A life lived alongside Christ doesn't mean it will be one free of pain, discomfort, or tough times. But it does mean that we can find contentment in it anyway because we have him in our hearts. He is the source of your strength.

Jesus, I have so many desires for more. I want more in my relationships, more in my career, more in my house. Help me to be content with what I have. Thank you that you have already given me so much.

What is your situation right now? Are you in need, or do you have plenty? Learn the contentment of just being in God's presence tonight.

Such a Time

When Esther's words were reported to Mordecai, he sent back this answer: "Do not think that because you are in the king's house you alone of all the Jews will escape. For if you remain silent at this time, relief and deliverance for the Jews will arise from another place, but you and your father's family will perish. And who knows but that you have come to your royal position for such a time as this?"

ESTHER 4:12–14 NIV

God never makes mistakes; his plans are intentional and he positions his people everywhere. Esther was a woman of noble and trustworthy character, and because of this, she was used to help God's people in one of their times of greatest need.

You may not know how you are a part of God's great plan, but if you remain true to God and keep your heart loyal to him, he is going to use you. As you go about your various duties today, remember that God has put you here for such a time as this.

Heavenly Father, I trust in the plan that you have for humanity and for my life. I want to be a part of doing your work on earth, so I pray you would give me the courage to do whatever you ask of me.

Esther sent this reply to Mordecai: "Go, gather together all the Jews who are in Susa, and fast for me. Do not eat or drink for three days, night or day. I and my attendants will fast as you do. When this is done, I will go to the king, even though it is against the law. And if I perish, I perish."

ESTHER 4:15-16 NIV

Esther did not act rashly. Instead she made it her intention to seek the Lord wholeheartedly.

At times, fasting is the right thing to do to gain clarity and focus when you need direction. For Esther, her life depended on approaching the king in the right way.

If you are facing some serious decisions in your life, consider fasting or doing something extreme that will allow you to be entirely dedicated to hearing God's voice.

God, I want to hear your voice in the times I really need your guidance. Give me a strategy to be able to focus on your words of truth and to understand the right way forward.

What big decisions are you facing at the moment? Commit these decisions to God tonight and choose to dedicate some time to asking for an answer.

Your Request

> *The king and Haman went to Queen Esther's banquet, and as they were drinking wine on the second day, the king again asked, "Queen Esther, what is your petition? It will be given you. What is your request? Even up to half the kingdom, it will be granted."*
>
> ESTHER 7:1-2 NIV

When Esther found out the king's plans to destroy the Jews, she must have thought that God made a mistake in having her marry him. She probably wished that someone else had been chosen to be queen. But God chose her.

You may feel like a situation in your life is impossible. You may wish you were somewhere else, or that someone else had been given your set of circumstances. God chose you, and he makes no mistakes. He chose you to be right where you are to accomplish the work he has for you.

Father, you make all things possible. I know that you created me for this time. Help me to use it wisely and with Godly ambition.

Queen Esther answered, "If I have found favor with you, Your Majesty, and if it pleases you, grant me my life—this is my petition. And spare my people—this is my request. For I and my people have been sold to be destroyed, killed and annihilated. If we had merely been sold as male and female slaves, I would have kept quiet, because no such distress would justify disturbing the king."

ESTHER 7:3-4 NIV

When you are living out the calling that God has for you, he will ensure that you find favor with the right people. Because of Esther's loyalty, the king wanted to do anything for her. When he realized that his laws were going to destroy the very person he loved, he used his power to change things for the whole nation.

Don't be discouraged if you have had a day of feeling fearful about what lies ahead. Find the bravery that comes from knowing that God is on your side. He will find a way to grant your request.

God, I bring you the situations where I am fearful. As I think about what may happen tomorrow, I ask for your peace to guide my thoughts and heart. Let me be assured that when you are on my side, all things will work together for good.

What do you need from God right now? Who do you need to make a request to? Trust that this person will be favorable toward you.

Gladness, Joy, and Honor

Mordecai went out from the presence of the king in royal apparel of blue and white, with a great crown of gold and a garment of fine linen and purple; and the city of Shushan rejoiced and was glad. The Jews had light and gladness, joy and honor.

ESTHER 8:15-16 NKJV

This picture of Mordecai shows a beautiful transformation from underdog to royalty. His transformation was a representation of what God, through Esther, had accomplished for the Jews.

You might be feeling like an underdog, not having any recognition for what you are doing and wondering when God is going to change things around for you. Mordecai remained faithful and respectable. Rather than seek out his own glory, he allowed goodness to shine through. Let God's goodness shine through your life and then trust that God can turn your situation around for the better.

Lord God, I submit my feelings of being overlooked or discouraged about my position in life. Help me to remain a faithful, trustworthy person and let this be the quality that turns things around for the better.

In every province and city, wherever the king's command and decree came, the Jews had joy and gladness, a feast and a holiday. Then many of the people of the land became Jews, because fear of the Jews fell upon them.

ESTHER 8:17 NKJV

The courage of Esther and the faithfulness of Mordecai had far reaching implications for their entire people. Even those who were not Jews, became Jews in order that they would be a part of the gladness, joy, and honor that the Jews were experiencing.

God wants to use his people in order to extend his kingdom. As you think back over your day, let yourself see the small and big ways that God is using you. Be encouraged that your character, good works, and love for others will be influential in times to come.

Jesus, give me courage and strength of character to continue to do your good works. I don't want to hold onto my salvation for myself, I want others to come to know you. Let me continue to expand your kingdom because of the love that is working in my life.

In what way, big or small, is God using your character and good works?

Friends in Silence

When Job's three friends heard of all this adversity that had come upon him, each one came from his own place—Eliphaz the Temanite, Bildad the Shuhite, and Zophar the Naamathite. For they had made an appointment together to come and mourn with him, and to comfort him. And when they raised their eyes from afar, and did not recognize him, they lifted their voices and wept; and each one tore his robe and sprinkled dust on his head toward heaven.

JOB 2:11-12 NKJV

We know that Job was a person who suffered tremendous loss. It might be easier to identify with Job than others in the Bible because we have all experienced suffering in our lives. But what about being a friend of a person that is suffering?

It can be tempting to try and give words of encouragement, comfort, and advice, but sometimes we just need to be near to those who need it. As you go about your day, remember that sometimes your support is shown in actions not words.

Jesus, help me to know when you just want me to be silent and sit with those who are suffering. Show me the needs around me today.

They sat down with him on the ground seven days and seven nights, and no one spoke a word to him, for they saw that his grief was very great.

JOB 2:13 NKJV

Occasionally, there really are no words. Someone you love is hurting, and you truly don't know what to say. Your presence says it all. Know that, in those moments you feel lost for words, if God occupies the central place in your heart, he'll make your heart known.

How easy or difficult would it be for you to simply be with someone in their sorrow and not try to fix them? Spend some time tonight reflecting on the friends who have done exactly that for you and be thankful for the support of good people.

God, I thank you that I can support my friends by just being near. Help me to be near to those who need me the most.

Do you know someone who would be blessed by the silent, loving presence of someone who loves them?

Right to Vent

"Who am I, that I should try to answer God or even reason with him? Even if I were right, I would have no defense. I could only plead for mercy."

JOB 9:14-15 NLT

Life's not fair. Think of games, or races, or even schooling. Someone always comes out on top, and there are always losers. We can influence some outcomes, but there are many things that are outside of our control.

We cannot guarantee that we will be protected from the troubles of this life. So, what do we do when we feel like complaining about our misfortunes? We often feel like we have no right to complain to God—we are told to be thankful in all things, right? Well, yes, but God can handle your complaints and your cry for answers.

God, I'm glad that you can handle my complaints and my honest heart. I know that this is the safest place to vent my frustrations, because only you can help me to change my heart from grumpiness to gratitude.

> *"Even if I summoned him and he responded,*
> *I'm not sure he would listen to me."*

JOB 9:16 NLT

It can be healthy to discuss your troubles with God, even if you aren't sure that he is listening. Using your voice is important to revealing what is going on in your heart.

Do you feel like making your complaints known tonight? Instead of voicing them to others, pour them out before the Lord. He is understanding and gracious, and he promises to be with you in all things.

God, I have a lot that I want to complain about. I know it is healthier for me to voice this to you than to others, and so I do that now, believing that you will help me get over my troubles.

What are the complaints that you want to bring to God tonight? He can handle hearing them.

Caring for You

"You guided my conception and formed me in the womb. You clothed me with skin and flesh, and you knit my bones and sinews together."

JOB 10:10-11 NLT

When you think about the amazing formation of a baby inside the womb, it can be mind-numbing to realize the growth process and all the intricate details that go into growing a baby.

God was careful about how you were formed. He was there right from the beginning of your time, even before you were consciously aware. As you get ready for your day, remember that he is in the details.

God, thank you for your amazing hand of grace that has been with me since I was formed in my mother's womb. I forget, sometimes, that I had nothing to do with my creation or growth. Give me a new appreciation for your care for me today.

> *"You gave me life and showed me your unfailing love.*
> *My life was preserved by your care."*
>
> JOB 10:12 NLT

We choose to be generous with our time and with our funds. We opt to consider others' feelings before our own.

The Bible talks about kindness quite a lot. Even Job, in his misery, recognized how generous and considerate the Lord was of him. When wave after wave of heartbreak took over Job, he still saw God's care for him.

God, I know that you are kind. I don't always acknowledge that you are good to me, but I know that you gave me this life and that you are watching over me. Help me to show kindness to others.

Who can you show kindness to this week?

When Nature Speaks

"There is hope for a tree, if it is cut down, that it will sprout again, and that its tender shoots will not cease. Though its root may grow old in the earth, and its stump may die in the ground, yet at the scent of water it will bud and bring forth branches like a plant."

JOB 14:7-9 NKJV

Job did not have the benefit of understanding humanity through Christ's resurrection. Christ showed us that death has been conquered and that life will be resurrected and restored. Job had seen a glimpse of this reality in nature. He knew that when trees were cut down they sprouted again; yet, he did not make the connection that nature exposes God's design for humanity.

There is hope in the light of Christ's resurrection that though we suffer, we will sprout again.

Jesus, I thank you that you rose again and showed us that there is eternal life for us to look forward to. Grant me the peace of knowing that your good and perfect purposes will be accomplished.

"A man dies and is laid low; he breathes his last and is no more."

JOB 14:10 NKJV

When Job was going through relentless suffering, he had a lot of opportunities to contemplate death. His pain was unbearable, he did not understand God's purpose for his misery, and he had no firm understanding of why God didn't grant him death. He was, for a time, with little hope.

Sometimes our lack of understanding God's greatness leaves us feeling hopeless about a situation. Remember that there is a greater plan unfolding that only God knows. Place your trust in his goodness today.

God, I bring my burdens to you and acknowledge those feelings of despair. Even though I am wearied by the end of the day, I trust in your goodness and hope for tomorrow.

What are you having difficulty understanding about your life? Allow Jesus to breathe hope into that place.

I Will See God

"I know that my Redeemer lives, and he will stand upon the earth
at last. And after my body has decayed, yet in my body I will see
God! I will see him for myself."

JOB 19:25-26 NLT

Job's faith has been weakened by the test, but he clutches
desperately to the one promise that can sustain him: no
matter what happens to Job in his earth-bound life, nothing
can take away the joy he will share with God in his eternal life.

Everything on earth is a fleeting treasure, a momentary
comfort that can be lost in a flash. But the assurance of your
eternal place in his kingdom, if you have submitted your life
to Jesus Christ, is indestructible.

*Jesus, you are my redeemer, and I thank you that even though I
have far less to complain about than Job did, I can still bring my
troubles before you and know that one day you will take it all
away. Let me find joy in that knowledge today.*

"Yes, I will see him with my own eyes.
I am overwhelmed at the thought!"

JOB 19:27 NLT

Job went through all the emotions expected of someone who has lost everything and is in deep pain. He mourns, and laments, and weeps. He is confused, hopeless, and weak. Yet even in his lament, Job speaks the truth about God. His heart is driven toward something beyond his present circumstance and as he lifts his eyes to the heavens, he exclaims, "Yes, I will see him with my own eyes."

If your day has been discouraging, lift your eyes toward the heavens and let your heart be confident that one day your troubles will be gone and you will see Jesus with your own eyes.

God, thank you for your joy that sustains me every day. Thank you that you have been good to me today, and that you will show your goodness tomorrow especially when I ask for it.

What eternal values can you bring into your day tomorrow?

Fountain of Youth

"Let their flesh be renewed like a child's; let them be restored as in the days of their youth."

Job 33:25 NIV

Think back to when you were a child. Do you remember what it was like caring only for the moment; moments of freedom and unpredictability, lost in make-believe and dreams? That was then, and this is now.

How do you feel about the past? What life has threatened to strip from you, God can restore and reshape. Forget today about the things which never really mattered all that much, and remember what it is to breathe life in your lungs.

God, restore to me the beauty of childlike faith. I want to find favor with you simply because I delight in being called your child.

> "That person can pray to God and find favor with him,
> they will see God's face and shout for joy;
> he will restore them to full well-being."

JOB 33:26 NIV

Responsibility eventually overtakes carefree spontaneity. Reality drowns out limitless dreams.

Restoration of full well-being can be ours. Doesn't that sound just like childhood? God can restore to you what's been lost.

God, I am so overcome with responsibility. Sometimes I want to go back to just relying and trusting on someone else to take care of everything. I thank you that there is also freedom that comes with responsibility. I ask you now for a simple restoration of a carefree heart.

Where do you need God to help you lighten the load? Let him release the burden on your heart and give you freedom in your spirit.

Things Too Wonderful

*Job replied to the L*ORD*: "I know that you can do all things; no purpose of yours can be thwarted. You asked, 'Who is this that obscures my plans without knowledge?' Surely I spoke of things I did not understand, things too wonderful for me to know."*

JOB 42:1-3 NIV

After a long time of silence, God finally answers Job, in one of the lengthiest records of God speaking in the Bible. In his speech there is a tone of frustration from the powerful Creator of the universe, and yet he speaks, personally, to the one who is suffering.

You may be in a situation where you feel like God has been silent. It is okay to question God, but consider that you were not there from the beginning of creation and are not seeing the world through the lens of the Almighty. Knowing his ways would be far out of our comprehension. Let God be God in your circumstances today.

Almighty God, Creator of the heavens and the earth, thank you so much that you are a God in control of everything. I am sorry when I have challenged the way you work. Help me to accept my current circumstances and to seek you for answers in all humility.

"You said, 'Listen now, and I will speak; I will question you, and you shall answer me.' My ears had heard of you but now my eyes have seen you. Therefore I despise myself and repent in dust and ashes."

JOB 42:4-6 NIV

There are moments in our life when we finally know that we have understood something of God's power and love in our life. Sometimes we hear about God, but we don't him for who he truly is.

As you take some time to read and reflect on God's Scriptures tonight, ask the Holy Spirit to illuminate something of his presence to you. When we see God's power and love, we are drawn to repentance.

God, I thank you for revealing yourself to me, sometimes in really big ways. Give me reverence and humility so when you do speak, I understand your greatness and your goodness. Your ways are all too wonderful for me, and I repent of pride and ask you to fill me with love.

What is God illuminating to you about his power and love in this moment?

Light the Way

We also pray that you will be strengthened with all his glorious power so you will have all the endurance and patience you need. May you be filled with joy, always thanking the Father. He has enabled you to share in the inheritance that belongs to his people, who live in the light.

COLOSSIANS 1:11-12 NLT

A sidewalk that is illuminated by many street lights is the best way to walk around safely at night. When we receive Christ, it is as though he has lit up our path so we can see our way home.

This is the blessing of belonging to his kingdom, and he longs that everyone would see the light. As you go into the world today, you will see others that are stumbling around in the darkness. Ask God for the strength and patience to guide others onto the right path home.

Father, I am so grateful that you have given me light so I can be led home. I know you care about those people who are still wandering around in the dark. Help me to lead others to the light so they, too, can share in this wonderful inheritance.

He has rescued us from the kingdom of darkness and transferred us into the Kingdom of his dear Son, who purchased our freedom and forgave our sins.

<small>COLOSSIANS 1:13-14 NLT</small>

When humanity was at its worst, falling into a pit of darkness, Jesus reached into the world with his hand of love and pulled us out; he rescued us. While we may accept that Jesus saved us, it does some good to consider the cost he paid for our freedom—his life.

There is no greater price than that of a life, and Christ willingly went to the cross for you. Today, as you have acknowledged his light in your life, thank him for his sacrifice that freed you from the wages of sin.

Jesus, you rescued me from death. When I feel tempted to dwell on my sin, remind me of my freedom. You paid such a great price in order to set me free and I want to live in the light of forgiveness.

How have you experienced the difference between those walking in the darkness and those walking in the light?

Creator Jesus

He is the image of the invisible God, the firstborn of all creation. For by Him all things were created, both in the heavens and on earth, visible and invisible, whether thrones or dominions or rulers or authorities—all things have been created through Him and for Him.

COLOSSIANS 1:15-16 NASB

The union of Jesus with God is a hard thing to grasp, but it helps us to understand Jesus as being part of the beginning of all things. This means Jesus was with God in creation and understood everything there is to know about humanity.

When Jesus came to earth, he represented God like no other being could. When you read about Jesus, remember that you are also seeing God the Father.

Jesus, it can be hard to comprehend all there is to know, but it is evident in your words and deeds that you came from heaven with all power and understanding and that you created all things, including me. Give me greater understanding as I think on these wonders today.

He is before all things, and in Him all things hold together.

Colossians 1:17 NASB

We can easily picture God being alone at the beginning of creation. Scripture clearly shows us that Jesus is central to creation and redemption as well. If he created the world, he knows how to redeem it.

Jesus came to earth to restore creation to its full potential. Rather than destroy, Jesus came to heal.

Jesus, this evening I feel tired and need to hand my day, and all that went on, to you. Thank you that you understand me because you created me and that you want to restore not only my life but the lives of those around me. Help me to share the hope that a life with you brings.

What is Jesus holding together for you right now?

True Philosophy

See to it that no one takes you captive through hollow and deceptive philosophy, which depends on human tradition and the elemental spiritual forces of this world rather than on Christ.

COLOSSIANS 2:8 NIV

There are plenty of theories and philosophies about our world: how it came to exist, what our purpose is, why we behave the way we do. We are intelligent beings, but we are not the supreme being who created the heavens and the earth.

The wisdom of God, shown through Jesus Christ, is the only truth and everything else should be understood through the message of his life, death, and resurrection. You will no doubt face various philosophies as you go through your day, but stand firm in your belief in God.

Jesus, when the world comes at me with a different truth to yours, help me to be discerning of right and wrong. Thank you for sending the Holy Spirit who can guide me with wisdom.

*In Christ all the fullness of the Deity lives in bodily form,
and in Christ you have been brought to fullness. He is the head
over every power and authority.*

COLOSSIANS 2:9-10 NIV

It is important to remember that Jesus was not only fully
human but fully divine. This means that he had all the
power given to him from above and that his words were not
confused with the world's.

When you see Jesus, you see God. When Jesus took our sins to
the cross, he defeated death. We are now on this side of that
victory. Claim the power that is yours through Jesus.

*Jesus, thank you for coming to earth so we could know about the
Father. Thank you for redeeming me from my old life and giving
me a new life, where I have been brought to fullness.*

In which areas of your life do you need to claim the authority
of Jesus?

Things Above

If then you have been raised with Christ, seek the things that are above, where Christ is, seated at the right hand of God.

COLOSSIANS 3:1 ESV

Social media: an escape, a gift, a communicative tool, a joy stealer, a comparison thief, a comedian, entertainment. Social media can be fun. But it can also become an idol when we don't recognize it as such.

God's desire for our life is that we chose him above all else. He wants to be our focal point, one we return to time and again, so we don't ever steer too far off course. Instead of seeking approval from others today, turn your eyes toward the one who loves you the most, whose voice should speak above the rest.

Jesus, I choose to listen to your voice, right now. Still my heart, calm my mind, and speak because I am listening.

Set your minds on things that are above,
not on things that are on earth.

COLOSSIANS 3:2 ESV

It takes a great deal of self-discipline to switch your mind from one thing to another. We often get trapped in letting media take our minds away from anything, which can be restful for a time, but it can also be a waste of time.

When we choose to dwell on meaningless things of the world, it is all the more difficult to let the things of the kingdom fill your thoughts. This time that you have set aside is a great way to dwell on things from above. Scripture elevates you to the right place and gives you the best frame of mind.

Holy Spirit, thank you for leading me to this moment of quieting my mind from the busyness of the day and switching it to thinking about your kingdom. Help me to take every opportunity to think of you.

Where do you choose to spend the majority of your time? What choices could you eliminate to stay centered on Jesus?

Clothed in Love

*As God's chosen people, holy and dearly loved, clothe
yourselves with compassion, kindness, humility,
gentleness and patience.*

COLOSSIANS 3:12 NIV

When we get up in the morning, one of the first things we do
is get dressed. We are usually pretty thoughtful about what we
put on, and a lot of it has to do with what we are going to do
during the day.

In the same way, take some time this morning to think about
how you want to display Christ's love. What will you put on to
ensure that people see his goodness? If you clothe yourself
with all these virtues, people are bound to recognize Christ.

*God, thank you that I am one of your precious children. Thank
you that because I am loved by you, I know how much others need
to be loved. Help me to be kind, patient, and gentle with everyone I
meet today.*

Bear with each other and forgive one another if any of you has a
grievance against someone. Forgive as the Lord forgave you.
And over all these virtues put on love, which binds them
all together in perfect unity.

COLOSSIANS 3:13-14 NIV

A day can start with really good intentions, until someone
does something that pushes you over the edge. We can quickly
get grumpy, discouraged, or stressed and forget about the
clothes of kindness and gentleness that we put on earlier.

If you have come home feeling disappointed with your day,
remember that God forgives you. Love can take time to put
into practice and God gives you plenty of grace to try again.
When you make love your goal, unity will be the result.

*Jesus, I am tired and at times feel worn down by other people who
have not been very kind to me. Give me the patience and humility
to forgive anyone that I am upset with. I want to start tomorrow
with a fresh attitude that brings unity in all my relationships.*

Who needs your forgiveness and patience tonight?

Lift your Spirit

*Let the message of Christ dwell among you richly as you teach and
admonish one another with all wisdom through psalms,
hymns, and songs from the Spirit, singing to God
with gratitude in your hearts.*

COLOSSIANS 3:16 NIV

A song or poem can lift your spirit and put you in a positive
mood, especially if it is describing the goodness and love of
God. When you dwell on encouraging words, your heart can
move from misery to gratitude.

When we are grateful, we start to see the light of God much
better. Allow Christ into your heart today, even though it will
be full of things to do, people to see, jobs to take care of. Be
thankful as you do the day-to-day things, and cultivate your
heart for giving thanks.

*God, be present in my life today so I can't help but think about you
and all the wonderful people and things you have placed in my
life. Help me to be thankful even in times of trial.*

Whatever you do, whether in word or deed, do it all in the name of the Lord Jesus, giving thanks to God the Father through him.

COLOSSIANS 3:17 NIV

A thankful heart is a heart that refuses to let the enemy in and deceive us. Suddenly, our circumstances seem not so terrible, our problems not so huge. A heart of gratitude glorifies God and keeps us centered on him.

You can have that same perspective every day—even in the most mundane circumstances. A heart of thankfulness keeps you grounded in Christ, in communion with him, and allows you to live the fullest life he's designed for you.

God, there was so much that went on in my day, and I want to thank you for all of it. Thank you for the ups that make me smile and the downs that build resilience. Thank you for the good and the bad. Help me to be thankful in everything.

What can you do to start cultivating a heart of gratitude?

Open Doors

Devote yourselves to prayer, being watchful and thankful. And pray for us, too, that God may open a door for our message, so that we may proclaim the mystery of Christ, for which I am in chains. Pray that I may proclaim it clearly, as I should.

COLOSSIANS 4:2-4 NIV

We should always pray that God will open doors for us to share his message. You might not be in a distant land to proclaim the gospel, or in chains for trying to preach the good news, but there are plenty of people who are.

Think of those people who are intent on furthering the kingdom, and devote yourselves to praying for them.

God, thank you that you are using people in other parts of the world to spread the gospel and to reveal the truth to all mankind. Protect them, keep them in good health, and guide them to those people who are the most receptive to hearing your Word. Open doors for me today, so I can share your message as well.

Be wise in the way you act toward outsiders; make the most of every opportunity. Let your conversation be always full of grace, seasoned with salt, so that you may know how to answer everyone.

COLOSSIANS 4:5-6 NIV

Did you make the most out of your opportunities today, or did you let them slip by? It's easy to begin with the right motivation, but we also need the courage to lead a conversation in talking about Jesus.

You don't necessarily have to start talking about the Bible, but let your conversation be gracious and life-giving to the person that you are talking with so they will see Jesus shining through your heart. Ask the Holy Spirit to give you the words and answers that you need.

Father, I need your courage as I go into my day tomorrow. I don't always have enough boldness to take the opportunities that I know you give me to speak to people about your love and grace for them. Holy Spirit, guide me as I speak so I will know how to answer.

How can you prepare yourself for the opportunities that may come your way tomorrow?

Sustain Me

*You, LORD, are a shield around me, my glory, the One who lifts my
head high. I call out to the LORD, and he answers me
from his holy mountain.*

PSALM 3:3-4 NIV

There is always something to worry about, isn't there?
Whether it's health, finances, relationships, or details, there
are many unknowns in life that can easily keep us worrying.
What if we could trust completely that God would take care of
us and our loved ones?

God is your rock and he alone will sustain you. There will be
many unknowns in your life. There will be moments when the
rug feels as though it's been pulled out from under you, and
there is nothing to do but despair. In those moments, you can
trust God. You can rest your soul, your mind, and your body in
the hands of the One who has the power to sustain you.

*God, today I face the unknown. Let me rest in the knowledge that
you will sustain me.*

*I lie down and sleep; I wake again, because the L*ORD *sustains me. I will not fear though tens of thousands assail me on every side.*

PSALM 3:5-6 NIV

The words in Psalm 3 can bring us comfort and peace when we are fearful. It speaks volumes about the grace of God: the protection and safety of his hand. But the verse goes beyond peace and comfort to the power of God. We only wake up because of his sustaining power.

When we trust and believe in this God who possesses the power of life and death, what do we have to fear? Our entire lives are in his hands. We can't change that fact, so we might as well rest in it.

God, tonight I need rest. I need to rest my body and I need to rest my soul. I believe you have the power of life and death, so I ask that as I sleep, you sustain me.

What is interfering with your ability to rest? Ask God to give you a solution so you can rest physically and spiritually.

Trust in Times of Trouble

The Lord also will be a refuge for the oppressed,
a refuge in times of trouble.

PSALM 9:9 NKJV

It feels easier to trust God in the big moments, the desperate moments. But what about the everyday moments? The times that we grab hold of control and want to do it all ourselves. In those moments, we can press into him without restraint.

Let go, cry out to God, ask him to carry you. And he will. The everyday moments that might feel crooked will be straightened. He will carry you as he promises.

Jesus, thank you for being my good shepherd. Help me to seek out your ways today, in all those everyday decisions. I know you don't need to tell me exactly what to do, but help me to be like you so I reflect your nature to others around me.

Those who know Your name will put their trust in You;
for You, LORD, have not forsaken those who seek You.

PSALM 9:10 NKJV

God has given us a huge gift in his faithful nature. He
promises us things and sticks to those promises without fail.

How beautiful is this God? He will give you a path to
confidently walk on if all you do is trust him.

Jesus, I have also been able to reflect on the truth that I know your
name. I do not live in darkness, but I have seen the truth of who
you are and what you have done for me and for this world. Help
me to trust you with what you are doing in my life, right now.

Where do you have the most difficulty trusting God? Practice
letting go in those moments and leaning on him for help.

Wondering

I call to you, God, and you answer me.
Listen to me now, and hear what I say.

PSALM 17:6 NCV

If only answers to prayer came so simply or quickly. Perhaps you want to know what courses to study, what job offer to accept, what school your kids should go to.

God's Word encourages us again and again to come to him with our questions, concerns, and deepest longings. He does promise a reply, though not necessarily in the form of a check in a box.

God, I call to you now, asking for answers. At times I am unsure if I am asking the right thing, but I know it doesn't matter because you will hear me and you will answer, even if it isn't the answer that I want.

Show me the wonders of your great love, you who save by your right hand those who take refuge in you from their foes.

PSALM 17:7 NIV

As you come to the end of another day, are there things that your heart is aching for? Do you have concerns, fears, or hopes for this week, or this year?

God is waiting expectantly for your prayers, and he will answer you. It may not be today, or even for a long time, but keep asking. Keep waiting for his reply. He hears you.

Jesus, I feel full of questions that I'm not sure you are answering. Give me confidence in remembering that your Word says that you do hear me and that you do answer. Answer me, and help me to discern what you are saying.

What are you longing to know? Just ask God.

Tangled

The ropes of death entangled me; floods of destruction swept over me. The grave wrapped its ropes around me; death laid a trap in my path.

PSALM 18:4-5 NLT

This is our faith walk. While Jesus' light never goes out, sometimes our sight does. We get so bogged down by circumstances, by sin, by our own agendas, we can't see a thing. So how do we keep moving?

We cry out, and then we follow the sound of God's voice. We must step more slowly now, but we can still walk. We just need to listen and have faith in his voice.

God, I know that you are always ready to rescue me, but I also know that I need to acknowledge my distress. I call out to you and plead with you to rescue me. Thank you for hearing my cry.

*In my distress I cried out to the LORD; yes, I prayed to my God for help.
He heard me from his sanctuary; my cry to him reached his ears.*

PSALM 18:6 NLT

Can you think of a time where you honestly couldn't see where you were headed? Perhaps that time is now.

Call out to the God who is listening for your voice. He knows where you are right now. He wants to help you avoid that tangle of roots, or a dangerous drop-off. You will not be unheard. God will answer you, and he will rescue you.

*God, I acknowledge tonight that my sin has blinded my path.
I have often chosen the way of this world over your ways.
Thank you for your forgiveness and ability to cleanse me from
all unrighteousness so I can see the way again.*

Are there steps you need to take in spite of your blindness to the path? Call out to God. Let his voice guide you home.

Lean on the King

The LORD rules over the floodwaters.
The LORD reigns as king forever.

PSALM 29:10 NLT

Picture a season in your life where you were knee-deep in busyness, swallowed in sadness, or buried in exhaustion. Picture that season and how you looked, acted, reacted, and survived.

Now picture the King of the heavens and earth. See how he rules over the entire earth. This powerful God wants you to lean on him, and that seems easy to do when you understand just how great and mighty he is. If you have woken up feeling tired, lean on the strength of your Savior.

God, I know what it is like to be weary and weak. Thank you that you have always been my strength and that you will be my source of power today.

The LORD gives his people strength.
The LORD blesses them with peace.

PSALM 29:11 NLT

Do you feel weary after a long day? Perhaps you have been dealing with children, or trying to work toward an important deadline for work or study.

It's hard to feel peace when you are so busy and so tired. Give your day to the Lord. Take this one moment to rest. Allow his peace to settle on your heart.

Jesus, I need rest. I need you to fill this tired mind and heart with your presence. Be my strength this evening, and bless me with peace.

Have you encountered a moment with Jesus where you understood more fully that he gets you to your very core? He knows your heart. He knows when your soul needs rest.

Praise, Always

I will extol the LORD at all times;
his praise will always be on my lips.

PSALM 34:1 NIV

It's relatively easy to sing God's praises when all is going well in our lives: when he blesses us with something we asked for, when he heals us, or when he directly answers a prayer. We naturally turn and give him praise and glory for good things.

What about when things aren't going well? What about in dry times, painful times, or times of waiting? Choose today to have praise readily on your lips instead of complaint. Whenever you feel discontentment or frustration, replace it with praise. By focusing on the goodness of God, the hardships will lessen, and your joy will increase.

God, this morning I choose praise. My day has barely started and I can already feel the stresses mounting, but I choose praise. Let my lips be full of joy instead of complaint.

I will glory in the LORD; let the afflicted hear and rejoice.
Glorify the LORD with me; let us exalt his name together.

Do we only praise God for something after he's given it, or do we praise him ahead of time in faith, knowing that he will always be good no matter what happens?

We should look at all difficulties in life as miracles waiting to happen—chances for God to show his goodness and bring us closer to his heart.

God, at times I admit that it is hard to praise you. Sometimes I don't see you in my life and I don't recognize you in other people's lives either. The news of the day can be depressing and there doesn't seem to be any joy. But I choose praise. The world might seem discouraging, but you are not. I will praise you at all times.

What is discouraging you right now? Praise God even in these circumstances, and let this praise lift your head and your heart.

Our Steps

The LORD directs the steps of the godly.
He delights in every detail of their lives.

PSALM 37:23 NLT

Just when we thought we wouldn't worry about asking God about the details, we read that he delights in the details. It makes perfect sense when you make the connection that your life is about all the small details, and that God wants to dwell in this life of yours.

God cares about the details. As you get up today and think about your activities, big and small, invite God into each and every one of them. This is how he is able to guide your steps—one by one.

God, thank you for being a part of all the little things in my life.
I invite you in to each thing that I do, not expecting you
to command my step, but expecting that you delight in the
small stuff.

Though they stumble, they will never fall,
*for the L*ORD *holds them by the hand.*

PSALM 37:24 NLT

There is someone who is ready to catch you when you fall. You may have stumbled throughout your busy day, but he will never let you hit the floor as you take a tumble.

God delights in you. He will direct your every step if you ask him to. He will gladly take you by the hand and guide you.

God, give me a really good rest tonight. I am weary at the end of the day, but I am not completely downtrodden because I know you have been there to uplift me in the times when I need it the most. Thank you for being so faithful to me.

How has the Lord lifted you up today?

Known

I am feeble and severely broken;
I groan because of the turmoil of my heart.

PSALM 38:8 NKJV

Have you ever been run so ragged that you just didn't know if you could take even one more step? Your calendar is a blur of scheduled activities, your days are full, your every hour is blocked off for this or that, and it's hard to find even a spare minute for yourself. Your very bones feel weary, and you fall into your bed at night, drained from it all.

Are you allowing the Lord to guide your days? Though you may be weary and heartbroken, he has enough energy to get you through. Hold out your hand to him today and walk side-by-side with Jesus.

Father, you know exactly where my heart is and how I am feeling right now. You understand me more than anyone in this life because you created me. Help me to know that I am understood today.

You know what I long for, LORD;
you hear my every sigh.

PSALM 38:9 NKJV

We love to be understood and long to be seen. For many of us it's how we know we are loved. How much, then, must the Father love us?

He who knows everything about us—who takes the time to listen to every longing and comfort every sigh—is waiting to give us his perfect gifts. We are known. We are loved.

God, there are a lot of things that I long for. I have a list that gets bigger and bigger by the day. Help me to know what is just selfish, and what is really a heartfelt desire that comes from a heart that is after yours.

What are you longing for tonight? Let God show you his great love by revealing how intimately he knows you.

Wait in Silence

For God alone, O my soul, wait in silence, for my hope is from him.

PSALM 62:5 ESV

If the radio were broken in your car, would you need to fix it immediately, or would you relish the silence? Perhaps you or someone you know keeps the TV on all day "for the noise."

What is it about silence that makes so many of us uncomfortable? Some of us even talk to ourselves to avoid it. Seek out silence today. Allow God to discern your needs, your questions, and then wait for him to answer.

God, allow me some time of silence. Right now, I wait on you. Even if you don't speak, let me feel your presence so I can be restored in silence.

He only is my rock and my salvation, my fortress;
I shall not be shaken.

PSALM 62:6 ESV

Our feelings about silence often connect directly to our feelings about being alone. The radio keeps us from realizing we are alone, or from leaving us alone with our thoughts. But alone with our thoughts is exactly where God most wants to speak to us.

How can we hear God if we're partially tuned in to a song, show, or commercial? How can we listen if we never stop talking?

Jesus, I have made the decision right now, to turn off or away from all the distractions so I can wait on you. I give you this time, right now, to experience your hope for my life.

What is God filling your heart with now?

Ask for Help

Bend down, O Lord, and hear my prayer; answer me, for I need your help. Protect me, for I am devoted to you. Save me, for I serve you and trust you. You are my God.

PSALM 86:1-2 NLT

In this world full of independence, we have not had to practice the art of asking for help. None of us want to impose ourselves on anyone. We don't want to make a fuss. We think we should be able to do things on our own.

God didn't create you to be on your own or have to do things by yourself. Today, ask him for answers, ask him for help, ask him for protection, and trust that he will save you.

Bend down, O Lord, and hear my prayer; answer me when I need your help, protect me when I feel afraid, save me when I feel I am falling. I serve and trust you today because you are my God.

Be merciful to me, O LORD, for I am calling on you constantly. Give me happiness, O LORD, for I give myself to you. O LORD, you are so good, so ready to forgive, so full of unfailing love for all who ask for your help.

PSALM 86:3-5 NLT

Even when life is humming along quite nicely, we include God in our day more than we realize. We constantly rely on his Holy Spirit, whether we audibly ask him or not.

We know we need wisdom, self-control, and love to guide our every step. When we walk with the Lord constantly at our side, we can't help but experience happiness. Approach your day with joy.

God, it is so refreshing to know that you care about my happiness. Sometimes I feel foolish or shallow wanting to be happy, but now I understand that you are good and so ready to give when we ask.

How is God bringing you happiness at the moment? Thank him for this feeling.

My Refuge

He who dwells in the secret place of the Most High shall abide under the shadow of the Almighty.

PSALM 91:1 NKJV

Have you ever been awake when you think no one else is? Maybe you had an early morning flight, and you feel you are the only person who could possibly be stirring at that hour. It feels kind of magical, doesn't it? It's like you have an unshared secret.

Regardless of you being a night owl, morning person, or somewhere in-between, there is peace that comes with meeting Jesus in secret—when your world has stopped for a bit. We need spiritual food to conquer each day.

Jesus, I'm glad to have this moment with you. Thank you that even a small amount of time with you gives me the courage to face this day with confidence and serenity.

I will say of the LORD, *"He is my refuge and my fortress;*
My God, in Him I will trust."

PSALM 91:2 NKJV

Relax, this is another moment in your day when you have chosen to be uplifted in time spent with Jesus. Whatever it looks like, rising early or staying up late, taking a work break, a study break, or a parent break, finding that quiet is where you actually acquire strength.

Jesus will meet you in that space, filling you with peace, strength, and love to go out and conquer the world. Carry this confidence into your day tomorrow.

Lord God, it is hard to prioritize time to escape with you, not just because of the demands of life but because of all the distractions. Holy Spirit, remind me that finding this time will provide a refuge for my soul.

Can you find daily quiet time to meet with Jesus?

Lasting Laws

You are near, O LORD, and all your commands are true.

PSALM 119:151 NLT

The sun will set tonight; it will rise tomorrow. This is truth. We have no reason to doubt what we've witnessed every day of our lives. But when experience tells us otherwise, or perhaps we have no experience to go on, doubts creep in.

It's going to snow tomorrow. "I doubt that," we say. Remember today, that God's truth is unchanging. It is as sure as the sun that rose this morning.

God, just as the Psalmist wrote, you are near me always, so close to me. Thank you that every one of your commands reveals truth. Let me trust in your truth as I go into my day.

I have known from my earliest days that your laws will last forever.

PSALM 119:152 NLT

When someone we trust says they'll be there for us, we have faith in their words. Someone who has repeatedly let us down can make the same promise, but we remain uncertain until they've shown up and proven themselves. We're unsettled. We doubt.

God wants to erase all our doubt and he will; we only need to have faith.

Lord God, I have faith in your words. Others may let me down. Sometimes I don't even keep true to my word. But your words are true and unchanging.

Examine your prayer life. Do you trust God, or do you doubt his promises to you? Why? Share your heart openly with him, and ask him for unwavering faith.

Good to All

The LORD is good to all; he has compassion on all he has made.
All your works praise you, LORD; your faithful people extol you.

PSALM 145:9-10 NIV

Have you ever laid in bed at night thinking over past wrongdoings and beating yourself up over decisions you made years ago? If so, you are not alone. We can be incredibly hard on ourselves.

There is good news for us all. Once we accept Christ as our Savior, we are made new. There is no need to continue to berate ourselves for the choices of the past. God has washed away our sins and made us clean. We don't have to look at life from our former point of view because our old lives are gone and new ones have begun.

Thank you, Almighty God, for your forgiveness. Thank you that the past is forgotten by you, and that I can move forward in this new day, this new life, that you have given me.

They tell of the glory of your kingdom and speak of your might,
so that all people may know of your mighty acts and the glorious
splendor of your kingdom.

PSALM 145:11-12 NIV

Is this one of those nights, filled with regret? Release your past to the Lord. If you struggle to get past a mistake you once made, ask him for help in forgiving yourself.

You have been made new in the eyes of God. There is so much freedom in this knowledge. Enjoy it and share it so people will know of God's great kingdom.

God, again, I can often dwell on the things that I have done wrong, or the things that have gone wrong in my life. I know this is not the life that you want me to live. I know that you want me to experience your grace, so my life can be a wonderful witness of your grace. Fill my heart with peace in this moment.

What are you regretting in this moment? Give it over to God and move on.

He Understands You

Praise the LORD! For it is good to sing praises to our God; for it is pleasant, and a song of praise is fitting. The LORD builds up Jerusalem; he gathers the outcasts of Israel. He heals the brokenhearted and binds up their wounds.

PSALM 147:1-3 ESV

Whether you are carrying pain and suffering from past abuse or tragedy, or you've more recently been hurt, run toward the one who heals.

There is no requirement or need too great; God will piece you back together. Your offering of praise to him is beautiful and he will turn your mourning into joy.

God, I come to you as a person who has been broken and hurt by others. Sometimes I feel this pain more acutely, but wherever I am at with this, you know the things that have really torn my heart. Give me peace today, knowing that you are helping me to forgive and become whole again.

He determines the number of the stars; he gives to all of them their names. Great is our Lord, and abundant in power; his understanding is beyond measure.

Psalm 147:4-5 ESV

It might take work. It will take constant communion with him to remind you of his healing power, but he will glue you back together until you are whole.

Broken souls, broken bodies, broken hearts, be reminded of God's power in these moments and do not turn away. He knows the stars by name and he understands you intimately.

Jesus, I need your healing. I choose to delight in you this evening because I know that you are doing a good work in my heart. Piece me back together. Let me release the bitterness, the resentment, and other things that are holding me back from moving on in this area of my life.

Are you experiencing pain and need God's healing power? Release everything you are holding onto and let him heal you.

Power of the Spirit

We know, brothers and sisters loved by God, that he has chosen you, because our gospel came to you not simply with words but also with power, with the Holy Spirit and deep conviction. You know how we lived among you for your sake.

1 THESSALONIANS 1:4-5 NIV

There are ways to know the sun is out without looking directly at it. We feel the warmth, we see the light, we experience the brightness of the day—we just know the sun is there.

Many people have heard about Jesus, but they will only truly believe when they feel and experience his presence. This is what the Holy Spirit was sent to do: to help people sincerely experience Christ. Remember the Holy Spirit is with you today, drawing you closer to Jesus and giving you a deeper understanding of him.

Holy Spirit, thank you for being near to me this morning. Guide my heart, thoughts, and behaviors today so I can share your presence, not only with words, but with the power of your Spirit.

You became imitators of us and of the Lord, for you welcomed the message in the midst of severe suffering with the joy given by the Holy Spirit.

1 THESSALONIANS 1:6 NIV

The Holy Spirit can break through in any situation and seems to be particularly near in times of suffering. There is something beautiful about drawing near to God in times of need.

If you are experiencing pain today, let the Holy Spirit minister to you. If you have seen others going through a particularly rough time, ask for God's presence to be very real to them. Continue to welcome the message of Christ, the message of hope, into all areas of brokenness and see him work powerfully in your midst.

Holy Spirit, I need you to work powerfully in my current circumstance. Renew the message of the cross in my heart and mind. I am forgiven, loved, and redeemed.

In what way do you need to experience the power of the Holy Spirit tonight?

Flattered

We speak as messengers approved by God to be entrusted with the Good News. Our purpose is to please God, not people. He alone examines the motives of our hearts.

1 THESSALONIANS 2:4 NLT

We have such good news as believers of Jesus Christ and we know that it is worth sharing. It is good, however, to consider how you speak of this good news to others. It can be tempting to water down the gospel, or to make it sound like every other religion. Equally, we can go overboard with trying to complicate the simplicity of the message with clever arguments.

Scripture says that God cares about your heart motivation. The next time you are able to share the good news, don't be anxious, just do it out of love and God will work out the rest.

Lord God, give me an opportunity this week to share the gospel. Help me to discern the best approach, the right words, and mostly, give me a heart of love for you so your grace is what stands out the most.

Never once did we try to win you with flattery, as you well know. And God is our witness that we were not pretending to be your friends just to get your money. As for human praise, we have never sought it from you or anyone else.

1 THESSALONIANS 2:5-6 NLT

The truth is people don't always want to know the truth. Sometimes we are over cautious about offending people or we say what people want to hear because we are worried about what they will think of us. We want to be accepted so we go to great lengths to cover up the truth.

Flattery might get people to like you, but it doesn't deliver the message of the cross. Don't seek the approval of people, seek the approval of your Creator.

God, I know that I am sometimes overly concerned about the approval of others. Help me to grow in confidence of your love and to know that your approval is the only thing that really matters. Thank you that you love me whether I get things right or wrong.

Are you trying to get people to like you in some way? Open yourself up to the scrutiny of whose approval you are seeking.

Quiet Work

Make it your goal to live a quiet life, minding your own business and working with your hands, just as we instructed you before.

1 THESSALONIANS 4:11 NLT

You might love the thought of a quiet life or you might think that it sounds like the most boring way to be. Whatever your personality, the apostle Paul knew the importance of being mindful and respectful of the people in our community.

We all know of people who spend too much time getting involved in other people's business and this kind of conduct doesn't win people over. Do the work that God has given you, whether paid or unpaid, easy or hard. God will bless your interactions with others when you live a respectful life.

Jesus, I want to be a diligent worker, applying myself to the tasks that I have each day, and not becoming someone who is lazy and gets involved in the affairs of others. Develop in me a character that is growing toward respect and consideration of others.

People who are not believers will respect the way you live,
and you will not need to depend on others.

1 THESSALONIANS 4:12 NLT

Nobody wants to feel like they are being taken advantage of. It can be frustrating when you see people who are not working hard depend on people who are. If you busy yourself with meaningful work, you won't need to be a burden on anyone else.

Christ can speak through you when you give people a reason to respect your conduct. If you have been working hard today, good job. Be encouraged that you are being a faithful witness for Jesus.

God, I'm sorry when I have been a little lazy and expected others to pick up the slack. I know that you want me to be diligent, and that you are pleased when I do make an effort to tend to important business. Let this virtue be built into my character.

What are some meaningful jobs that you could do this week?

Rejoice Always

Rejoice always; pray without ceasing.

1 THESSALONIANS 5:16-17 NASB

It is easy for us to get weighed down with negative things. Our lives, and the lives of those around us, are full of troubles that make us weary.

Some days it can be difficult to find joy in the middle of our own chaos. We wonder what God's will is, especially in the hardships. We can't see his master plan, but feel as though if we could, maybe we could make it through. We wonder what God wants us to do in the middle of our difficulties. According to this Scripture, we rejoice and keep praying.

God, you have given us Scripture to help us in our lives. I will rejoice, pray, and give thanks to you today, for at least I know that this is your will.

In everything give thanks;
for this is God's will for you in Christ Jesus.

1 THESSALONIANS 5:18 NASB

These three things: constant rejoicing, prayer, and
thanksgiving are the formula for doing God's will in our lives.

Take this moment, this evening, to think about what you're
thankful for. Rejoice continually in what God has done for
you. Thank God intentionally for those things.

*Father, I have a big list of things to be thankful for. I choose to
dwell on these things because they bring me joy and it reminds
me of what a blessed life you have given me. God, you know that
things have been difficult and there are times when I have doubted
your goodness. In this moment, I see your care for me in so many
ways. Thank you.*

Who would be thinking about you right now and being
thankful for you in their lives? Acknowledge that you are a
blessing to others.

Faith Prompts

We keep on praying for you, asking our God to enable you to live a life worthy of his call. May he give you the power to accomplish all the good things your faith prompts you to do.

2 THESSALONIANS 1:11 NLT

Have you ever been afraid of what others will think of you when they learn that you are a Christian? Do you worry that people might treat you differently if you proclaim your faith?

It can be hard enough to fit in without giving society another reason to shun you. Shake off your timidity. Be prepared to share your faith without fear. God has sent his Holy Spirit to give you power when you lack it. Take advantage of it.

God, I have been timid in sharing my faith to others who don't know you. Put opportunities to share your goodness into my life today, and give me the boldness to proclaim your name.

The name of our Lord Jesus will be honored because of the way you live, and you will be honored along with him. This is all made possible because of the grace of our God and Lord, Jesus Christ.

2 THESSALONIANS 1:12 NLT

Be assured, there is no reason to be afraid of your faith. God has given you his Holy Spirit to guide you through tough conversations; he has equipped you with all the talent you need to share his love with those around you.

There will be some who will laugh, and there will be some who will mock you for your beliefs, but most will see the way you conduct yourself and will know that your goodness comes from your faith.

God, thank you that while I may not have had the opportunity to share you with someone today, you will give me more opportunities. I pray I would be more intentional and confident to share your good news with someone tomorrow.

What is stopping you from sharing God's good news with others? Reflect on how you can take down that barrier.

Strong Mind and Heart

Stand firm and hold to the traditions which you were taught, whether by word of mouth or by letter from us.

2 THESSALONIANS 2:15 NASB

When you hear a really good speaker, you are often quick to get out your notes and jot a few of the good points down. Sometimes you hear something so good that you have to share it through social media or save it to your files.

When God speaks to you through others, make sure to keep these words near. It is important that we continue the traditions of our faith handed down from one generation to the next.

God, thank you for the provision of your Scripture which has many of our core beliefs written down in one place. Thank you also, for people that you have appointed to speak the truth. Help me to be someone who listens, takes note, and holds these things dear to my heart, so I can pass them on when the time comes.

May our Lord Jesus Christ Himself and God our Father,
who has loved us and given us eternal comfort and good hope
by grace, comfort and strengthen your hearts in every
good work and word.

2 Thessalonians 2:16-17 nasb

This evening is a time to rest. Even if you have other things to do tonight, remember that God wants you to have time to be comforted and strengthened. God doesn't want you to burn out from overdoing it.

Find a way to do something that is uplifting, whether it is being around people who you love or an activity that refreshes your soul. Give yourself space and time so God can strengthen you for tomorrow.

Heavenly Father, I do feel weary at times from all my work.
Sometimes I do not feel appreciated or valued for what I do.
Remind me that I work for you, and that you are truly pleased
with me. Refresh my heart and mind tonight.

What can you do this evening that will refresh your heart, mind, or body?

Earn It

Even when we were with you, we gave you this command: Anyone
unwilling to work should not eat. For we hear that some of you are
living in idleness, mere busybodies, not doing any work.

2 THESSALONIANS 3:10-11 NRSV

When people are full of self-importance, they often care more
about talking about their good works than actually doing any
good works. This seemed to be happening in Paul's day and
the principle is simple: if you don't work, you don't eat.

God didn't intend for us to take his provision for granted.
He wants us to use our skills and good character for the
benefit of the community. This often means hard work.
When people see your hard work, they will have no reason to
make accusations against your faith. Diligent work is a great
witness of our Creator.

God, thank you for the work that you have put in front of me. Help
me to be diligent with this work so I am not accused of being lazy
or a busybody. Help me to be a witness to the servanthood that
comes with living as you did.

Such persons we command and exhort in the Lord Jesus Christ to do their work quietly and to earn their own living. Brothers and sisters, do not be weary in doing what is right.

2 Thessalonians 3:12-13 NRSV

Do you feel like you worked extra hard today? Be encouraged that your Father in heaven is so pleased with the job you have done today.

We are very tempted at the end of a long day to complain about so many aspects of our job, but a better example is just to quietly continue to earn your living. God doesn't want you to be miserable, but he does want you to do what is right.

God, sometimes I fail to recognize that I am being a witness of Christ just by being a diligent worker. Please give me energy to continue to work hard and do what is right.

What complaints do you have about your various jobs? Turn these complaints into thanksgiving for God's provision.

Directed Paths

Trust in the LORD with all your heart,
and lean not on your own understanding.

PROVERBS 3:5 NKJV

Trust can be a hard word to put into action mostly because our experience with others tells us that we can be sorely disappointed. People let us down in many ways. We can even be disappointed in ourselves.

Remember the trust game that involved standing with eyes closed and falling back into the hands of a few peers in hopes that they would catch you? There was risk involved in that game, and it didn't always turn out well. Nothing can truly be guaranteed in this life, can it? It depends on where you place your trust. There's no risk in trusting in God, he will never fail.

Jesus, today I choose to trust you with all the details. Whether it is in getting a lot of jobs done, or in my meetings with other people, I ask for your guidance and trust that you will help me.

In all your ways acknowledge Him,
and He shall direct your paths.

PROVERBS 3:6 NKJV

God watches over us, cares for us, and is involved in our lives. When we acknowledge that every good thing comes from him, our faith is strengthened, and we are able to trust him more.

Make a point of noticing how God has directed your path today, and thank him for being trustworthy.

God, I know that you have been involved in everything that has gone on today. I know that you have been a constant presence in my decisions and conversations. I know that you are with me in the good and difficult times and I will continue to trust you to lead the way.

What are you finding hard to trust God with at the moment? Share this with God and acknowledge that his goodness in your life will lead you in the right way.

Highway of Light

The path of the righteous is like the light of dawn,
that shines brighter and brighter until the full day.

PROVERBS 4:18 NASB

Have you ever walked through your home at night, thinking that you could make it without turning a light on, only to stumble on something unexpectedly set in your path? When you cannot see where you are going, you are likely to get tripped up. On the other hand, your way is obvious when you simply turn on a light.

Are you choosing the light? Is your path brightly lit? Or are you standing in total darkness? If so, then flip the switch. Pray that you will make wise choices. Seek his wisdom for your life. He wants to shine brightly for you. Let him in, and he will gladly be your eternal light, illuminating your days.

God, give me wisdom so I can walk in your light today. Keep my feet from stumbling.

The way of the wicked is like darkness;
They do not know over what they stumble.

PROVERBS 4:19 NASB

The Bible tells us that walking in righteousness is just like walking in the bright light of day. But choosing rebellion is like stumbling around in a deep darkness.

In the dark, you'll never know what hit you until it's already too late. When you walk in the light, you expose the darkness, even in the lives of others around you.

God, let your light in me be a positive influence on the life of others around me. I often see darkness in the world around me and I get discouraged. Holy Spirit, encourage my soul tonight as I prepare to bring your light to the world in the morning.

How can you bring light in a world of darkness?

Wisdom's Value

Receive my instruction, and not silver,
and knowledge rather than choice gold.
PROVERBS 8:10 NKJV

If you were granted the one thing that you desire most, what would it be? We can probably answer this question better if we think of who or what we idolize. Whose life do we want, or what quality do we most admire? Beauty, intelligence, creativity, recognition, or love?

Silver, gold, and rubies are rare and precious elements. They are beautiful, strong, and valuable. Perhaps you own, or are even wearing, jewelry with precious metal and stone. Remind yourself of the greater value of wisdom, and be encouraged to seek Godly understanding above anything else.

Jesus, I am going to need wisdom today. Every situation that I find myself in is better if I let you speak into them. Give me direction and understanding as I walk into my day.

*Wisdom is better than rubies, and all the things one may desire
cannot be compared with her.*

PROVERBS 8:11 NKJV

King Solomon understood the value of wisdom better than
any other. When God offered him anything he desired, King
Solomon responded with a request for wisdom. He could
have asked for fame, or riches, or success in warfare; instead,
he asked for understanding.

King Solomon sought knowledge and instruction first, and
ended up being the wisest, wealthiest, most famous, and
successful king that ever lived.

*Father, you have provided wisdom to guide me and lead me into
a blessed life. Help me to ask for your wisdom in all my situations
and to desire Godliness above the other precious things in this life.*

In what situations do you need to seek God's wisdom?

Doorway to Wisdom

Blessed is the one who listens to me,
watching daily at my gates, waiting beside my doors.
PROVERBS 8:34 ESV

The word wisdom is used hundreds of times in the Bible. Time and time again, we are instructed to use good judgment, to make sound decisions, to use prudence and circumspection.

King Solomon made a special point to ask God to give him wisdom throughout his time as Israel's leader. Because of this, God honored and blessed him.

God, I long for your wisdom. I cannot trust my own wisdom, or even the wisdom of those around me because I know that the world can be so foolish. Give me joy as I respond to your words of truth today.

Whoever finds me finds life and obtains favor from the Lord.
Proverbs 8:35 esv

The interesting thing is that wisdom is often referred to in Scripture as a "she." In Proverbs, she beseeches us to find her, to choose her. She tells us that if we do, we will find favor with God.

Spend some time at her doorway this evening. True happiness is found there, and the Lord will honor your decision.

God, thank you for giving me wisdom today. I know that my decisions are more enriched and rewarding because your wisdom is guiding me. As I get into bed tonight, let me dwell on this secret of growing delight, knowing that I have found your favor.

Are you choosing wisdom? Are you seeking her out?

Gossip Is Never Good

Whoever derides their neighbor has no sense,
but the one who has understanding holds their tongue.

PROVERBS 11:12 NIV

Neighbors are a good target for gossip, aren't they? We can get irritated by the small things and we observe comings and goings without ever really getting to know people. We are quick to make judgments of people we barely know.

It might feel good in the moment to tear people down because then we are not alone in the many ways we fall short. But it is a lie. We were designed to lift one another up. Be a good neighbor today. Give people the benefit of the doubt, hold your tongue, and let Christ's love shine out of your heart and actions.

Jesus, give me the wisdom and grace to hold my tongue today. Help me to be a good neighbor—whether at home, work, or school.

A gossip betrays a confidence,
but a trustworthy person keeps a secret.

PROVERBS 11:13 NIV

Have you been more aware of gossip today? It's an easy trap to fall into, but be encouraged to continue to allow the Holy Spirit to shape your response to gossip.

The next time you are tempted to share what isn't yours to tell, take a deep breath and pause. Ask yourself if betraying a confidence is worth letting down a friend. Instead, allow yourself to be the type of friend that the Lord has designed you to be.

God, help me not to give into temptation and share personal things with others that don't need to hear them. Help me, also, to be careful about who I choose to share my secrets with. Let me discern what friends are faithful and worthy of trust.

Have you been able to keep from gossip today, or this week? Commit to a strategy that will help you to avoid sharing gossip.

Give Freely

Give freely and become more wealthy;
be stingy and lose everything.

PROVERBS 11:24 NLT

There is need everywhere we look. Families need homes, missionaries need support, food shelves need donations, and non-profit organizations need finances. How can we even begin to meet those needs? How could we possibly give enough to make a difference?

Generosity can be scary. Giving might mean that we will have to do without. Giving costs us something. We think that we need to have less in order to do more. But in God's economy, he who gives generously will be repaid lavishly. He who holds nothing back will inherit everything.

God, give me an opportunity to be generous today. It feels a little scary for me to say that, but I know that you want me to be a generous giver, and I know that it will be good for me to give, and good for someone else to receive.

The generous will prosper;
those who refresh others will themselves be refreshed.

PROVERBS 11:25 NLT

Were you able to give to someone today? Remember that God will provide for your every need, no matter how much you give to others.

God doesn't measure wealth the way we do. He doesn't operate on our economic system. He gives with rewards that will last forever and wealth that will never run out.

God, give me another chance to give to someone. Thank you that each new day brings another opportunity to serve you and others. I look forward to whomever I might meet tomorrow that has a need.

What or who is God asking you to be generous to?

Sharp Tongues

Whoever speaks the truth gives honest evidence, but a false witness utters deceit. There is one whose rash words are like sword thrusts, but the tongue of the wise brings healing.

PROVERBS 12:17-18 ESV

Words can cut deeply. Throughout the Bible, God characterizes a person of wisdom as one of few words, one who is slow to respond. Perhaps this is because a careless word can do so much damage.

None of us can deny that words carry power. They can easily leave a mark that is not quickly erased. In the same way, words can bring healing. We can encourage, comfort, and even redeem our wrong with honest and gracious communication.

Holy Spirit, I am going to need your help as I speak today. I know that I don't always carefully watch what I say, so please remind me instantly when I am about to say something that is not good. Let wise and kind words come from my mouth.

Truthful lips endure forever,
but a lying tongue is but for a moment.

PROVERBS 12:19 ESV

We can't underestimate the power of our words. The beautiful thing about this verse is that truth endures forever. If you have spoken careless words today, you have the power to bring healing with new and lasting words of wisdom.

If you have been pained by someone else's words or lies, turn to the wise words of Scripture to find healing to the scars in your own heart.

Jesus, heal those wounds that have come from hurtful words. Forgive me when I have said wrong things, and give me the boldness to make things right.

Are you hurt from unkind words? Do you need to be forgiven for saying something unkind? Bring it all to Jesus in heartfelt prayer.

Walk with the Wise

Walk with the wise and become wise,
for a companion of fools suffers harm.

PROVERBS 13:20 NIV

Humans were created for relationship; we are hardwired to want and need others. Because of our design, friendships are vitally important to our lives and also to our walk with God.

Friends either bring us up or drag us down. Likewise, friends can either encourage or discourage us in our pursuit of godliness.

As we seek counsel from our friends for the decisions we make in life, it is important that those friends are pushing us to follow Christ and not our own desires.

Jesus, I know that you desire that I have good friends. Give me discernment, even today, to spend time with those people who are good and uplifting and to keep away from the company of the unwise.

> *Trouble pursues the sinner,*
> *but the righteous are rewarded with good things.*

PROVERBS 13:21 NIV

Your friends have the power to lead you closer to God or push you away from him. Surround yourself with people who will echo God's words to you rather than lead you off course with their advice.

Evaluate yourself to make sure you are being the kind of friend who will lead others closer to Christ by your influence and your advice.

As I reflect on my day, God, I can see those people who have been very encouraging to me. I want to be with people who are wise and able to lift me up in my faith. I also ask for grace to be a good and wise friend to others.

Who have you spent time with today? Are they people who are wise and encouraging?

Guided Steps

A man's heart plans his way,
but the LORD directs his steps.

PROVERBS 16:9 NKJV

There are so many things in our lives that we simply don't get. We aren't sure why some things happen and other things don't. We have our own lofty dreams and treasured plans, and when they don't work out the way they did in our hearts, we feel lost, angry, and confused.

God doesn't want you to just stop planning, but he wants to be involved in your decisions. Invite him in and see how much better it feels to have him guide your way.

Father, thank you that you want to partner with me in this life. I know this takes communication and an ultimate submission to your will. Give me the grace to let go and let you direct my steps.

Pride goes before destruction,
and a haughty spirit before a fall.

PROVERBS 16:18 NKJV

When everything goes wrong and the plans in our hearts don't work out, God knows what he's doing. He sees what we do not.

We can have the best ideas in the world, but if God is not directing us, our plans will falter. Trust in him with all your heart. Dedicate your plans to him, and allow him to keep you from falling.

God, thank you for the dreams and desires that you have put in my heart. Thank you that I can trust you to get me there, without me having to work out all the plans. I'm grateful that you are navigating this life for me and that you are working things out for my good.

What are some of your plans for the future? Commit them to the Lord, asking him to direct your steps.

Welcome Reconciliation

Love prospers when a fault is forgiven,
but dwelling on it separates close friends.

PROVERBS 17:9 NLT

When a close friend does something that offends us, our hurt can cause us to look for validation from someone completely outside the issue. We feel the need to process our pain, so we find a listening ear who will confirm our feelings.

The next time someone offends you, instead of finding someone to commiserate with you, run to God and ask him for the strength to forgive. Choose to forgive the fault and protect your friendship rather than extending the pain by sharing it with others.

God, I know I need to be wiser about who I choose to share my heart with. I know that sometimes I indulge in gossip, even if it is about myself. Give me self-control when I am tempted to overstep the boundary. Help me to keep my integrity intact.

Anyone who loves to quarrel loves sin;
anyone who trusts in high walls invites disaster.

PROVERBS 17:19 NLT

By mulling a matter over both in our minds and with our words, we allow our anger to build. And the more we repeat the offense to listeners who validate us based on our side of the story, the further we travel from reconciliation.

In order for love to prosper in our relationships, we must choose forgiveness over offense. We have to lay down whatever rights we felt we had in the situation and put love first—because love is of God.

Jesus, I know that you chose love to cover all our sins. Help me to choose love instead of retribution when I have been wronged. I don't want to put walls up and shut people out of my life, so let my heart be full of grace for others.

What offense are you holding on to? Bring it to God and leave it there.

Humble Wages

Humility is the fear of the LORD;
its wages are riches and honor and life.

PROVERBS 22:4 NIV

God values humility over pride and earthly success. That is why sometimes God makes us wait before revealing his plans for us. In the waiting is where he grows us in humility. When things don't work out perfectly, our pride is dismantled and we learn the most valuable lessons.

God being glorified in our lives doesn't make sense to our humanity because his plan isn't our plan and his ways are different. The entire message of the Gospel is upside-down from what we know here on earth. In God's kingdom, humility is elevated, and pride is made low. Those who are poor are rich, and those who are weak are strong. Humble yourself in his presence today.

Jesus, thank you that my success isn't something that I accomplished on my own. I have seen a lot of failures along the way, and I have also recognized how many people you have put into my life to help me. I recognize you in my success today.

In the paths of the wicked are snares and pitfalls,
but those who would preserve their life stay far from them.

PROVERBS 22:5 NIV

Maybe your day has not felt like a success. God is more concerned with having your heart fully devoted to him so you avoid the traps of sin.

God wants you to serve him, and he loves when you prosper in kingdom work, but those things aren't his main goal. He wants you to have a life that avoids evil and loves goodness, so you experience peace and joy.

God, let my main goal be one of eternal value. I know that I pursue earthly success and I know that this isn't wrong, but help me to avoid the usual traps of sin so I can enjoy life.

What kind of success are you pursuing right now?

A Good Heart

My child, if your heart is wise, my heart too will be glad.
My soul will rejoice when your lips speak what is right.

PROVERBS 23:15-16 NRSV

As Christians who have knowingly received so much from God, we want to give something back. We see people around us who are giving back—they either have dedicated their lives to bringing the message of the Gospel to remote locations, or they are donors who fund entire ministries and give thousands to the poor.

Surely these people are much further along than we are in the repayment of their debt to God, we think. These are excellent works, but what God really desires is our hearts.

Jesus, thank you that you think that my heart is so valuable. You created me, you know me, and now you want me to know you. I give you my heart today, knowing that you will show me your ways.

Do not let your heart envy sinners, but always continue in the fear of the LORD. Surely there is a future, and your hope will not be cut off.

PROVERBS 23:17-18 NRSV

More than anything extravagant that you wish you had to offer God, he wants the one thing you already have—your heart.

Christ didn't die on the cross so we would faithfully tithe to our church, or sell everything we own for the sake of his name. He died simply to be with us, to make a way for us to know him and enter into pure relationship with him.

Thank you, God, for pursuing me like no one else can. You are such an awesome God, and yet you deeply care for me. I have so many things going on in my life, even just for today, and often I forget to let you in. As I lay in bed tonight, help me to see hope for a blessed future.

Are there people in your life who need to know Jesus? Pray for them tonight, asking that they would understand how valuable their heart is to Jesus.

Friendship

The heartfelt counsel of a friend is as sweet as
perfume and incense.

PROVERBS 27:9 ESV

When you sign up for a competitive team sport, you have a basic understanding that you're going to have to work hard and that emotions will run high to win and succeed. You know that you'll win some, you'll lose some, and that somewhere along the way you'll start to feel good about playing the game whether you win or lose.

Playing a competitive team sport sometimes feels the same as building relationships with others. We rely on our friends to cheer for us when we are doing well, and to share in the disappointment of losses. It's a valuable thing to find a friend who is on your team.

Father God, thank you for creating friendship. It is truly a
beautiful thing. I am so grateful for the wonderful friends in my
life. Help me to share my love, patience, and kindness with a
friend today.

Never abandon a friend - either yours or your father's. When disaster strikes, you won't have to ask your brother for assistance. It's better to go to a neighbor than to a brother who lives far away.

PROVERBS 27:10 ESV

When we do find amazing friends, those precious few who make us better people by encouraging us and making us laugh, we need to hold on tight and enjoy the rare gems they are. If you're still looking for a close friend, don't lose heart. Pray for God to bring people into your life.

Friendships can span generations. You can find them in older and younger people. Look for reliable, trustworthy people who will be there, even when things go wrong. Remember that your friends are relying on you to be a good friend too.

Jesus, thank you for the sweetness of my close friends. Help me to find ways to bring them joy and care for them as they care for me. Where I feel lonely, I ask that you bring the right friends into my life to craete that amazing fragrance that I need.

Do you have a friend that holds you accountable but also lifts you up when you need it?

Clean It Up

Whoever conceals their sins does not prosper,
but the one who confesses and renounces them finds mercy.

PROVERBS 28:13 NIV

When we make a mess on the floor, the worse thing to do is to sweep it under the rug and leave it there. Dirt doesn't go away. It needs to be cleaned, or it will stain, stink, and create mold.

When we fail to examine our hearts in situations—even arguments where we think we are right—we allow some buildup that isn't healthy for anyone. We need to search out our sin and clean it up. Mercy will always follow the humble.

God, give me the humility to admit when I am wrong today.

Blessed is the one who always trembles before God,
but whoever hardens their heart falls into trouble.

PROVERBS 28:14 NIV

Have you had an argument recently, perhaps even today, and left convinced that the other person was the one in the wrong? Consider what part of it you could have done better: there are always two sides to a fight.

Even if it is small, confess your wrongdoing, and be prepared to forgive. Don't let your heart be hardened. Let God's mercy toward you become your strength to forgive.

God, I thank you that there is great blessing in humility. I forgive those who have wronged me today, and ask for you to continue to soften my heart.

Who needs to experience your forgiveness right now?

Pray for Leaders

I urge you, first of all, to pray for all people. Ask God to help them; intercede on their behalf, and give thanks for them. Pray this way for kings and all who are in authority so that we can live peaceful and quiet lives marked by godliness and dignity.

1 TIMOTHY 2:1-2 NLT

When you think of the leaders of our day, you can either be full of respect or have no regard for them at all. We have good world leaders and terrible world leaders, we have great managers and appalling managers. Either way, God wants us to pray for all of them.

Ask God to help them. The person who is struggling to lead well needs all the help they can get. When we have people who lead well, we have better countries, schools, and workplaces. Start praying.

God, I'm sorry when I have tried to undermine people who are in authority. I know that it is a harder job than it might seem at times, so I pray for your courage, integrity, and peace to be in the hearts of all of our leaders—from presidents and church leaders, to principals and executives. Give me a chance to encourage one of these leaders today.

*This is good and pleases God our Savior, who wants everyone
to be saved and to understand the truth.*

1 TIMOTHY 2:3 NLT

Good results come from having good people in leadership. As
you have prayed and perhaps even encouraged a leader today,
remember that this isn't just for the benefit of that person, it
is for the benefit of a community of people.

God finds all kinds of ways to show himself to others, and
one of these ways will be through Christ-like leaders. Be
confident that your support encourages the gospel to spread.

*Father, as I reflect on the people who are currently in leadership in
my community and in the world, I pray that you would continue to
raise up Godly leaders. Protect them from all forms of hardship and
strengthen them to lead in a way that shows people your truth.*

What leaders can you commit to praying for more often?

Spiritual Fitness

Bodily exercise profits a little, but godliness is profitable for all things, having promise of the life that now is and of that which is to come.

1 TIMOTHY 4:8 NKJV

We know the value of exercise; it benefits the body and the mind. We also know that exercise requires determination and discipline. There is, however, exercise that is more beneficial than physical exercise. Scripture compares godliness with bodily exercise.

Godliness is not just something that we instantly receive when we accept Christ as our Savior. Godliness is a work in progress. It requires discipline and commitment to understanding what it means to be like Jesus.

Father, I need that discipline in my life. I don't just want to make a plan, I want to have the strength and stamina to carry through on that plan. I look toward the higher goal of eternity.

*This is a faithful saying and worthy of all acceptance.
For to this end we both labor and suffer reproach,
because we trust in the living God, who is the Savior of all men,
especially of those who believe.*

1 TIMOTHY 4:9-10 NKJV

Do you accept that you are going to have to put in the time and effort to prioritize spiritual practices in the same way you try to with physical exercise?

Godliness has benefit beyond this life. Be encouraged that you will be rewarded in both this life and the life to come.

Jesus, I want to be spiritually fit. I know the benefits of having you in my life daily. Thank you that I have had the opportunity to read a Scripture this morning and now this evening. Help me to keep this discipline of spending time with you.

Where do you need extra spiritual training? Ask the Holy Spirit to be your personal trainer.

Show Respect

All who are under the yoke of slavery should consider their masters worthy of full respect, so that God's name and our teaching may not be slandered

1 TIMOTHY 6:1 NIV

While we don't like to think of ourselves as servants, many of us are involved in employment or some type of service. The Bible says much about those who have shown diligence and respect to those who are in authority.

We don't want to give people an opportunity to think of us as lazy or uncaring. When we work hard, we represent the servant nature of Christ. Show people that you are capable of putting others first today.

God, as I think about getting on with my usual day-to-day tasks, I pray that you would give me renewed energy to respect people who I work for, or those who have a position of authority.

Those who have believing masters should not show them disrespect just because they are fellow believers. Instead, they should serve them even better because their masters are dear to them as fellow believers and are devoted to the welfare of their slaves.

1 TIMOTHY 6:2 NIV

There is a higher purpose to us respecting our employers. When we show diligence, commitment, and effort, we are honoring God's name as a witness of Christian living.

Be encouraged as you go into your place of work (whether home, study, or employment), knowing that as you show good service, you are positively representing the name of Jesus.

Jesus, thank you for this time of rest tonight. Give me the will to do a really great job tomorrow and to show respect for those who are in leadership.

Who can you pray for tonight who is in a position of authority over you?

A Different Kind of Rich

Teach those who are rich in this world not to be proud and not to trust in their money, which is so unreliable. Their trust should be in God, who richly gives us all we need for our enjoyment.

1 TIMOTHY 6:17 NLT

We think that more money will get us what we want, and sometimes it does, momentarily. All too often, when we finally buy that thing we have been waiting for, we don't feel that much better and we begin to look at the next thing.

Wealth in this life won't give us what our heart really desires. We won't find lasting peace or lasting joy. God is the one who fulfills these desires because he brings a better kind of richness to our relationships and situations. Ask his for love, not money, today.

God, let me be generous today, but not just with money. Challenge me to be generous with my time, energy, or a kind word.

Tell them to use their money to do good.
They should be rich in good works and generous to those in need,
always being ready to share with others.

1 Timothy 6:18 NLT

Have you fallen into the trap of thinking that spending will give you enjoyment? The Scripture says that God is the source for our enjoyment. He would rather we use our money to do good.

Gifts are wonderful, but allow yourself to dwell on the goodness that you can share with others, particularly those in need.

God, give me an opportunity to give to someone in need. I pray that you will give me a more generous heart and expose the times when I am buying something of little value.

Have you felt challenged to spend wisely lately? Who can you be generous to this week?

Flames

*I remind you to fan into flame the gift of God, which is in you
through the laying on of my hands. For the Spirit God gave us does
not make us timid, but gives us power, love and self-discipline.*

2 TIMOTHY 1:6-7 NIV

We are called to use our gifts to advance God's kingdom. In
order to feel confident in what that looks like, we need to
draw from courage that is given through the Spirit of God.
The same Spirit that lives in him is alive in us.

Fanning the flame is powerful and involves loving
extravagantly. Today, you have the opportunity to touch lives
in ways that may seem small, but are really part of the flame
that will eventually burn brighter.

*Jesus, I take a step closer to you this morning and ask that you
continue to give me power and self-discipline to keep pressing
closer into you. Help me to push aside the distractions and to be
focused on the gospel.*

Do not be ashamed of the testimony about our Lord or of me his prisoner. Rather, join with me in suffering for the gospel, by the power of God.

2 TIMOTHY 1:8 NIV

If we are being fed by a spirit of power, love, and self-discipline, we will have all that we need to testify about God, and to endure suffering of all kinds, just as Paul did. In order to see the fullness of God's Spirit, we need to take a step toward igniting the hearts of people who God has put across our paths.

A step might be taking a colleague to coffee, asking your waiter if they belong to a church, or reaching out to that neighbor you've always wondered about.

Holy Spirit, I need your power in me to mention the name of Jesus in a world that is seemingly so hostile. Give me opportunities to talk about you. Grant me boldness where I feel timid, and peace when I feel anxious.

What are you afraid of when sharing the gospel? Ask God for boldness.

Convinced

Of this gospel I was appointed a herald and an apostle and a teacher. That is why I am suffering as I am. Yet this is no cause for shame, because I know whom I have believed, and am convinced that he is able to guard what I have entrusted to him until that day.

2 TIMOTHY 1:11–12 NIV

Have you ever tried to wade upstream through a river, or swim against a strong current? It is hard. Sometimes this is how we feel as Christians in a world full of unbelievers. Our culture is full of political correctness and accepting all beliefs, but when it comes to Christianity, it feels like anything we say is offensive.

Paul was put in prison a number of times for offending the people of his time. He seemed to suffer gladly because he was convinced that Jesus was the Savior and that his mission was to share the good news with the world. Paul was convinced of the truth, and because of this, he was not ashamed.

Jesus, you are worth suffering for because you are the good news that the world needs to hear. Holy Spirit, give me power to share what I believe, being convinced that it is the truth.

*What you heard from me, keep as the pattern of sound
teaching, with faith and love in Christ Jesus. Guard the good
deposit that was entrusted to you—guard it with the help
of the Holy Spirit who lives in us.*

2 TIMOTHY 1:13-14 NIV

Do you tend to keep quiet about your faith in Jesus? Are you
worried about suffering, or being mocked for your beliefs?

Take time each day to develop your relationship with him; the
more you know Jesus, the more confident you will be in what
you believe. Imitate Paul's dedication to sharing the gospel,
guard its truth, and trust God to protect you.

*God, give me ways to spend more time with you so I become as
convinced as Paul was that you are the way, the truth, and the
life. Give me the confidence to be a good witness of who you are.
I don't want to worry any more about words, because I know you
care more about a genuine heart.*

Why are you convinced that Jesus is the good news? See if you
can share this soon.

God's Inspiration

Continue in what you have learned and have become convinced of, because you know those from whom you learned it, and how from infancy you have known the Holy Scriptures, which are able to make you wise for salvation through faith in Christ Jesus.

2 TIMOTHY 4:14-15 NIV

We don't just stop at salvation—there is so much more to learn about God. While you may be assured of the message of the gospel, it is important to continue to incorporate the Scripture into your daily life so it is always on your heart and ready to guide you in all your situations.

In the days of this Scripture, people had to rely on their memory and public readings of the Scripture. Our job is really much easier as we have the Scripture available at the touch of a button. Use this to your advantage, and soak yourself in the Word today.

God, give me creative ways to incorporate Scripture into my daily life. I don't want to stop at just being saved, I want to learn how to live a life that is wholly guided by your principles.

*All Scripture is God-breathed and is useful for teaching, rebuking,
correcting and training in righteousness, so that the servant of
God may be thoroughly equipped for every good work.*

2 TIMOTHY 4:16-17 NIV

Were you able to read a bit more Scripture today or have there
been too many things on your to-do list? Remember that
reading Scripture isn't about completing a task, it's there
because God wants you to be inspired by the words that he
has breathed life into.

God's Word is living, which means that he can speak into your
situations and heart at the moments when you need it the
most. Let him encourage you tonight, so you are equipped for
the day ahead.

*Holy God, your Word really is a lamp to my feet and a light to my
path. Thank you for your incredible words that can help to correct,
train, and equip me to continue to do life with your guidance.
Holy Spirit, encourage my heart each day to remember these words
of life.*

What is God speaking to you through his Word this evening?

Days Ahead

When times are good, be happy; but when times are bad,
consider this: God has made the one as well as the other.

ECCLESIASTES 7:14 NIV

It's easy to be happy on a sunny day, when all is well, the birds are singing, and life is going along swimmingly. But what happens when waters are rougher, bad news comes, or the days feel just plain hard? Is your happiness determined by your circumstance?

Pray that you will discover true joy in our Creator. Ask him to give you a deep and abiding satisfaction in each day that goes beyond human understanding.

God, you created this day. It might be raining or sunny, it might be full of troubles, or full of peace. Whatever the circumstance, help me to know your joy and your peace in everything.

No one can discover anything about their future.

ECCLESIASTES 7:14 NIV

God wants us to feel gladness when times are good. He has made each day. We are called to rejoice in all of them whether good or bad. Happiness is determined by our circumstances, but true joy comes when we can find the silver linings, hidden in our darkest hours—when we can sing his praises no matter what.

We don't know what the future holds for us here on earth, but we can find our delight in the knowledge that our eternity is set in beauty.

God, I want to be a happy person. I know that too often I am grumpy, stressed, or serious. Thank you for those who make me laugh. Thank you for all the good things in my life. Let me choose to dwell on those good things this evening despite my circumstances. Give me joy beyond measure.

What is the source of your happiness? Do you need to readjust what makes you truly happy?

Waiting for Perfect

Farmers who wait for perfect weather never plant. If they watch every cloud, they never harvest. Just as you cannot understand the path of the wind or the mystery of a tiny baby growing in its mother's womb, so you cannot understand the activity of God, who does all things.

ECCLESIASTES 11:4–5 NLT

Even in our modern age with all our scientific advantages, our weather still remains one of the most unpredictable phenomena. There are many unknowns when we set about to make decisions that we can often paralyze ourselves from doing anything. We try to wait for everything to line up and make sense, but how often are circumstances ideal? How often do we think we need to wait until they are?

We cannot control or predict much in life, but God can. Instead of putting trust in your ideas, trust in God's direction for you today.

God, sometimes I wait too long for the perfect timing. Help me to be realistic that there hardly ever is a "best time" to do things. Help me to do my very best today.

*Plant your seed in the morning and keep busy all afternoon,
for you don't know if profit will come from one activity
or another—or maybe both.*

ECCLESIASTES 11:6 NLT

We rarely get to the end of the day and feel like we have
accomplished everything. What matters is that you have done
something. The advice of Scripture is to decide that a few
minutes late is better than absent. Let's acknowledge our
collective fatigue, and know that we can only do our best.

Reflect on today and realize that waiting for a burst of
creativity, or a break in the weather, is not the only thing you
need to get on with work. Ask God to help you attack your
projects, and see what happens.

*God, I am tired and don't know if I was very productive today.
Help me to stop waiting for the right time to get things done and
instead work diligently toward the things that matter.*

What are you waiting for? What do you need to start moving on?

Nothing Better

I know that there is nothing better for people than to be happy and to do good while they live. That each of them may eat and drink, and find satisfaction in all their toil—this is the gift of God.

ECCLESIASTES 3:12-13 NIV

It cannot be put more clearly. There is nothing better than to be happy in your life. Your life is made up of now. Each moment you live, each breath you take, it's right this very second.

To find happiness in your life is to find the best thing. And to find satisfaction in your effort is to find the gift of God. Treasure your life. Be satisfied with where you are. Satisfaction is living each day as if it were the dream.

God, I want to be content with where I am in life. Even more than that, I want to be happy. Thank you that you still care about my dreams, and thank you that life is a journey and process of shaping and re-shaping those dreams. Thank you for every moment, including right now.

I know that everything God does will endure forever;
nothing can be added to it and nothing taken from it.
God does it so that people will fear him.

ECCLESIASTES 3:14 NIV

Pretending we are someone else, or somewhere else, begins early in childhood and more subtly continues as we age. We still allow imagination to transport us to other places, and other circumstances.

Somehow it is easier for us to embrace the wonder of "what if" than the reality of "what is." Know who you are and where you are today, and embrace it all with faith.

Father, as I look back on some of my childhood dreams, I realize that it was nice to dream and it made me feel happy. But today is my reality and I pray that you would help me to see my life as a gift. Stir joy in my heart once again.

What dreams are you still holding on to? Enjoy the process of getting to those dreams and remember that God wants your happiness.

Eternal Workings

*What do people really get for all their hard work?
I have seen the burden God has placed on us all.*

ECCLESIASTES 3:9-10 NLT

Much emphasis is placed on figuring life out. We so easily become caught up in the here-and-now that we lose sight of the fact that life on earth is really only a blink compared to what our life will be in eternity.

You have the unique opportunity to determine how you will spend your forever life. Serve God well with your one life on earth, so you can live endlessly with him in glory.

I want to serve you well today, God. I get caught up in all the distractions of this life, but I know that eternity sits in my heart. Help me to uncover your eternal workings in my life today. Reveal something of long lasting worth to me.

God has made everything beautiful for its own time. He has planted eternity in the human heart, but even so, people cannot see the whole scope of God's work from beginning to end.

ECCLESIASTES 3:11 NLT

Our entire agendas will shift when we begin to live with eternal perspective. Once we understand that the only things that will last are those of spiritual worth, we suddenly realize that our priorities must be adjusted. Our eternal worth must supersede our earthly value.

We can be among the world's most wealthy here on earth but be headed for eternal destruction. Or we could be living paycheck to paycheck in this life and be governor of half a kingdom in the next.

Thank you, heavenly Father, that you are preparing a place for me. Thank you that you have started to make me beautiful and you will continue to make me beautiful right into eternity. I don't know what you are doing from beginning to end, but I trust that you know all things.

How is what you are doing right now preparing you for eternity?

The Winter Is Past

My beloved speaks and says to me: "Arise, my love, my beautiful one, and come away, for behold, the winter is past; the rain is over and gone."

SONG OF SOLOMON 2:10-11 ESV

Some say that romance is dead. It's not for God: the lover of our souls. He desires nothing more than time with his creation. You are his beautiful one. And he does, indeed, want to bring you out of the cold winter.

He's finished the watering season and it is finally time to rejoice in the season of renewal. Your day may look like it is full of dark clouds, but look for the silver lining; the sun is ready to come out.

God, thank you that you help me to get through the difficult seasons and that you long to bring me out of those times because of your great love for me. Help me to follow you into this next season with a heart full of trust.

The flowers appear on the earth, the time of singing has come,
and the voice of the turtledove is heard in our land.

SONG OF SOLOMON 2:12 ESV

When the rain is falling and the sun is hidden behind dark clouds, it is hard to imagine yourself having fun or enjoying life. This evening, as you reflect on the season you are in, consider the "flowers" that are beginning to show through in the areas that you have least expected them.

See that God is calling you into spring. The time has come. He is calling you, regardless of how ready you may think you are. Will you arise and come away with your beloved? He is waiting for you.

God, it is hard for me to realize how much you love me. Thank you that you are with me in all seasons. Give me the courage to follow you into the next.

What things do you need to leave in the winter? Bring yourself into the promise of spring.

Little Foxes

*Catch for us the foxes, the little foxes that ruin the vineyards —
for our vineyards are in blossom.*

SONG OF SOLOMON 2:15 NRSV

Foxes are known for their cunning. They're sneaky little things, hunting their prey on the sly. They're known for their ability to camouflage themselves, hiding as they circle, and then suddenly pouncing on their intended target.

Our enemy is a cunning one, and he uses our sin and temptations in the same sly way. They're camouflaged in the corners of our minds where we don't even notice until it's often too late. We see it when we're already caught, and our sin is shaking us to the point where we're ready to give up and give in.

God, give me an alert mind today, so I can be aware of the little things that try to creep in and destroy my relationship with you and with others. Let me catch the foxes before they cause harm.

My beloved is mine and I am his;
he pastures his flock among the lilies.

SONG OF SOLOMON 2:16 NRSV

God wants us to be like vineyards that are in bloom. This lush and beautiful field is where true relationships can develop, but we always need to be on guard for the foxes. It can be hard to know when a little fox has snuck into your heart.

Sometimes we are caught off guard and realize that we have let something unwanted come into our lives. Look for the ways that sin might be hiding in your heart, and give it over to God so he can prevent the unnecessary shaking in your life.

God, search my heart and give me wisdom and strength to get rid of the annoying little foxes that might be running amuck—I only want your goodness in my heart so I can truly bloom.

Can you identify the foxes in your situations? Ask for God's wisdom to discern what is from him and what is not.

Fierce Love

*Place me like a seal over your heart, like a seal on your arm;
for love is as strong as death, its jealousy unyielding as the grave.
It burns like blazing fire, like a mighty flame.*

SONG OF SOLOMON 8:6 NIV

God's love is not weak. When we think of love in a romantic
way, it can seem like a delicate concept. Yet love is the thing
that holds people together through storms; it is the force that
compels us to act impulsively or irrationally. It drives almost
all our decisions and behaviors.

Love is as strong and real as death, and God is the author
of this powerful emotion. As you consider his love this
morning, think about the power of love, and let your faith be
strengthened because of this power.

*God, I am grateful for your love that gives me so much purpose.
Help me to live today in the strength of your love, and to let the
power of love emanate from me to others.*

Many waters cannot quench love; rivers cannot sweep it away.
If one were to give all the wealth of one's house for love,
it would be utterly scorned.

SONG OF SOLOMON 8:6 NIV

There is, quite literally, nothing that can compare to love. Humans have been trying to explain love from the beginning of creation, yet it doesn't seem as though words are enough. When we see true love in action, it illuminates God, because he is love.

When you see love that changes lives, situations, and relationships for the better, you know that is God's power. We can't get enough of love, and love won't go away. Embrace it, accept it, and give it without limit.

God, let me be a person who loves fiercely. Let me give all that I can because I know you have given me everything out of your great love for me. Allow my heart to be full of this love tonight, and let me be ready to give without limits tomorrow.

Have you experienced God's love today? Be ready to give it away tomorrow.

Rebirth

At one time we too were foolish, disobedient, deceived and enslaved by all kinds of passions and pleasures. We lived in malice and envy, being hated and hating one another. But when the kindness and love of God our Savior appeared, he saved us, not because of righteous things we had done, but because of his mercy.

TITUS 3:3-5 NIV

Since sin entered the world in the Garden of Eden there has been a divide between the holy God and humanity. But throughout history, God has created ways for us to still have fellowship with him despite our inability to save ourselves.

God created temples and priests in the Old Testament, and then Jesus lived, died, and was resurrected, and he changed that system so it is no longer in places but in our hearts that God dwells.

God, dwell in my heart today. I am not worthy but I know that through your Son, Jesus, I have been made worthy.

*He saved us through the washing of rebirth and renewal by the
Holy Spirit, whom he poured out on us generously through Jesus
Christ our Savior, so that, having been justified by his grace, we
might become heirs having the hope of eternal life.*

TITUS 3:5-7 NIV

God wants to be with us. He didn't shrug his shoulders when
sin entered the world and reconcile himself to the fact that
he wouldn't be able to have a close relationship with us any
longer. Rather, he went to the greatest lengths to still be with
us because his love for us is that intense.

God wants to dwell among us. Not just visit. Not just talk
sometimes. He wants his presence to be constantly among us.

*God, I long for your presence. I know you are here with me as I
spend this time reflecting on my day and on my heart toward
you. Dwell in me, right my wrong, and create in me a clean and
genuine heart.*

How can you let the Holy Spirit speak to you tonight? Let his
hope wash over you as you rest in his presence.

Appreciate the Faithful

I am praying that you will put into action the generosity that comes from your faith as you understand and experience all the good things we have in Christ. Your love has given me much joy and comfort, my brother, for your kindness has often refreshed the hearts of God's people.

PHILEMON 1:6-7 NLT

If you could write a letter to someone who has been a loyal, faithful, servant of Christ, would it sound a lot like what Paul has written to Philemon? Encouraging people with your words is a good habit to get into.

If you think about a time when you have been extremely generous or kind, you will know that it feels right to be appreciated. Take note today of people who have demonstrated kindness, and remember to show your appreciation.

Jesus, thank you for your loyal servants that are all around. Their generosity and kindness is what keeps your church encouraged and refreshed. Refresh those people who are selflessly doing your work, and remind me to appreciate them as often as I can.

*That is why I am boldly asking a favor of you. I could demand it in
the name of Christ because it is the right thing for you to do.
But because of our love, I prefer simply to ask you.
Consider this as a request from me—Paul, an old man
and now also a prisoner for the sake of Christ Jesus.*

PHILEMON 1:8-9 NLT

Trust between friends is a wonderful thing. Paul could
have placed an obligation on Philemon to help him out, but
instead he knew that as a faithful friend, all he needed to do
was ask.

Do you have friends that you can trust like this? Everybody
needs that kind and generous person in their life who
they can trust will help them out when they need it. More
importantly, are you someone that a friend could ask to help
them in time of need?

*Jesus, thank you for the generosity of friends in my life. I pray that
you would increase my love for others so I can also be someone
who is relied upon to do the right thing. Help me to be a person who
is trusted to take care of others.*

Will you respond generously to a request from a friend?

The Sword

The word of God is alive and active. Sharper than any double-edged sword, it penetrates even to dividing soul and spirit, joints and marrow; it judges the thoughts and attitudes of the heart.

HEBREWS 4:12 NIV

Sometimes it can feel as though the Bible doesn't really speak to our modern lives. After all, these stories took place thousands of years ago. It doesn't always seem relevant. Old Testament people lived for hundreds of years. We can't fathom being swallowed by a fish when we try to avoid God's presence. Rainbows are beautiful, but it's hard to picture the entire earth being covered in water, so we forget that rainbows are a symbol of his covenant with us.

The Word of God is alive today and just as relevant as it was for the original readers. Dive in and seek out what he is speaking to you today.

God, let me take your Word out into the world today.

Nothing in all creation is hidden from God's sight.
Everything is uncovered and laid bare before the eyes of him
to whom we must give account.

HEBREWS 4:13 NIV

As you read the stories of the Bible, search for the truth woven throughout every word in Scripture, and make sure to pay attention. When we increase our knowledge of the stories of Israel, the warnings of the prophets, the sayings of the wise, and the life of Jesus, we are more connected to our faith.

Don't be ignorant in this Christian walk, use the sword (the Holy Scriptures) to arm yourself to fight for the faith.

Holy Spirit, give me inspiration as I read your Word. Allow me to see the deeper truth and to get life from what I read.

Are you giving yourself time to read God's Word? Challenge yourself to read a bit deeper this week.

Our High Priest

Since then we have a great high priest who has passed through the heavens, Jesus, the Son of God, let us hold fast our confession.

HEBREWS 4:14 NKJV

One of the most beautiful things about the God we serve is that he knows exactly what we are going through at any given time. How does he know? Because he has been there himself.

When Jesus came to earth in the form of a human, he was tempted by the same everyday things we are. Whether it's lust, unkind thoughts, unwarranted anger... you name it, he had to face it. Just like we do.

Thank you, Jesus, that you can relate to my weakness. Thank you that you went to the cross for my weakness and wore it yourself so I can have newness of life in you. Help me to resist temptation today.

*We do not have a high priest who is unable to sympathize
with our weaknesses, but one who in every respect has
been tempted as we are, yet without sin.*

HEBREWS 4:15 NKJV

You can bring your temptation and confessed sin to the Lord
without fear; he knows exactly how you're feeling. He is not
some far off God in the sky who cannot relate to you and your
life.

Pray for protection from temptation just as he did, and he
will answer you.

*God, I may have failed you today, but I know that you forgive me.
Help me to rely on your strength to resist sin the next time I am
tempted to follow the way of the world.*

In what ways are you being tempted? Ask Jesus to come into
those areas of your life.

Spiritual Growth

You have been believers so long now that you ought to be teaching others. Instead, you need someone to teach you again the basic things about God's word. You are like babies who need milk and cannot eat solid food.

HEBREWS 5:12 NLT

It would be frustrating to go to school and never learn a thing. The point of learning is to gain understanding so we can be better skilled and prepared for what is ahead.

In the same way, our goal is to become mature in Christ. Maturity brings a sureness to your faith and steady trust that Christ is working through you. You might not reach this goal today, but you are on your way.

God, thank you that you allow me to grow in you each day. Help me to be a little more mature in you today than I was yesterday.

Someone who lives on milk is still an infant and doesn't know how to do what is right. Solid food is for those who are mature, who through training have the skill to recognize the difference between right and wrong.

HEBREWS 5:13-14 NLT

Not too long after our bones finish growing, we realize the real growth is just getting started. We start to experience relationships, working, and responsibilities. In each of these things, we need Godly wisdom—the ability to discern what is right and wrong in our decision making.

No matter what our age today, most of us are still working on wisdom. When we are growing in Christ, it's a process that never really ends. Scripture says this is the way he made you, to grow in your humanity, becoming physically and spiritually mature.

Jesus, I ask that you will help me to grow in wisdom each day as I am stretched and challenged.

Reflect on your growth tonight. Where is God stretching and challenging you?

Good Work

God is not unjust; he will not overlook your work and the love that you showed for his sake in serving the saints, as you still do.

HEBREWS 6:10 NRSV

When we accept the gift of Christ's salvation, we can be assured that we will live for eternity with our Father in heaven. There is nothing that we can do by our actions alone that ensures a place for us. But that doesn't mean the buck stops there.

Though not a requirement for admittance through the pearly gates, a life lived doing good deeds is something every Christ follower should seek to attain.

Thank you, Jesus, for showing me how to live a life a love and humility. Help others to see my good works and to recognize that my life has been marked by you.

We want each one of you to show the same diligence so as to realize the full assurance of hope to the very end, so that you may not become sluggish, but imitators of those who through faith and patience inherit the promises.

HEBREWS 6:11-12 NRSV

You may not have thought today was much different from the last, and perhaps you don't see the good deeds that you have done as being particularly spiritual. Remember that God created you as an image-bearer, that just by choosing to follow Jesus you are being like him.

Be encouraged that you are a shining example of his love and that others will see how a life with Christ is a beautiful one.

Jesus, I choose to believe in your light and your love, and I choose to follow you. There are people I saw today, and there will be people I see tomorrow; I ask that I will continue to influence them with the truth of a life in Christ.

What is different about your life? Can others see that you love Jesus by the choices you are making?

Process of Sanctification

When Christ had offered for all time a single sacrifice for sins,
he sat down at the right hand of God, waiting from that time until
his enemies should be made a footstool for his feet.

HEBREWS 10:12-13 ESV

You are complete. When he chose to die on the cross for our sins, Jesus took away every flaw. He finished what we never could; he made us perfect. Jesus didn't do half a job, he finished it.

Even when you find yourself trapped in sin, or feeling the consequence of a mistake, remember that the penalty of death has been taken away for good. Every day that you draw closer to him, you are walking in the completion of the work that he finished for you.

Jesus, please take my negative thoughts about myself today and help me walk into my day with a confidence of knowing that I am completely loved by my Creator.

By a single offering he has perfected for all time
those who are being sanctified.

HEBREWS 10:14 ESV

You are perfect. Looking in the mirror, or thinking back over your week, it is easy to forget or disbelieve those words. Don't let that happen.

A wrinkle here, a bulge there, an unkind word, or a jealous thought cannot change the way the Father sees you. And it's how he wants you to see yourself.

Jesus, I thank you that even though I do not feel perfect, I know that I am perfect because of you in me. I choose to think the best of myself because of what you have done for me. Help me to live in the confidence of knowing I am being the best that I can be.

What imperfections do you need to hand over to God this evening?

Confidence in Christ

Do not throw away this confident trust in the Lord.
Remember the great reward it brings you!

HEBREWS 10:35 NLT

Do you remember when you first decided to follow Christ?
Maybe you felt like a huge weight was being lifted off you, or
that the peace and joy you'd been searching for was finally
yours. You were filled with excitement in your newfound life,
and you felt ready to take on the world in the name of Jesus.

Following God may come easy at first. We accept him into our
lives and are swept into his love with incredible hope. But as
time goes on, old temptations return and threaten to shake
our resolve. The confidence we felt in our relationship at first
lessens as we wonder if we have what it takes to stick it out in
this Christian life.

Jesus, sometimes I doubt who you are and what you have done.
I know that you don't mind that kind of honesty. Please come
alongside me in times of doubt so even if I don't understand this
faith, I can be assured of your nearness to me. Let me live another
day for you.

Patient endurance is what you need now, so that you will continue to do God's will. Then you will receive all that he has promised.

HEBREWS 10:36 NLT

Perhaps you have lost the confidence you had at first. Or maybe you are still in that place of complete confidence and trust. Either way, step boldly forward into all that God has for you.

Remain confident in him; he will accomplish what he has promised. When following him gets hard, press in even harder and remember that you will be richly rewarded for your perseverance.

God, it seems like right now I have to take things day by day. I know that this is enduring in the faith, but sometimes I just want to enjoy it. Give me the patience and peace to know that I am still in your will and that good things are just around the corner.

What are you waiting on God for? Pray for patient endurance, and wait in hope and expectation.

Money Love

*Keep your lives free from the love of money,
and be content with what you have; for he has said,
"I will never leave you or forsake you."*

HEBREWS 13:5 NRSV

Sometimes money can feel like water in our hands. It slips right through our fingers, and is gone as soon as it's acquired.

As Christians, we know that we should trust God with our every need. But do we really? Are we confident that no matter what circumstances come our way, God is going to take care of our finances? Or do we become consumed with worry that we will not have enough?

Holy Spirit, I invite you into my financial life today. I know that you are involved in all parts of life and that you know the wisest way about everything. Please guide me in wisdom with money; let me not fall into the trap of spending more than I need to.

We can say with confidence, "The Lord is my helper;
I will not be afraid. What can anyone do to me?"

HEBREWS 13:6 NRSV

Right after God tells us not to love money, he reminds us that
he'll never leave or forsake us. He knew that we would worry
about our finances. He knew that fear would come far more
easily than contentment.

Remember that no matter how little or how much money you
have, God is control. He is more than able to provide for all
your needs and he will never forsake you.

Jesus, teach me contentment. I have a lot of things that I feel like I
need right now, and I need perspective to know that a lot of these
things are just a matter of wanting. Help me to prioritize generosity
over consuming.

What are you spending your money on? Are you content with
what you have?

This Is the Way

Your ears shall hear a word behind you, saying,
"This is the way, walk in it."

ISAIAH 30:21 NKJV

Decisions, decisions. It seems a week never goes by without our needing to make at least one important choice. Whether job related, relationship motivated, or something as seemingly innocent as how to spend a free Friday, wouldn't it be nice to have an arrow pointing us in the right direction—especially if we are in danger of making a wrong turn?

According to the Word, we have exactly that. When we truly desire to walk the path God sets us on, and when we earnestly seek his voice, he promises to lead us in the right direction. Stay on his path today.

God, I need your help with some important decisions today. Let my ears hear your voice to guide me in the right direction.

*Whenever you turn to the right hand
or whenever you turn to the left.*

ISAIAH 30:21 NKJV

Consider the decisions you have had to make today. What
decisions will you need to make tomorrow? Whether you
choose the right or the left, know that God is able to guide you
into his best for the situation.

You might not get it right every time but his ever-present
Spirit is right there, ready to put you back on the path each
time you wander off.

*Holy Spirit, thank you that you are the guiding voice behind me.
Help me to become more aware of what you are speaking to me.*

What guidance do you need right now?

Look Up

Lift up your eyes on high and see who has created these stars,
the One who leads forth their host by number,
He calls them all by name.

ISAIAH 40:26 NASB

If you have ever had the chance to be in a remote location on a clear night, you will know what it is like to look up into the sky and marvel at the magnificent display of stars. It is such a breathtaking view—one that reminds us of the greatness of our God.

Do you feel insignificant in God's great world today? Remember that God has a perfect plan for this world, and you complete the plan. Lift up your eyes and know that God knows your name and that you are not missing from his plan.

God, you are so great. When I think of everything you created,
I am amazed that you care about a plan for my life. Thank you
that I can trust that you are in control.

Because of the greatness of His might and the strength
of His power, not one of them is missing.

ISAIAH 40:26 NASB

Many times, in the Bible, humanity is compared to the stars.
We are reminded of how many people God has created. Yet,
God says that he both leads and calls them by name.

If the stars appear magnificent, then how much more
magnificent is the One who created them? We worship a God
who is able to remember each of us by name, and to know that
not one of us is missing.

God, I am blessed that you know my name. As I go to sleep tonight,
I am reminded of the wonderful life that you have planned for me.
Even when things get hard, I know that you lead and call me into
your light.

Can you look back on your life and recognize God's hand in
significant moments? Thank this great and almighty God for
his specific care for your life.

Getting Through

> *"When you go through deep waters and great trouble, I will be with you. When you go through rivers of difficulty, you will not drown!"*
>
> ISAIAH 43:2 TLB

Some see God as distant, vengeful, or condemning. Others see God as kind, affectionate, and attentive. Sometimes circumstances become too overwhelming. Mountains of anxiety rise up and we feel isolated and alone.

Let no doubt take root; he is a God who cares deeply, loves fully, and remains faithful, ever at our side in times of trouble. Though our sorrows overwhelm us, he is the comfort that we need.

God, thank you so much for your care for me. I choose to take your love into my day.

"When you walk through the fire of oppression, you will not be burned up—the flames will not consume you."

ISAIAH 43:2 TLB

Will you take his hand, offered in love, and receive his comforting touch? Will you remember his faithfulness and let it calm your heart?

God is with you. You will not drown. The flames will not consume you. Cling to his promises and the mountains, as high as they may seem, will crumble at your feet.

God, tonight I am tired and weary. I feel like I have been through deep waters and at times I have even been afraid of drowning. Please protect my heart and my thoughts from fear and give me peace in the middle of it all.

What are you concerned about right now? Trust in God and put your hand in his tonight.

New Paths

"I am about to do something new. See, I have already begun!
Do you not see it?"

ISAIAH 43:19 NLT

The clean slate of a new day is filled with an air of
expectation. It's like deep down inside, there is something
built into our heart and mind that longs to start afresh.

This morning is that chance for you to start again. You may
have had a day yesterday or felt like you didn't complete
what you needed to, but today is a new day. Whether you
are a goal setter or someone who approaches the day with
a "whatever may come" attitude, you have God's mercy and
grace to help you achieve it.

God, thank you for letting me start new today and every day.
I pray for the faith to see what you have already begun.

*"I will make a pathway through the wilderness.
I will create rivers in the dry wasteland."*

ISAIAH 43:19 NLT

This day, and every one that follows, is yours. It is yours to
choose who and how to love, to serve, and even to be.

The choice you made in reading this page represents the
choice to take this journey in the company of your heavenly
Father. This is how you give him space to create pathways and
rivers in those dry areas of your life. That is a beautiful place
to start.

*God, thank you for remaining faithful to me today. Help me to
make space for you to create paths and rivers in areas that I feel
tired and dry.*

What new thing would you like to do? What pathways do you
need God to clear?

Never Too Late

Behold, the LORD's hand is not so short that it cannot save.

ISAIAH 59:1 NASB

When Jesus hung on the cross, there were two thieves hanging beside him. One of those thieves, as he hung in his final moments of life, asked Jesus for grace and a second chance. That thief—minutes before death—was given forgiveness and eternal life.

The very same day he entered paradise as a forgiven and clean man. In light of his story, how can we ever say that it's too late to turn it all around?

Give me a fresh start today, God. I need to remember that your mercy and forgiveness awaits me every single morning. I trust in that forgiveness today and ask for a renewed sense of purpose.

Nor is His ear so dull that it cannot hear.

ISAIAH 59:1 NASB

Do you have regrets in your life that you wish you could take back? Things that you aren't proud of? You lay awake at night thinking about mistakes you've made and you wonder if you've gone too far to ever get back.

If you feel like it's too late to change something in your life for the better, remember the story of the thief on the cross. There is always hope in Jesus. The God we serve is the God of second chances. That might sound cliché, but it couldn't be truer. His love has no end and his grace knows no boundary. It is never too late for you to follow him with your life.

God, thank you for reminding me that your love is always ready to save me from worry, fear, or self-doubt. Help me to rest tonight in the knowledge that you are willing and ready to rescue me.

What do you need saving from this evening? Ask God to help you and trust that he will listen.

Bring the Nations Back

Now the LORD speaks - the one who formed me in my mother's womb to be his servant, who commissioned me to bring Israel back to him. The LORD has honored me, and my God has given me strength.

ISAIAH 49:5 NLT

Jesus didn't confine his ministry to the Jewish people and believers of his day. He extended his ministry to the Gentiles and everyone "outside" the law of the Scribes and the Pharisees.

You are included in God's great plan to extend salvation to the ends of the earth, so all nations would come back to him. As you go into your community today, remember the great commission that God has given all of us.

Jesus, thank you that I have been included in the great big family of God. I have seen the light and now I want others to see that light too. I pray that the church would rise up and share your glory to the ends of the earth.

> *"You will do more than restore the people of Israel to me.
> I will make you a light to the Gentiles, and you will
> bring my salvation to the ends of the earth."*
>
> ISAIAH 49:6 NLT

It was always part of God's plan to bring salvation to his entire creation. We know the people of Israel are the chosen ones through whom God brought salvation, but we need to remember that God wanted his message to go to the ends of the earth.

God doesn't want us to keep him to ourselves. He wants us to be a light that shines for all to see so salvation can reach the ends of the earth. Are you willing to be that light for Christ?

God, I am willing to be your light in the days ahead. Help me to spread your truth to my part of the world.

What can you do to extend your light to the world around you?

Rebuilding

To all who mourn in Israel, he will give a crown of beauty for ashes, a joyous blessing instead of mourning, festive praise instead of despair. In their righteousness, they will be like great oaks that the LORD has planted for his own glory.

ISAIAH 61:3 NLT

You will have a lot of thoughts about your day ahead: grocery lists, dentist appointments, song lyrics, or lost keys. We are so consumed with our thoughts of all the details of the day ahead that we forget to think on the greatness of God.

When we allow our thoughts of God to take over, we see our despair and mourning fall away. You are not a weak sapling, limited by inadequate light and meager nourishment. You are a strong and graceful oak, resilient for the glory of God. Ashes and mourning and heavy burdens are relieved. For those burdened by their brokenness it is of great comfort. Jesus came to give us new life.

Father God, thank you that mourning is not a weakness. Thank you that in those times of deepest need, you are the water of life that I can draw my strength from. Help me to drink of your living water today.

They will rebuild the ancient ruins,
repairing cities destroyed long ago.
They will revive them,
though they have been deserted for many generations.

Isaiah 61:4, NLT

Sometimes we look back on our past and wish we could be in that place again, with so much hope and future ahead of us. Life can be incredibly difficult as we go along and our hearts, emotions, and even bodies can begin to break down. Dreams that we once had seem a distant memory, buried under the rubble of the rest of our lives.

It's okay to mourn for those things but now is the time to seek God and ask him to rebuild and restore the broken areas. Let him breathe new life into places that have been deserted and dry. Trust him to revive you.

God, thank you that I was able to get through another day. I am encouraged that I am strong because of you. Help me to stand tall and be proud of the person that you have made me to be. Thank you that you are in the process of rebuilding and reviving me.

In what ways has God been rebuilding your life or restoring past hope to you?

Ask for Wisdom

If any of you lacks wisdom, let him ask of God, who gives to all liberally and without reproach, and it will be given to him.

JAMES 1:5 NKJV

Sometimes it feels like life is tossing you around. Remember that it is not your circumstances that determine your anxiety, it is your faith. Pray for wisdom. But when you do, make sure you are ready to receive it.

Believe the word that the Lord has for you, and do not doubt. If you get stuck on a task or decision today, ask for God's wisdom. He promises to give it to you, and to give liberally.

Jesus, thank you that I can have faith in your love and care for me in the middle of life's storms. Keep my heart steady and peaceful today.

Let him ask in faith, with no doubting, for he who doubts is like a wave of the sea driven and tossed by the wind.

JAMES 1:6 NKJV

There's nothing quite like the feeling of riding on a boat on a beautiful day. It's incredibly relaxing, leaning back and enjoying the gentle rocking of the waves.

Have you ever been out on the water during a storm? It's anything but relaxing. In fact, being tossed around by dangerous winds as the waves grow larger is downright scary. This is what it is like when we are stuck in a tricky situation without asking God for help. Ask God to help you figure it out, and trust him with his guidance.

God, forgive my unbelief. It can be hard to believe that things will get easier or calmer, but I pray that as I rest this evening, you would bring faith and peace into my thoughts. I ask tonight, believing in your answers.

How is your faith in your current circumstances? Have you remembered to ask God for help?

Think First

Take note of this: Everyone should be quick to listen, slow to speak and slow to become angry, because human anger does not produce the righteousness that God desires.

JAMES 1:19-20 NIV

For some, listening comes naturally; for others, it is something that has to be worked on. There is an art to listening, especially when you are upset. If this happens today, be intentional about being slow to speak.

Take time to think through what others are saying to you. Try to understand where they are coming from. Discern if they just need to talk. Wait for them to ask your opinion and consider if your response will be helpful.

God, help me to take the time to listen to others today. Help me to try to understand the heart of the matter and give me the grace to keep the peace.

*Get rid of all moral filth and the evil that is so prevalent and
humbly accept the word planted in you, which can save you.*

JAMES 1:21 NIV

Have you been willing to tune in to what others are saying
today, despite your emotions? It may have been a gentle
rebuke, some great advice, or an encouraging word.

Whatever it is, allow God's grace in your conversations, and
humbly listen to what he wants you to hear, so evil does not
find a way in to your relationships.

*Jesus, thank you for the people I was able to talk with today. I pray
that I made them feel understood and truly heard. Bring to mind
those conversations where I was distracted by my own emotions
and help me to rely on your gentle reminders to listen better
tomorrow.*

Who is God bringing to mind that you need to listen
graciously to?

Address the Need

*What good is it, dear brothers and sisters, if you say
you have faith but don't show it by your actions?
Can that kind of faith save anyone?*

JAMES 2:14 NLT

What is your faith worth? How far are you willing to go to
express the love of God to a dying world? Will you give of
yourself when it isn't convenient? Will you love on someone
who is unlovable and give to someone who can never repay you?

The cost may seem great, and the work insignificant, but God
sees your heart and what you have done, and he counts it as
work done directly for him.

*God, let me show my faith in action toward those in need. Holy
Spirit, guide me to the needs of others, whether it is someone close
to me or needs of people in another country. Help me to respond
quickly to help others today.*

Suppose you see a brother or sister who has no food or clothing, and you say, "Good-bye and have a good day; stay warm and eat well"—but then you don't give that person any food or clothing. What good does that do? So you see, faith by itself isn't enough. Unless it produces good deeds, it is dead and useless.

JAMES 2:15-17 NLT

As Christians, we are called to be the representation of Christ to the world; we are the visible expression of an invisible God. In order to express the heart of the Father, we have to know what is on his heart.

God tells us in Scripture that he cares deeply about the least of these: the orphan, the widow, the poor, the needy. We cannot preach Christ to someone who is needy while leaving them in their need. Our words will not communicate the love of our Father unless accompanied by the actions that make him tangible to them.

God, I see needs all around me. I saw a lot of needs in the people around me today. As I go to sleep tonight, I ask that you show me what I can do to help. I pray that you would give me ideas and courage to give to those who most need it.

What needs did you see around you today? What are the needs that are tugging at your heart the most and how can you respond to those?

Steering the Ship

When we put bits into the mouths of horses to make them obey us, we can turn the whole animal. Or take ships as an example. Although they are so large and are driven by strong winds, they are steered by a very small rudder wherever the pilot wants to go.

JAMES 3:3-4 NIV

It doesn't take long to realize the power of the tongue. Words can be our strongest device. There is no doubt that we are good at talking; the question is, do we talk good?

Who will you be talking to today? Can you exercise self-control when trying to organize your family? Can you show restraint when you get upset with a colleague? Can you steer your words away from gossip or untruth?

Heavenly Father, thank you for giving me the gift of communication. Help me to use my words for good and not for harm today.

The tongue is a small part of the body, but it makes great boasts.
Consider what a great forest is set on fire by a small spark.

JAMES 3:5 NIV

The words we allow to come out of our mouths can have great consequence. Once they are spoken, we cannot take them back. It is not only the words that we choose to say, sometimes it is the fact that we say them at all.

As the Scripture says, even a small spark can set a great forest on fire. Ask God to forgive you for the times when you have sparked a fire. Allow the Holy Spirit to guide your heart and your thoughts so the words you speak are truthful, encouraging, and life-giving.

God, guide my heart and thoughts so I can speak truth and life.
Forgive me if I have not used my mouth for good today. Thank you
for your grace.

As you reflect on your conversations today, have you been able to speak God's truth?

Quarrels

What is causing the quarrels and fights among you? Don't they come from the evil desires at war within you?

JAMES 4:1 NLT

Quarreling is as common for adults as it is for children; it just looks different in action. The heart behind fighting is the same, and the reactions stem from the same provocation.

James cuts right to the heart of sin. We have an internal war going on of selfish motives; we want to rise to the top and when we feel the need to fight for our pride, we quarrel until we feel we have won. If you run into an argument today, examine your heart motive for fighting back and resist the urge to let pride get in the way.

Jesus, I don't like fighting with others, but sometimes I get so angry and frustrated that I do and say things that I don't intend to. Give me the strength to gain control over wrong things that might come into my heart and keep me from wrong actions today.

You want what you don't have, so you scheme and kill to get it. You are jealous of what others have, but you can't get it, so you fight and wage war to take it away from them.

JAMES 4:2 NLT

Praise God for his amazing grace, which is extended to us for this very reason.

Let us submit to God's forgiveness and draw near to him for his cleansing and purifying grace. It washes over us, and our quarrels are forgiven. When we humble ourselves, he promises to exalt us.

God, thank you for your grace in my life today. Thank you that I have been more aware of my anger and that you have been with me, giving me the strength to do the right thing. Help me to bring this right attitude into my day tomorrow.

How have you dealt with conflict today? Ask God to help you with a strategy to overcome your desire to win arguments.

Favor Humility

He gives us more grace. That is why Scripture says:
"God opposes the proud but shows favor to the humble."

JAMES 4:6 NIV

Some of the most substantial and ultimately wonderful changes in our lives come from moments of vulnerability. But vulnerability takes one key ingredient: humility. And humility is not an easy pill to swallow.

Isn't it sometimes easier for us to pretend that conflict never happened than to face the fact that we made a mistake and wronged another person? It's not always easy to humble ourselves and fight for the resolution in an argument—especially when it means admitting our failures.

Jesus, show me grace for people in my life who have wronged me. In the same way, help me to be humble when I have wronged others, and prompt me to be quick to apologize when I am wrong.

Submit yourselves, then, to God.
Resist the devil, and he will flee from you.

JAMES 4:7 NIV

When you face a dilemma of integrity, God is there waiting for you to ask him for the strength to resist the temptation of pride. We need to resist the habit of making excuses or blaming others for situations instead of simply being honest.

Who are you in the face of conflict? Do you avoid apologizing in an attempt to save face? Does your pride get in the way of vulnerability, or are you willing and ready to humble yourself for restoration in your relationships? God says that he will give favor and wisdom to the humble.

God, I know that often I let pride win in my life. I don't like to be vulnerable or to show my weakness. I ask for confidence in the wonderful person that you have made me to be. I submit myself to you, knowing that it is through your power that I can resist the temptation of pride.

What can you do this week to humble yourself for the sake of a restored relationship?

Come Close

Come close to God, and God will come close to you.
Wash your hands, you sinners; purify your hearts,
for your loyalty is divided between God and the world.

JAMES 4:8 NLT

Do you ever feel like you can't feel God? Like you've lost sight of him somehow? Sometimes we aren't sure how to get back to that place where we feel his presence strongly and hear his voice clearly.

God will not push himself on you. He will not share his glory with another, and he will not try to compete with the world for your heart. But if you draw near to him, he will wrap you in the power of his presence. Welcome him into your life today.

God, be close to me today. There have been times where I don't know where you are or what you are doing, but I recognize that those are probably the times when I am not drawing close to you. Let me feel your presence surround me in all that I do.

Let there be tears for what you have done. Let there be sorrow and deep grief. Let there be sadness instead of laughter, and gloom instead of joy. Humble yourselves before the Lord, and he will lift you up in honor.

JAMES 4:9-10 NLT

We go through seasons where we feel distant from God, possibly because of our own sin. We may make decisions to turn away from God and this is something to be mourned.

The beautiful truth is that he has never gone anywhere; God is unchanging and unwavering. His heart is always to be with us, and he never turns his back on his children. When we humbly admit our need for his forgiveness, his promise is to restore us again to him.

God, I accept your forgiveness in those times that I have chosen things of this world over you. I thank you that you give me the grace to start afresh tomorrow, and I ask for a sense of your presence in every part of my day.

Where has your loyalty been recently? Have you been so consumed with this world that you have forgotten to allow God into your day-to-day life? Let him back in tonight.

Excuses

*"O Sovereign Lord," I said, "I can't speak for you! I'm too young!"
The Lord replied, "Don't say, 'I'm too young,' for you must go
wherever I send you and say whatever I tell you."*

JEREMIAH 1:6-7 NLT

You will, undoubtedly, have various seasons in your
life: seasons of longing and contentment, seasons of
discouragement and joy, seasons of more and less. Being a
grown-up means stretching into new ways of living, and this
usually doesn't happen until the season hits.

Don't make excuses for why you can't do what God is calling
you to do. Be brave! God will not move you into something
without giving you the grace you need to make it through.

*God, thank you for the calling you have placed on my life. Please
give me the courage to know that you are with me now as you call
me forward.*

"Don't be afraid of the people, for I will be with you and will protect you. I, the LORD, have spoken!"

JEREMIAH 1:8 NLT

Sensing God has called you forward can be challenging. It requires bravery, obedience, dedication, and sometimes total upheaval of everything comfortable.

If we feel that impending change in our hearts, it usually means God is preparing us for something different. In those times, the One who won't change, won't back down, and won't leave us stranded is our heavenly Father.

Father God, I take this time now to ask you if you are calling me into something new. If this is where you want me right now, then sustain me and help me to be content. If you are calling me to move forward, then help me to brave knowing that you are with me.

Do you see an impending change approaching? How is God calling you forward?

By the Water

"Blessed is the one who trusts in the LORD,
whose confidence is in him."

JEREMIAH 17:7 NIV

If you live in a cooler climate, then you've probably experienced the gorgeous season that is fall. Each year, the leaves slowly turn to shades of golden yellow, orange, and red. It's a thing of beauty, but eventually, the leaves wither and die, then fall to the ground.

All too often, the same can happen with our relationship with the Lord. We get that initial fire for him; we burn brightly with it, but then fall away from him. If we keep our trust in him, he tells us that our spiritual leaves will never wither. He wants our lives to be like trees that continually bear fruit.

God, I want to burn forever bright for you. Help me to stand up to the heat and the wind if that's what faces me today. Give me the assurance that I won't fall.

"They will be like a tree planted by the water that sends out its roots by the stream. It does not fear when heat comes; its leaves are always green. It has no worries in a year of drought and never fails to bear fruit."

JEREMIAH 17:8 NIV

Did your day resemble an evergreen, or did you feel like you began to wither? Take this evening to replenish your soul by spending time in the Lord's presence. Plant your roots deeply in him, and let him water your soul.

Be thankful that you can come to God at the end of the day and draw from his living waters. He is your joy and solid foundation, so choose to walk in his ways as he leads.

Jesus, show me where my goodness is bearing good fruit. Thank you that I carry your love and your grace in my heart and that this keeps me grounded with a deeper understanding of who you are, and who I am because of you.

Where is your heart health today, spiritually speaking? Do you need persistent watering and nourishment?

Fulfilled

*"O Lord, if you heal me, I will be truly healed; if you save me,
I will be truly saved. My praises are for you alone!"*

JEREMIAH 17:14 NIV

Examine your scars, and recall the wounds that gave them to
you. Depending on the severity of the injury, and how long
ago it occurred, running a finger along the scar may bring
back vivid memories of the pain you felt. You are healed, but
also changed.

It may be painful, but explore your old heart wounds, the
ones that never seem to entirely heal. Begin the process of
releasing them to God, and claim the promise of his true
healing.

*God, I have pain in my life. I'm thankful that you have healed me,
but sometimes remembering the hurt brings the pain back. Please
remind me that I was saved from pain and help me to dwell on
your healing.*

> *"They keep saying to me, 'Where is the word of the Lord?*
> *Let it now be fulfilled!'"*

JEREMIAH 17:14 NIV

Broken bones mend, but a limp or occasional twinge may remain. So might our fear; it can take a lifetime to fully trust our healing is complete—except for when God does the healing.

When we ask God to remove old hurts, betrayals, and disappointments from our hearts, he removes them completely.

Jesus, I am thankful that just as you have healed my pain, you have also healed me from the pain of my sin. Thank you that you provided the way for me to be completely restored to you. I praise you for my salvation tonight.

What has God healed you or saved you from? Thank him.

Authentic Prayers

*"Then you will call on me and come and pray to me,
and I will listen to you."*

JEREMIAH 29:12 NIV

It's easy to go about our day, crossing our many to-do items
off our lists and making sure we accomplish all our tasks.
Sometimes spending time with the Lord can become just
another box to check off. Toilets? Cleaned. Groceries?
Purchased. Scripture reading? Done.

Are you holding back in your relationship with the Lord, or
have you given him all your heart? Don't reserve anything.
Give all of yourself to him. Seek him in all areas of your life.
He is there wherever you look, waiting for you, wanting to
connect with you.

*God, I desire a real relationship with you. Let me seek you with all
my heart so I can find you. Thank you that you are always near.*

*"You will seek me and find me when
you seek me with all your heart."*

JEREMIAH 29:13 NIV

The Lord wants so much more out of his relationship
with us than to be merely another chore to accomplish or
another bullet point on our checklist. He is so much more
than a small portion of your day, forgotten after you've
closed your Bible. Search for him—he wants to be found. He
wants to show you all that can be had when you desire true
relationship with him.

You might not have had time in your day to pause and think
about your relationship with God, but you can change that
right now. Be still and allow him to speak to you this evening.

*God, I take these quiet moments to reflect on my relationship with
you and how much I want to pursue what you want for my life.
Speak to me in this moment.*

What do you feel God is saying to you?

Long Ago

> *"Long ago the LORD said to Israel: 'I have loved you,*
> *my people, with an everlasting love.*
> *With unfailing love I have drawn you to myself.'"*

JEREMIAH 31:3 NLT

We were originally created to bear the mark of our Creator.
We were masterfully designed to reflect his image and
to reveal his glory. The corruption of sin has masked us,
disguising our initial intended purpose.

When we respond to salvation and give ourselves back to God,
he begins reworking us to once again appear as he intended.
Sanctification is a process that can be painful. But its end
result is beautiful. God empties our hearts of the things that
could never satisfy to make room for himself—the only thing
that will always satisfy.

God, you continue to show me kindness and I need that as I am
figuring out how to live out my faith well. I accept your grace
today, for the times when I don't reflect you, and I ask you to
empower me to be more like you.

"I will rebuild you, my virgin Israel. You will again be happy and dance merrily with your tambourines."

JEREMIAH 31:4 NLT

There are times in life, perhaps even today, where you feel like God has taken a wrecking ball to your life. He has flattened everything you had—your desires, your interests, your pursuits—but fear not. He will rebuild you.

God is creating a masterpiece with your life that will bring him glory and honor. Everything he removes he will restore to mirror the image of his likeness: your intended created purpose.

God, I feel like a broken wall. I don't feel like I have a lot left to give. I feel like there is not a lot to look forward to. Thank you for this Scripture that reminds me that you are a God that rebuilds his people and turns their sorrow into joy. Turn my heart to joy so I can dance and sing once again.

What do you feel has been broken in your life? Can you trust God to build you up in this area again?

Display of Power

"Thus says the LORD who made it, the LORD who formed it to establish it (the LORD is His name): 'Call to Me, and I will answer you, and show you great and mighty things, which you do not know.'"

JEREMIAH 33:2-3 NKJV

God is more than able to give us miraculous signs as we have seen countless times throughout the Bible and throughout history. But he is so much more than experience. We mistakenly think experience is the peak of his power.

Other gods can perform miracles and deliver experiences, but the one true God continues to show his power in the valley. He is even in the valley of the shadow of death where miracles seem non-existent. Those other gods have nothing to offer us in despair.

God, thank you for showing your power at times, but help me not so seek those out to validate who you are. Let my faith be enough to be assured of your presence and goodness in my life and your continued work in this world.

"It shall be to Me a name of joy, a praise, and an honor before all nations of the earth, who shall hear all the good that I do to them; they shall fear and tremble for all the goodness and all the prosperity that I provide for it."

JEREMIAH 33:9 NKJV

God was present with you today and will continue to show himself to you in different ways. He will show you things you don't even know. Don't limit him to your experience or what you presently know of him or of life.

God will show us great and mighty things. He is not limited by time, space, or human understanding. Put your hope and faith in the God who is.

Show yourself to me tonight, Lord Jesus. I know you are with me, and I don't need any signs or wonders. Fill me with the knowledge of your presence and the peace of your nearness.

How has God shown himself to you in the small things today?

My Daily Portion

Remember my affliction and my wanderings, the wormwood and the gall! My soul continually remembers it and is bowed down within me. But this I call to mind, and therefore I have hope: The steadfast love of the Lord never ceases; his mercies never come to an end; they are new every morning; great is your faithfulness.

LAMENTATIONS 3:19-23 ESV

Some days it is good to reflect on exactly what God has saved us from. As a nation, Israel knew what it was to fail God time and time again. They rebelled against him and they deserved punishment; yet, God chose to redeem them, over and over again. His love for his people compelled him to show mercy.

We are not unlike the Israelites in our rebellion and turning away from God's purposes. We are also not unlike the Israelites in that God has incredible compassion for us. In sending his Son, Jesus Christ, God proved once and for all that his compassion will never fail.

Thank you, Father, that this morning I get to start again with your mercy. Let your love flood my heart so I can face this day with determination and strength.

"The LORD is my portion," says my soul, "therefore I will hope in him." The LORD is good to those who wait for him to the soul who seeks him.

LAMENTATIONS 3:24-25 ESV

Why does God's compassion have to appear new every morning? Because we can barely go a day without failing, and yet every day he is all we need. We need to be reminded of God's faithfulness so we can turn toward him daily.

Do you feel like you have failed God today? Thank him for his compassion every single morning, confess, and be ready to start the next day new. His Word promises that his goodness is ready for you when you seek him.

God, forgive me again. I am so glad that your mercy is waiting for me again tomorrow, because I will need it.

What do you need God's mercy for? Ask him, knowing that he is faithful to you.

Unseen Love

*Though you have not seen him, you love him; and even though you
do not see him now, you believe in him and are filled with
an inexpressible and glorious joy.*

1 PETER 1:8 NIV

It's hard to reconcile the fact that you love Jesus immensely
even though you have not seen him. This amazing love is a
testimony of Jesus living in your heart and you being able to
communicate directly with him.

You have developed and deepened a relationship with Christ
and even though you haven't seen him the way the disciples
have, you know him and know that he understands you. What
a blessing to have such joy because of this relationship. Keep
walking and talking with him today.

*Jesus, I really do love you, and even though I haven't seen you with
my eyes, I have seen you with my heart. Stay close to me today.*

You are receiving the end result of your faith,
the salvation of your souls.

1 Peter 1:9 NIV

The joy that we have from knowing Jesus comes from the hope of realizing that the future is more beautiful than we can imagine. We can experience pain and suffering in this life, but with Christ we expect a much better end result.

This is why faith can be hard and easy at the same time. It can be hard to endure our current circumstances, and yet we know that at the end is salvation. What great news to share with others.

Holy Spirit, thank you that I have sensed you near to me today. I love that you are walking with me and that this faith is not futile. I have a hope in an amazing future that goes beyond the trials of this life. Keep my faith strong.

Have you experienced the joy of knowing that your faith has led to salvation? How can you share this good news with the people in your life?

Imperishable Inheritance

You know that it was not with perishable things such as silver or gold that you were redeemed from the empty way of life handed down to you from your ancestors, but with the precious blood of Christ, a lamb without blemish or defect.

1 PETER 1:18-19 NIV

Money can get us a lot of things: nice cars, clothes, and homes, and it can buy us enjoyable experiences like vacations and entertainment. Money is so important it can even get some people out of prison.

God has access to all the money in the world, but this isn't what our humanity or our eternity is about. No amount of money could create us, and no amount of money can save us. Our souls are an entirely different price; a price that Christ paid for with his life. Let this eternal perspective guide your ambitions today.

God, thank you for the reminder that my life isn't about money or gaining wealth. None of these earthly riches are going to matter in the end. Thank you for shedding your precious blood so I would have eternal life.

He was chosen before the creation of the world,
but was revealed in these last times for your sake.

1 PETER 1:20 NIV

Our need for redemption was no surprise to God; Jesus was his plan from the beginning. It's important to read and know about Jesus because he was the way that God chose to reveal himself to humanity.

Instead of handing us an inheritance in the way that we expect from our relatives, God gave us an eternal inheritance. Through Jesus, you have become a part of God's kingdom forever.

Jesus, thank you for revealing God through your Word and works.
Thank you for leaving me with your Holy Spirit so I could know
you personally. Help me to share this revelation of who God is with
others around me this week.

What do you know and believe about Jesus that reveals the Father to you?

Chosen by the King

You are a chosen people, a royal priesthood, a holy nation, God's special possession, that you may declare the praises of him who called you out of darkness into his wonderful light.

1 PETER 2:9 NIV

We all want to believe that we are special. Most of us grow up being told that we are, and it feels good to believe it. But over time, we look around us and realize that, really, we are just like everyone else. Doubt begins to creep in, making us second guess ourselves and damaging our self-confidence.

Long before you were born, you were set aside and marked as special. You were chosen to be God's special possession, and that's a pretty amazing thing.

God, help me to accept that I am special and chosen today. Give me confidence that I can make an influence in this world, even today, because you have chosen me to be in this place for a purpose.

Once you were not a people, but now you are the people of God; once you had not received mercy, but now you have received mercy.

1 PETER 2:10 NIV

God sees you as special. Revel in that knowledge this evening. He is calling you out of the darkness of the ordinary, and bringing you into the light of the extraordinary.

He picked you. He loves you. He wants you. Trust in that.

Thank you, God, that you have brought me into your light. Thank you that you shone a light into my heart and that I am now a chosen follower of you. Thank you for your mercy that can cover any wrongdoing in my day and start me afresh for tomorrow.

How did God shine his light into your heart? Be thankful that you now experience his mercy every day.

Cornerstone

You are coming to Christ, who is the living cornerstone of God's temple. He was rejected by people, but he was chosen by God for great honor.

1 PETER 2:4 NLT

The cornerstone, otherwise known as a foundation stone or setting stone, is the first stone set in the construction of a building's foundation and vitally important since all other stones will be set in reference to this stone. The position of this stone determines the position of the entire structure.

When Christ is referred to as the cornerstone, we know that his life, death, and resurrection is our reference point for how we are to live. When we align ourselves with Christ, we are building up that living temple to be used for great honor.

God, I know that many rejected you, but thank you for all of us who have gladly received you. Help me to see how I can be used as part of your spiritual temple today.

You are living stones that God is building into his spiritual temple.
What's more, you are his holy priests. Through the mediation of
Jesus Christ, you offer spiritual sacrifices that please God.

1 PETER 2:5 NLT

You might not feel as though any of your day has resembled anything like a priest, or even felt remotely holy, yet the Scriptures say that because you have Christ in you, all that you have to offer God is pleasing.

Remember that your efforts are not what counts, but your love for Christ and his kingdom is what matters. Let God use you as a piece of this beautiful building that he calls his temple to dwell in.

Jesus, thank you that you have made my feeble attempts to honor God be something that really does please God. I know that I am a part of something greater than myself, so please keep using me as a living stone in this spiritual temple.

How can you think about your day in reference to seeing yourself as a living stone?

Repay with Blessing

*All of you, have unity of spirit, sympathy, love for one another,
a tender heart, and a humble mind.*

1 PETER 3:8 NRSV

Have you ever been shown kindness that you didn't deserve?
What did it feel like to be given love when you deserved hate?
We will wrong one another and we will be wronged by others.
It's the human condition. But that is why the love of God is
the only perfect solution for us.

When we choose love and kindness over anger and revenge,
the sins that seemed so intense suddenly fade away. Love
is the presence of Jesus in us, and Jesus is the only true
anecdote for sin.

*Jesus, thank you for your grace, I am going to need it today. I pray
that you would give me your love for the people who I interact with
today. If I am wronged, I pray I will choose kindness.*

Do not repay evil for evil or abuse for abuse; but, on the contrary, repay with a blessing. It is for this that you were called— that you might inherit a blessing.

1 PETER 3:9 NRSV

As you reflect on your day, did you find yourself challenged to choose love instead of anger? It might have been a hard day and you may have struggled to see Jesus working in your life.

Constant love won't come naturally to you. Your humanness will cry out from within you and anger and rage will bubble forth without conscious invitation.

When you rely on the Spirit of God to intervene in your life and in your relationships, he can make kindness your response and love your reaction. Ask him to fill you with his Spirit and release his love in your heart so you can walk fully in his presence.

Holy Spirit, fill me with your presence. Renew your love in my heart so I can be ready for tomorrow. I need your guidance in my actions and decisions. Thank you for your grace.

Who can you identify in your life that needs to see the heart of God? Can you commit to showing them love this week?

Various Gifts

God has given each of you a gift from his great variety of spiritual gifts. Use them well to serve one another.

1 PETER 4:10 NLT

We all have something we feel most alive when doing. Call it a hobby, a talent, a passion—our niche. When we find that thing we both enjoy and excel in, it's one of the most special discoveries.

God has created us each with a unique skill set. He blessed us with talents that both distinguish us from others and complement us to others. He gave us these gifts so we, as a whole, created body of believers, could further his purposes and advance his kingdom.

God, I am thankful for the gifts that you have given me. Help me to recognize that without you I wouldn't have these gifts, and that you want me to use them for your kingdom.

Do you have the gift of speaking? Then speak as though God himself were speaking through you. Do you have the gift of helping others? Do it with all the strength and energy that God supplies. Then everything you do will bring glory to God through Jesus Christ. All glory and power to him forever and ever! Amen.

1 PETER 4:11 NLT

Think for a moment about the specific gifts God has given you. Don't be modest—God gives us gifts so we can be confident in them for his glory. Now think about your gifts in direct relation to the kingdom of God.

Sometimes it is hard to know what your talents are, especially if they don't seem "spiritual." Be confident that all of our skills have been given to us by a good God, so ask him where he wants to use you and then believe him to supply you with the energy for it.

God, show me the gifts that you have given me to use for your kingdom. Sometimes I cannot see how certain talents or ambitions of mine have much to do with your kingdom. Give me wisdom to discern what is the best way to submit my talents to you.

How can you use your gifts to benefit the church, the community, and the world?

Battle Weary

Be sober, be vigilant; because your adversary the devil walks about like a roaring lion, seeking whom he may devour. Resist him, steadfast in the faith, knowing that the same sufferings are experienced by your brotherhood in the world.

1 PETER 5:8-9 NKJV

There is a war going on right in front of you. A deep, big, all-in battle for you—for your heart. The war is raging and has been since you were born.

There is One who desires goodness for you. One who loves you unconditionally and wants to see you become who he designed. One who has sacrificed for you, bled for you, and died for you. There is One who not only takes but also gives away freely.

Jesus, give me the discernment and boldness today to resist the devil when he seeks to tempt me. Help me to call on your name and to defeat darkness with your light.

May the God of all grace, who called us to His eternal glory by Christ Jesus, after you have suffered a while, perfect, establish, strengthen, and settle you.

1 PETER 5:10 NKJV

It is hard work to resist the temptation of the world, time and time again. Battles are not fun, and they take their toll on your emotional and spiritual strength. This is part of the suffering of following Christ—that we continually lay down our old life, in order to walk in the new life.

There is a promise in the middle of your struggle, and this is that Christ will cause things to settle and he will strengthen you once again. Rest tonight, knowing that there is hope for your weary soul.

Tonight, God, I choose your goodness. I see words of grace, peace, and love in my house and in my heart. Thank you for loving me. I know that you will never separate me from your love, but I pray that I would also always dedicate my heart to you so I can stand firm when I need it the most.

Do you grasp the spiritual warfare that goes on in your life and recognize it for what it is? Continue to press into God and his Word to create your armor.

A Description of Glory

Above this surface was something that looked like a throne made of blue lapis lazuli. And on this throne high above was a figure whose appearance resembled a man. From what appeared to be his waist up, he looked like gleaming amber, flickering like a fire. And from his waist down, he looked like a burning flame, shining with splendor.

 EZEKIEL 1:26-27 NLT

When we think of Jesus, we are familiar with the descriptions given in the gospels—a man just like us who was born and raised as a Jew and walked with ordinary people. When we hear of Jesus having descended from glory and then being raised again to glory, we can begin to get a glimpse of this glorified Jesus with the vision that Ezekiel had.

Human words can only begin to describe the magnificence of Christ. We serve a risen Lord who is now on the throne and he is as consuming and beautiful as an amber flame, ready to shine through your life today.

Jesus, thank you that although you humbled yourself to become like us on earth, you also defeated death and now stand victorious, awaiting the day when we will become fully like you. It can be too glorious for words, but I choose to be encouraged by this future as I go into my day.

All around him was a glowing halo, like a rainbow shining in the clouds on a rainy day. This is what the glory of the LORD looked like to me. When I saw it, I fell face down on the ground, and I heard someone's voice speaking to me.

EZEKIEL 1:28 NLT

When we finally meet Jesus face to face, we might have a different way to describe what he looks like, but Ezekiel's description is pretty magnificent. The human language is limited, yet we need to appreciate the beauty of descriptions.

It is true that Jesus is our hope for the future; he is like that promise represented by a rainbow on a rainy day. Yes, he is our friend, but he is also the King of kings, and he is worthy to be worshipped.

Jesus, you are more wonderful than words. Thank you that I can use all kinds of ways to describe the person that you are to me. I worship you as my Savior and as the Lord of all.

How can you describe what Jesus is like to you? In what way can you worship him tonight?

Call and Commission

"Son of man, do not fear them or their words. Don't be afraid even though their threats surround you like nettles and briers and stinging scorpions. Do not be dismayed by their dark scowls, even though they are rebels."

EZEKIEL 2:6 NLT

When God calls us to speak, it isn't always an easy mission. Sometimes God has you placed in an environment where people are openly hostile to the Christian faith. There is a lot of negativity and navigating the balance between tolerance and taking a stand for Christ.

Remember that you carry the truth and this is not something to be afraid of. People may look at you differently, or accuse you of being narrow-minded, or stop inviting you to events. Don't be dismayed. God has called you to speak; leave the rest to him.

Lord God, you are more powerful than the threats or scorn of humankind, yet I still seem to fear the rejection of others. Please give me the assurance that you are speaking to me and through me. Allow me to discern the right time to speak up for you.

"You must give them my messages whether they listen or not. But they won't listen, for they are completely rebellious!"

EZEKIEL 2:7 NLT

How often do you walk away from a conversation feeling like it was unresolved, or that you never really got around to the right point? When we talk about Christ, we can feel a little underprepared or inadequate—like we don't have all the right answers.

Sometimes we just get caught up in an argument that nobody seems to win. Don't worry if that has been your story today. God loves you and wants to speak through you. He knows that many will not listen, but he still encourages you to share him with all.

Jesus, I feel like I don't always communicate your words well. I get shy or intimidated or just don't want to be rejected. Thank you that there are many people who you trust with your Word and that the same is true for all. Help me to make my peace with the fact that many will not listen but that you want me to speak anyway.

What message might God be asking you to share this week?

Gathered In

"I, the Sovereign LORD, will gather you back from the nations where you have been scattered, and I will give you the land of Israel once again. When the people return to their homeland, they will remove every trace of their vile images and detestable idols."

EZEKIEL 11:17–18 NLT

God had a purpose to fulfill through the people of Israel. He intended this community of people to be part of revealing his plan for humanity. They needed to reconnect with one another so they could be unified in their covenant with the one true God.

There is a certain specialness to reuniting with our family and friends on those occasions when you can all be together in one place. When we are together with people who share the same values, shared stories, and even similar humor, it makes life feel more meaningful. Think about the community that you feel closest to, and make an effort to get in touch today.

Thank you, God, that you don't want us to do life alone. Thank you that there is strength and unity in the gathering of people who love one another. Give me a chance today, to connect with others so we can enjoy and encourage each other.

"I will give them singleness of heart and put a new spirit within them. I will take away their stony, stubborn heart and give them a tender, responsive heart, so they will obey my decrees and regulations."

When we turn back to God, we are once again in unity with the rest of the body of Christ. We all have different ways of expressing our faith, yet we all have the same purpose to glorify God. This is the spirit that God wants you to carry.

When you think over your day, have you approached life with stubbornness, unwilling to move or let someone else get their way? God desires unity so he can work through you.

Holy Spirit, I am sorry when I have let my pride get in the way of unity with others. Remove the stones from my heart this evening, and let me be open and responsive to your ways as I move into this week.

Have you ignored the gentle whispers of the Holy Spirit, or have you allowed you heart to be open and responsive to his guidance?

God's Restraint

"They rebelled against me and would not listen. They did not get rid of the vile images they were obsessed with, or forsake the idols of Egypt. Then I threatened to pour out my fury on them to satisfy my anger while they were still in Egypt. But I didn't do it, for I acted to protect the honor of my name. I would not allow shame to be brought on my name among the surrounding nations who saw me reveal myself by bringing the Israelites out of Egypt."

EZEKIEL 20:8-9 NLT

God cares about how he reveals himself to the world. His name was made great because of the favor he showed Israel in releasing them from slavery in Egypt. There were many times that God could have allowed the people of Israel to destroy themselves, but instead he protected them, and in doing so, he showed the nations his nature of mercy.

You are God's chosen representative of earth. Today you have the opportunity to reveal some of his merciful nature to others. It is not something to feel pressured about; rather, it is a privilege that you carry to be able to honor his name.

God, you are a God of mercy and I have witnessed that in your Scriptures and also in my life. Let me reveal this nature to others as I act in kindness and goodwill toward people today.

"I brought them out of Egypt and led them into the wilderness. There I gave them my decrees and regulations so they could find life by keeping them. And I gave them my Sabbath days of rest as a sign between them and me. It was to remind them that I am the LORD, who had set them apart to be holy."

EZEKIEL 20:10-12 NLT

We wouldn't necessarily recognize God's mercy when he brought the Israelites into the wilderness, but this was a better alternative than allowing them to come to complete destruction.

When we put all our energy into the things of this world, and into pleasing ourselves without following God's ways, we are bound to end up miserable. God has better things for you, even if you don't recognize that he has brought you out of harm's way. Give God the glory tonight for his mercy in your life.

Father, I am sorry when I have complained about my current circumstances. Thank you that you are always offering me a way out of a life of destruction. I am glad that I am saved by your merciful hand.

In what ways have you seen God's mercy in your life or in the life of others?

God Is Just

"If I say to a wicked person, 'You will surely die,' but they then turn away from their sin and do what is just and right— if they give back what they took in pledge for a loan, return what they have stolen, follow the decrees that give life, and do no evil—that person will surely live; they will not die."

EZEKIEL 33:14-15 NIV

God gives us opportunities to right our wrongs. When we make mistakes, it is all too easy to carry on and ignore the consequences. We avoid confrontation because we are embarrassed or feel badly and don't know what to say or do.

If you have been in this kind of position lately, it is not too late to restore what you can. Ask for forgiveness, give back the money you owe, make sure you do that job you said you were going to do, or admit that you haven't been honest. You are free from condemnation through Christ, so don't let your intention to make things right be out of guilt; instead, let your intentions be to show others love.

God, I am sorry when I have knowingly done something wrong and not looked back to see if I could make it right. Bring things to mind that I can do something about. Thank you for grace that sets me free to love without guilt.

"None of the sins that person has committed will be remembered against them. They have done what is just and right; they will surely live. Yet your people say, 'The way of the LORD is not just.' But it is their way that is not just."

ᴇᴢᴇᴋɪᴇʟ 33:16-17 ɴɪᴠ

We will never understand the ways of God, but we need to always stand firm in our belief that he is a just God. We rarely see all the sides of a story, so we can never be a true and accurate judge of right and wrong.

It is more important that we concern ourselves with trying to live in a way that shows unconditional love to others, and then let God deal with the issue of fairness. Give your heart and mind some peace tonight, and let God take over.

Heavenly Father, thank you that your mercy says that you won't remember my sins against me, but that your justice will ultimately let things work together for good. When I begin to think that you are unfair, let me realize that it is humans that are wrong, not you.

What have you been judging lately that you need to hand over to the God of true justice?

Numbers

"This is what the Sovereign LORD says: 'I am ready to hear Israel's prayers and to increase their numbers like a flock.'"

EZEKIEL 36:37 NLT

Have you ever seen or experienced a city or town that has been completely deserted? These are sometimes referred to as ghost towns. They used to be thriving but became uninhabitable because of some usually dramatic reason.

It is sad to see a once thriving community become nothing. Perhaps you have experienced that kind of a desertion in your lifetime, and you like to remember the days when things seemed to be more alive. God wants to restore what has been lost. He is ready to hear your prayers and bring life back into your environment.

Sovereign God, thank you for hearing my prayers. Restore those times when I felt energized by your Word. Thank you for the experiences that I have had of you working wonderfully through my life. Bring me a glimpse of that again today.

"They will be as numerous as the sacred flocks that fill Jerusalem's streets at the time of her festivals. The ruined cities will be crowded with people once more, and everyone will know that I am the Lord."

EZEKIEL 36:38 NLT

Have you felt a sense of stirring in your day that God is about to do something new in your life? It is time for celebrating what the Lord is doing and what he promises to do with you.

Spend some time this evening preparing for the flourishing times ahead. Pray for passion, pray for others to join you, pray for the lives that will be changed. Let God fill your heart with joy in the hope of a new season.

God, thank you for giving me joyful thoughts of what you have in store for me. I want to dwell on the goodness and blessing that you have already shown me and let this bring hope into my heart for tomorrow.

How can you prepare for God to bring a new season into your life?

Temple Glory

Then the Spirit took me up and brought me into the inner courtyard, and the glory of the LORD filled the Temple. And I heard someone speaking to me from within the Temple, while the man who had been measuring stood beside me.

EZEKIEL 43:5-6 NLT

The Israelites expected that once God had shown up in the temple he would never leave. It would have been devastating then, when the temple was ultimately destroyed. The problem with their expectation is that they had placed their hope in a physical building.

How wonderful that God kept his promise of dwelling forever with his people by allowing Jesus to put that temple into our hearts. You are now a beautiful dwelling for God's presence and he is willing to fill you with his glory. Receive his presence this morning and let it influence all that you do today.

Holy Spirit, I receive your presence right now. Thank you for the refreshing sense of peace that will help me have a blessed day. Let people recognize that my peace comes from you.

*The LORD said to me, "Son of man, this is the place of my throne
and the place where I will rest my feet. I will live here forever
among the people of Israel. They and their kings will not defile my
holy name any longer by their adulterous worship of other gods or
by honoring the relics of their kings who have died."*

EZEKIEL 43:7 NLT

God is a jealous God in that he wants your whole heart. His
presence is within you and if you fill your life with things that
are not honoring to him, you will crowd out this presence.

If your day has been consumed with wanting the things of this
earth, ask God to remove the wrong desires and then fill you
with the desires of the Spirit. Let God rest in your heart and
give you rest.

*God, take your rightful place in my heart again tonight. Allow me
to let go of the distractions that I have let into my mind today. Give
me the peace of knowing that you are dwelling within me.*

What have you allowed to crowd your heart today?

Excellence

His divine power has granted to us all things that pertain to life and godliness, through the knowledge of him who called us to his own glory and excellence.

2 PETER 1:3 ESV

Each of us is keenly aware of our own weaknesses. We know all our flaws too well and we make eliminating them our goal. But no matter how much effort we put in, we can never and will never achieve perfection.

Despite most of us realizing that we will never be perfect, we still put unreasonable pressure on ourselves. Whether in a task, in our character, or in our walk with Christ, we easily become frustrated when we reach for perfection and can't grasp it. If we allow perfectionism to drive our performance, then we will quench our own potential and inhibit our effectiveness.

God, thank you that this life is not about my perfection but yours. I will do my best to imitate your glory and excellence, but I know that this only comes by your grace. Help me to experience this today.

He has granted to us his precious and very great promises, so that through them you may become partakers of the divine nature, having escaped from the corruption that is in the world because of sinful desire.

2 PETER 1:4 ESV

God gives you the freedom to not be perfect. In fact, his power is all the more perfect when displayed in your weakness because it's not about you, it's about Jesus in you.

When you mess up, God's mercy takes over and the result of forgiveness is always perfection.

God, I wasn't perfect today. I'm pretty sure I'm not perfect any day. But I can rest tonight, knowing that your power is made perfect in my weakness. Forgive my sins. Thank you for a fresh start tomorrow.

Where can you see God's perfection shining through your imperfection?

Add to Faith

Make every effort to add to your faith goodness; and to goodness,
knowledge; and to knowledge, self-control; and to self-control,
perseverance; and to perseverance, godliness; and to godliness,
mutual affection; and to mutual affection, love.

2 PETER 1:5–7 NIV

If you see this list of virtues as a checklist, then you are
looking at it the wrong way. You know that God isn't about a
list of right things to do. Instead look simply at where it all
starts: with faith.

When you build your faith through reading God's Word and
spending time in his presence, you will notice the other
virtues begin to be added to your faith. With belief comes
goodness, knowledge, and self-control. Where is your faith
this morning? Remind yourself of your salvation through
belief in Christ, and let the rest work itself out from there.

Jesus, I believe in you. I know that this belief is what saves me, not
all the good or right things that I do. Help me to build those other
characteristics as my faith increases. Give me knowledge, self-
control, godliness, and love.

If you possess these qualities in increasing measure,
they will keep you from being ineffective and unproductive
in your knowledge of our Lord Jesus Christ.

2 PETER 1:8 NIV

The point of good news is that we share it. There are a lot of
reasons as to why we don't share the gospel with others, and
some have to do with whether we are building from our faith
with qualities like perseverance and mutual affection.

Developing these qualities gives us the right tools to share
effectively with those who don't know Christ.

Holy Spirit, I need more of you in my life so my faith increases,
and along with it, all these other forms of godliness that will help
me to show people about this faith. As I continue to read your
Word, help me to increase my understanding of you.

Are you seeing these qualities increase in your life?

Ways to Remember

I will always remind you about these things—even though you already know them and are standing firm in the truth you have been taught. And it is only right that I should keep on reminding you as long as I live.

2 PETER 1:12-13 NLT

It is so important to continue to stand in the truth of the gospel of Jesus. These days, there are so many other ideas that are competing to tell us what is best for us. We read about health trends, ways to improve our mental agility, time management strategies—anything for self-betterment.

None of these are inherently wrong, but they can distract you from a focus on the truth found in God's Word. This is why you need to find ways to remind yourself of the truth: reminders that are set for the rest of your life. Be encouraged that you are being reminded of God's truth every day.

God, I know that your truth should be above what the world finds important. Thank you for the big and small things that you will present me with today to remind me of your great love and my salvation.

*Our Lord Jesus Christ has shown me that I must soon leave this
earthly life, so I will work hard to make sure you
always remember these things after I am gone.*

2 PETER 1:14-15 NLT

It is as important to remind others of Christ's love as it is to
be reminded of it yourself. Each generation of Christians that
have gone before us have left their mark on the world because
they shared Jesus through their actions and deeds.

In the same way, you are able to pass on Christ's love through
what you say and do. This isn't to be experienced as a burden
but as a joy.

*God, let me be more aware of the impact of my faith on those
generations to come. I am encouraged that you work through me
so others will know of your love. Keep me motivated to pass on the
blessing that was handed to me.*

How can you see your faith being passed down through
generations?

God's Interpretation

*We have the prophetic word more fully confirmed, to which you
will do well to pay attention as to a lamp shining in a dark place,
until the day dawns and the morning star rises in your hearts,
knowing this first of all, that no prophecy of Scripture comes from
someone's own interpretation.*

2 PETER 1:19-20 ESV

When the people of God tried to interpret the prophecies
from Scripture, they didn't have full understanding. When
we read the words of these prophesies today, they seem to
make a lot more sense in light of Christ's life, death and
resurrection.

The best way to interpret Scripture is to come from the
knowledge that what is written is from God. He knew what
he intended, and he meant for it to be written that way. Trust
God's words and marvel at the plan that he has made from the
beginning.

*God, thank you for your Scripture that was read thousands of
years ago and finally came true. Help me to pay attention to your
Word, knowing that it can be a lamp to light my path.*

No prophecy was ever produced by the will of man, but men spoke from God as they were carried along by the Holy Spirit.

2 PETER 1:21 ESV

We have all forms of foretelling in our day, from horoscopes to psychics. The search to know the future is a quest that humans will never conquer because the future is not for us to know.

God guides us into understanding what is to come by telling us some things in Scripture. These are the prophecies that the Holy Spirit put in the heart of people to write down, and they are words that you can trust because they are from God.

Jesus, help me to stay away from the temptation of trying to interpret prophecy or trying to determine exactly what the future will be like. Give me greater understanding and insight into the prophetic word that is in Scripture.

What promises can you find in Scripture about the future?

Don't Go Back

When people escape from the wickedness of the world by knowing our Lord and Savior Jesus Christ and then get tangled up and enslaved by sin again, they are worse off than before.

2 PETER 2:20 NLT

If we don't surrender everything to Jesus in the first place, we are at risk of being caught back up into the sin that had us trapped. What does a life fully-surrendered to Christ look like? It's holding nothing back from God, and surrendering every single part to him.

If there are things from your past that you are still holding onto, hear the caution of what it is like to go back—it can get worse. Be encouraged that you have been set free, so keep yourself in that freedom.

God, I don't know how to fully surrender myself to you, but I know that I don't want to get tangled up in sin again. I really want to have a life that is dedicated to you and even though I fail, I still want to give it all up for you. Give me a chance to show you that today.

It would be better if they had never known the way
to righteousness than to know it and then reject
the command they were given to live a holy life.

2 PETER 2:21 NLT

Being a disciple of Christ requires complete and total
surrender of everything you have and everything you are. He
is not asking you to give up anything that he wasn't willing
to give for you. When he gave up the glory and rights of his
heavenly throne, he surrendered more for you than you ever
could for him.

Jesus never sold this life as being casual, simple, or inexpensive.
But he did promise that the reward would be great.

Jesus, let me remember the rewards that I have for a life
surrendered to you far outweighs any earthly treasure. I choose to
serve you today and every day. Give me the strength and grace to
pursue you with all my heart.

What is God asking you to surrender to him? Trust that he
knows what is best for you.

Differing Times

Do not forget this one thing, dear friends: With the Lord a day is like a thousand years, and a thousand years are like a day.

2 Peter 3:8 NIV

Time is an interesting human phenomenon. Even though it is constant, one minute can seem different depending on the context. If you are running on a treadmill at a really fast speed at the highest incline, one minute feels excruciating. If you are talking on the phone to one of your closest friends, that minute goes insanely fast.

God isn't fooled by time; he knows how to work in and outside of it. If you are feeling like it is taking a long time for God to bring some of his promises to fruition, remind yourself that his timing is right.

God, it seems like I have been waiting a really long time to see your promises come true. Give me patience, knowing that you have it all under control. Remind me of the promises that you have already fulfilled, and fill me with joy for the day ahead.

The Lord is not slow in keeping his promise, as some understand slowness. Instead he is patient with you, not wanting anyone to perish, but everyone to come to repentance.

2 PETER 3:9 NIV

Have you felt like your day has been rushed along by all the activities and need to get things done? We are so used to rushing through life that we find waiting hard. God is not slow. He is patient because he is waiting for us.

Jesus will return when the timing is right, but his heart is all about his love for those who still need his revelation to reach them. Respect God's need to do things in his timing and continue to wait expectedly for his return.

God, thank you for your great love that compels you to wait for those who you love. Thank you that you seek out the lost and celebrate when they are found. Help me to be part of furthering your kingdom by bringing those lost sheep to you.

Who do you know that needs to come to repentance? Pray for their salvation.

Perfection

*According to his promise we are waiting for new heavens
and a new earth in which righteousness dwells.*

2 PETER 3:13 ESV

We are drawn to want new things. There is something about
the freshness of an untouched, unmarked item that we long
for.

The idea of a new heaven and earth should fill your heart with
hope. It is not that God's creation needs to be undone—he
called it very good. It is simply that he needs to make this
place new, just as he is in the process of making us new.

*God, thank you for a new day where I can start fresh. Give me a
renewed sense of hope for the world and people around me that
you have created. Help me to endure the here and the now knowing
that all things will be made perfect in your time.*

Since you are waiting for these, be diligent to be found
by him without spot or blemish, and at peace.

2 PETER 3:14 ESV

It seems unreasonable to ask us to be spotless considering we make mistakes every day. Remember that Jesus took your place so you will be found without blemish. It is not about living a perfect life, it is about knowing and believing that he has made you perfect.

Continue to put your trust and faith in Jesus, knowing that one day your wait for full perfection will be over.

Jesus, thank you for your blood that has washed away every single sin. I know that I am forgiven, so remind me to stop striving for perfection and instead receive it by your grace.

Are you striving to be perfect on your own merit? Put your trust in Jesus and let him wipe all your sins away.

Healthy Habits

Daniel said to the steward whom the chief of the eunuchs had assigned over Daniel, Hananiah, Mishael, and Azariah, "Test your servants for ten days; let us be given vegetables to eat and water to drink. Then let our appearance and the appearance of the youths who eat the king's food be observed by you, and deal with your servants according to what you see."

DANIEL 1:11-13 ESV

The king in Daniel's time wanted his men to eat in a way that he thought would benefit their strength, but it went against the way that Daniel and his friends had been taught to eat. When Daniel challenged this with God's way, it resulted in them becoming healthier and more mentally alert than the other men who had eaten from the king's table.

You will no doubt be challenged in the course of your Christian walk to conform to the patterns of this world: what to eat and drink, or what will make you successful. In the end, you need to hold true to your values that were given to you from God and know that his ways will give you strength.

Holy Spirit, there will be so many influences in my day. Give me the strength of mind to know that your ways are better than the world's; help me to hold fast to what I know is right and good for me.

He listened to them in this matter, and tested them for ten days. At the end of ten days it was seen that they were better in appearance and fatter in flesh than all the youths who ate the king's food.

DANIEL 1:14 ESV

The way you live will be a standard for others. When you stay true to your convictions, you may not feel good at first but you will feel better knowing that you are a stronger, more capable person.

When others see this, it will testify to the goodness and wisdom of God.

Father, I am thankful for your wisdom and how that applies to my life. Let this wise living be a positive influence on people who know me and let them know that my ways are directed by you.

Have you been challenged lately to conform to the world? Ask God to help you rise to his standard.

God Reveals

Daniel answered and said: "Blessed be the name of God forever and ever, for wisdom and might are His. And He changes the times and the seasons; He removes kings and raises up kings; He gives wisdom to the wise and knowledge to those who have understanding."

DANIEL 2:20-21 NKJV

Life can be a lot like a maze sometimes; we're unsure of where each turn will lead and never know when we will find ourselves at the end of a path. God is not a God of confusion. He is always ready to reveal the next step for us, we just need to be ready to ask.

God can see it all from a much broader perspective and can intervene when he wills. Trust him today for his guidance and insight into your day's tasks and situations.

God, I come to you seeking clarity for my situation and what is around the next corner. Help me to prepare well for what is ahead and increase my knowledge of you as I see you revealed in big and small ways.

"He reveals deep and secret things; He knows what is in the darkness, and light dwells with Him."

DANIEL 2:22 NKJV

Have you felt confused today or at peace, knowing that God is in control? Either way, it is good to acknowledge that God holds the light for us in those dark times and shows us the way through. Sometimes he leads us through darker tunnels to find hidden treasure.

When you are going through something difficult, God always reveals more about his nature, and more about you. You might learn that you are stronger than you think and that he is more powerful than you knew. Let him light your path tonight.

God, reveal those deep and secret things that will help me gain insight into my heart and mind and into those situations where I have felt helpless or lost. Let peace rule in this space tonight.

In what ways have you felt like you have been in the dark? Ask God for revelation.

A King's Dream

Daniel replied, "There are no wise men, enchanters, magicians, or fortune-tellers who can reveal the king's secret. But there is a God in heaven who reveals secrets, and he has shown King Nebuchadnezzar what will happen in the future. Now I will tell you your dream and the visions you saw as you lay on your bed."

DANIEL 2:27-28 NLT

Daniel could have presented himself as some kind of skillful mind reader, but he gave all the glory to God. He could have used his gift of interpretation to make himself great in the king's palace, but with sincerity of heart he directed the king toward the one true God who knows all things.

There are times when you might be tempted to take the glory for yourself. Remember who gave you your gifts and allow your accomplishments to point toward the magnificence of your God.

Lord God, there really are no wise men, enchanters, magicians, or fortuneteller's who speak the truth. You are the God who created humanity and knows all that there is to know. If I have any success today I acknowledge you as the source of that success.

"While Your Majesty was sleeping, you dreamed about coming events. He who reveals secrets has shown you what is going to happen. And it is not because I am wiser than anyone else that I know the secret of your dream, but because God wants you to understand what was in your heart."

DANIEL 2:29-30 NLT

Have you heard exorbitant prophecies from people who claim to be full of God's wisdom? To speak God's words in a prophetic manner is a wonderful gift but often people get it wrong because they claim the fame and power for themselves; this kind of prophet should be challenged.

Anyone who is speaking God's words must have the humility, as Daniel did, to admit that they're not wiser than anyone else, but that they are speaking only because God wants to give understanding.

God, I know that you speak through your people even today. Give me discernment to understand the motivation behind those who are claiming to speak on your behalf. Help me to recognize your truth.

Where do you need to give God the praise instead of relying on your own wisdom?

The Final Kingdom

"In the days of those kings the God of heaven will set up a kingdom that shall never be destroyed, nor shall this kingdom be left to another people. It shall crush all these kingdoms and bring them to an end, and it shall stand forever."

DANIEL 2:44 NRSV

Sometimes the Israelite won and sometimes they lost. This meant that their kings and kingdoms would often be abundant, but they would also be annihilated. All along, Israel awaited a kingdom that would never fail or come to an end; a kingdom where God was eternally present.

In life, you will have experienced successes and failures. Be assured today that you are part of God's eternal kingdom that will stand forever.

God, I thank you that I can endure my failures knowing that ultimately I am part of a kingdom that will succeed. I put my hope in you and not the things of this world today.

> *"Just as you saw that a stone was cut from the mountain not by hands, and that it crushed the iron, the bronze, the clay, the silver, and the gold. The great God has informed the king what shall be hereafter. The dream is certain, and its interpretation trustworthy."*

DANIEL 2:45 NRSV

When Israel pictured an eternal kingdom, they were thinking of a physical kingdom, something like they had known but stronger and more powerful. God, however, had a plan that was beyond a kingdom made with human hands. His kingdom was not made from iron, bronze, clay, silver, or gold, but in the person of Jesus Christ, who started a kingdom that could never be destroyed.

Remember that this is the kingdom you are a part of now and praise God that the best is yet to come.

Jesus, sometimes it's hard to lift my eyes from a human perspective to look at things from an eternal one. As I grow closer to you, I pray I would see more through your eyes than the eyes of this world.

How can you shift your perspective from earthly things to things of the eternal kingdom?

A Blazing Furnace

Shadrach, Meshach and Abednego replied to him,
"King Nebuchadnezzar, we do not need to defend ourselves
before you in this matter. If we are thrown into the blazing
furnace, the God we serve is able to deliver us from it,
and he will deliver us from Your Majesty's hand."

DANIEL 3:16-17 NIV

Wouldn't it be incredible to have such an unwavering faith? These three men were so convinced that God would save them from the fire that they didn't even try to plead their case before the king.

You are unlikely to face a literal fiery furnace, but when you are challenged about your faith, think of this situation and remember to stand up for what you believe and who you believe in. God is the only God who truly saves.

God, thank you that you find ways to show your power and reality in big and small ways. Give me opportunities to declare my faith to others today.

"Even if he does not, we want you to know, Your Majesty, that we will not serve your gods or worship the image of gold you have set up."

DANIEL 3:18 NIV

Would you be willing to risk your life so as not to compromise God's truth? We would like to think that we are brave enough, but it would be the hardest thing we would ever have to do.

Thankfully, most of us aren't put through a life and death situation when it comes to speaking God's truth, but our faith should be just as strong nonetheless. Surprise yourself with the boldness that comes from knowing you serve the one and only living God.

Holy Spirit, you are with me all throughout the day, but often I don't draw from the power and strength that you so freely give. Remind me tomorrow of your presence so I can step out in boldness if the situation calls for it.

As you think over your day, are there things that have challenged your faith? Ask for a renewed vigor to defend what you know is true.

The Lion's Den

*At the first light of dawn, the king got up and hurried to the
lions' den. When he came near the den, he called to Daniel in
an anguished voice, "Daniel, servant of the living God, has your
God, whom you serve continually, been able to rescue you from
the lions?" Daniel answered, "May the king live forever! My God
sent his angel, and he shut the mouths of the lions. They have not
hurt me, because I was found innocent in his sight. Nor have I ever
done any wrong before you, Your Majesty."*

DANIEL 6:19-22 NIV

Daniel must have worried when he was placed in the lion's
den, and yet his eternal salvation was never in question.
Although there were those who hated his dedication to God,
Daniel knew that he was innocent before God.

We have nothing to fear when we know that we are not
deserving of blame. The next time you feel trapped because of
your service to God, remember that God will rescue you from
harm. Just as Scripture says, "When God is for you, who can
be against you?" Don't be afraid; God is on your side.

*Jesus, when I find myself in a lion's den kind of situation, I ask for
your peace and courage, knowing that I am innocent. Thank you
that no one can take away my salvation. I choose to live in that
assurance today, knowing that you will always come to my rescue.*

The king was overjoyed and gave orders to lift Daniel out of the den. And when Daniel was lifted from the den, no wound was found on him, because he had trusted in his God.

DANIEL 6:23 NIV

Have you felt tested today with people who have mocked the Christian faith? Sometimes it is not a personal attack, but when we see the media bent on destroying the name of Christians it can be discouraging.

God will not be defeated. Look forward to that moment when you, and other Christians, will be pulled out of the den, without a scratch, and will become a glorious witness to the goodness and power of God.

Great and mighty God, you are worthy of all praise. Thank you that one day everyone will see that you are the victorious King of heaven and earth. Help me to trust you each day, knowing that I have this eternal inheritance.

Meditate tonight on the fact that God is the victorious King of heaven and earth.

Petitions

"Now, our God, hear the prayers and petitions of your servant. For your sake, Lord, look with favor on your desolate sanctuary. Give ear, our God, and hear; open your eyes and see the desolation of the city that bears your Name. We do not make requests of you because we are righteous, but because of your great mercy."

DANIEL 9:17-18 NIV

Are you waiting for a breakthrough in your circumstances? Maybe you have been praying for an unbelieving family member, a strained relationship, an answer to your financial stress, or clarity for a big decision ahead.

Fasting doesn't often top the list of what to do when you really need that breakthrough, and it's not that hard to guess why it isn't a popular option. It takes self-control and determination to pray and petition God for an answer, but it will be worth it.

Lord God, I turn my face toward you today and I again ask for a breakthrough in my circumstances. Help me to think about you during my day and to continue to pray for your strength and endurance. If I need to fast, bring that conviction to my heart.

> *"Lord, listen. Lord, forgive! Lord, hear and act!*
> *For your sake, my God, do not delay, because your city*
> *and your people bear your Name."*
>
> DANIEL 9:19 NIV

Consider what the Bible says about fasting and notice how it goes hand in hand with prayer.

There is a certain humility that accompanies fasting; it requires sobriety of heart, reflection, and focus. It brings your impulses into submission and gives you confidence in your self-control. More importantly, it seems to let the Lord know that you mean business—that you are ready to receive his revelation and guidance.

God, I know that you might be calling me to petition you in some way. If it's not food, then give me something to give up so my heart can really press in toward what you want for my life.

Can you commit to make fasting and deep petition a spiritual discipline in your life? You may just get the answers you were looking for, and perhaps even ones that you were not.

As Jesus Did

If anyone obeys his word, love for God is truly made complete in them. This is how we know we are in him.

1 JOHN 2:5 NIV

It can be difficult to obey God. When life throws hard tasks our way, we want to flee. We want to submit to our own desires and ignore what God is asking of us.

When the child in you threatens to rise up and make choices for you, stop and pray. Lean in closer to the Lord and ask him for his help in choosing obedience. It's only with his guidance that we are able to be made complete.

Heavenly Father, you are such a wonderful God. Guide me into your truth today so I live by what is right. Give me understanding of what it means to live in you.

Whoever claims to live in him must live as Jesus did.

1 JOHN 2:6 NIV

Scripture says that obedience will make us whole in our relationship with God. We will truly know what love means when we choose obedience. We cannot claim to know him and love him if we are not living by his Word.

When we live in God, as Jesus did, we are surrendering our hearts to him. We are allowing an open and truthful communication with our Heavenly Father. Jesus spoke of living in the Father, and the Father living in him. We are invited to join in this intimate union.

God, I need your wisdom to do the right thing, so I am living in obedience to your Word. Help me to understand how Jesus related to you so I can do the same.

What are you being asked to obey God in this evening?

Lasting Love

Do not love the world or anything in the world.
If anyone loves the world, love for the Father is not in them.

1 JOHN 2:15 NIV

It's so easy to fall prey to the wants and desires of the world. There's the latest this, and the coolest that, and we have a hunger to own it all. We see a neighbor with a shiny new car, and suddenly ours seems old and unappealing. A friend shows up for coffee with a high end new phone, and we instantly want a better one, too.

There's nothing inherently wrong with new things, and we're not sinning simply by making an acquisition. It's more about the priority we give our purchases than the purchases themselves. It's about our hearts.

God, let me love you with my whole heart and put you above anything else in this world.

*Everything in the world—the lust of the flesh, the lust of the eyes,
and the pride of life—comes not from the Father but from the world.*

1 JOHN 2:15-16 NIV

Are you coveting all that the world has to offer, or is the ache
in your heart a yearning for Jesus' presence?

Pray for protection from the desires of the world.

*It's hard, God, to put you first in such a busy and demanding
world. Sometimes I just want to do it the world's way. I pray that
you would forgive me for missing the mark and help me to set my
eyes on you this evening, so I wake up with you on my mind.*

What are you putting first in your life?

Love Perfected

We have come to know and have believed the love which God has for us. God is love, and the one who abides in love abides in God, and God abides in him. By this, love is perfected with us, so that we may have confidence in the day of judgment; because as He is, so also are we in this world.

1 JOHN 4:16-17 NASB

We represent Jesus Christ to the world through love. If we know how high and wide and deep and long his love is for us, then we have no choice but to pour out that love on others.

The intrusive becomes welcome, the offensive becomes peaceful, rudeness gives way to grace, and the insufferable is overshadowed by the cross and all that Jesus suffered there.

God, you are love. That truth needs to sink into my heart this morning. I want to trust that love more than I have before, so much that it lives in me and overflows out of my life into the lives of those around me.

There is no fear in love; but perfect love casts out fear, because fear involves punishment, and the one who fears is not perfected in love. We love, because He first loved us.

1 JOHN 4:18-19 NASB

It's a wonderful cycle that is hard to break. You love God, he lives in you, you love him more, he lives in you more fully. We love because he is in us, and he is in us because we love him. It's amazing and wonderful, and you can rest assured that today you are not judged for what you have done, you are judged for the love of God that is in you.

Are you afraid to be fully known? Lay down your need to be perceived as perfect and allow yourself to be loved for who you truly are. Let your fear be washed away by the perfect love of a perfect God.

Jesus, I know that you love me, and I am so grateful for your love. It fills my heart up. When I think about your love for me, it enables me to be more loving toward others. Thank you for a day of acknowledging your love. Let your love shine through my deeds and words to others around me tomorrow.

In what situations are you finding it difficult to love others? What can you do to show love to these people tomorrow?

Brothers and Sisters

Whoever claims to love God yet hates a brother or sister is a liar.
For whoever does not love their brother and sister, whom they have
seen, cannot love God, whom they have not seen.

1 JOHN 4:20 NIV

The harsh reality is that if we have hardness in our hearts
toward a fellow believer, we cannot truly claim to love God.

God told us to love our neighbors as ourselves. He calls us to
be one with the body of Christ. Yet, we often find fault with
our brothers and sisters in the church—to the point where we
can't find love for them at all. It's not what God wants for us.

Jesus, I love you and I know that this means that I need to love
others. Forgive me for the times when I have not acted in love
toward a brother or sister. Help me to love you through my love to
others around me. Give me an opportunity to put this into practice
today.

He has given us this command: Anyone who loves God
must also love their brother and sister.

1 JOHN 4:21 NIV

Have you been able to show someone love today, even if you feel like they don't deserve it?

If there is someone within your community of believers whom you struggle to love, pray that the Lord will give you the supernatural power to do so. It's only through him that we can find the strength to love those we couldn't otherwise love.

God, you know who the people are that I struggle to love the way that I should. I get frustrated and upset with these people a lot. I ask that you give me a measure of your grace, so I can change my heart attitude toward them.

Who do you need to change your heart attitude about? In what ways will you show them love?

Bold Requests

This is the confidence we have in approaching God:
that if we ask anything according to his will, he hears us.

1 JOHN 5:14 NIV

Sometimes it can feel as if God is far away: an elusive man in the heavens who is so high above us that surely he cannot be interested in our day-to-day lives. Our desires and requests are so small by comparison that it seems unworthy a task to even ask him for help.

Allow yourself to be filled with God's presence today. He loves you and wants the best for you. If you ask in his will, he will answer you.

God, give me the boldness to ask for things in your name and to trust that you hear me and will respond.

If we know that he hears us—whatever we ask—
we know that we have what we asked of him.

1 John 5:15 NIV

God loves his children. He wants us to be happy, to feel fulfilled. When we approach him with our wants and needs, he truly hears us.

The next time you feel as if your requests are too unimportant to bother God about, remind yourself that he is always listening. Though he may not answer you in the way you expect, he is right there beside you ready to lend an ear.

God, I know that you love me as my loving Father. I know that some of my requests seem selfish or small, but I also know that you can sort out my requests in the ways that you know best. I choose to ask you for everything that I hope for and then trust you with however you choose to answer.

What do you need to ask God for right now? Ask him in boldness this evening.

Don't Lose It

Watch out that you do not lose what we have worked for,
but that you may be rewarded fully.

2 JOHN 1:8 NIV

Imagine gathering all your hard-earned wages for a week's
work, putting it in your back pocket and then losing it all on
your way home. It would be so frustrating to have nothing to
show for all your efforts; it would be a waste.

There is an urgency to the gospel that the apostles wanted us to
catch on to. The preservation of the truth, the demonstration
of Christ's love, and the spreading of the Word are paramount
to seeing his kingdom advance. Be part of this good work so we
can experience the reward of seeing people saved.

Jesus, I want to see your love spread to as many people as it can get
to. Help me to not let go of the truth that is in my heart. Give me a
chance to spread your love today.

Anyone who runs ahead and does not continue in the teaching of Christ does not have God; whoever continues in the teaching has both the Father and the Son.

2 JOHN 1:9 NIV

There are a lot of people who proclaim to know the truth about the world, but it is crucial that we know the gospel of Jesus Christ. Jesus revealed who God is, and he said there is no other way to the Father.

If you want to know God, you have to stick close to knowing Jesus and being diligent with remembering and putting into practice all that he said and did. Anything less than Christ is not the Father at all. Cling to the truth and let it all be about Jesus.

God, I never want to run ahead with teaching that doesn't encompass the work of Jesus. Continue to reveal yourself to me so I know the Father more and more.

Have you been tempted to follow teachings that don't mention Christ? Make sure to examine what you are hearing for the truth and presence of Jesus.

Strong and Healthy

Dear friend, I hope all is well with you and that you are as healthy in body as you are strong in spirit. Some of the traveling teachers recently returned and made me very happy by telling me about your faithfulness and that you are living according to the truth.

3 JOHN 1:2-3 NLT

Good news can make our day go from dreadful to amazing, especially when it is about something that we have been stressed or worried about, like a medical result, or a test score. When the early church was being established, there was no real way of knowing whether they were surviving or living by the truth until someone delivered a report. How relieving it must have been to hear that the church was indeed doing very well.

As you head into your day, can you think of something encouraging to report back to those who are thinking about you? Make someone's day by giving them a glowing report.

God, I am blessed to be growing strong and healthy in you. Remind me of someone to share my good news with so they can be encouraged as well.

*I could have no greater joy than to hear that
my children are following the truth.*

3 John 1:4 NLT

Teachers are encouraged when they know that the hard work they have put into helping kids learn has been put to good use.

Think of the teachers that have seen their children go on to become scientists, world leaders, or missionaries. What joy to know that we can pass down our knowledge and truth to others, so they can do something good with it.

Jesus, bring people into my life that I can teach about your Word. I want to be effective for your kingdom, so I pray that you would bring me opportunities, even this week, to do something meaningful that will last for many years to come.

What kind of knowledge and faith can you pass on to the next generation?

Rescue Others

You must show mercy to those whose faith is wavering.
Rescue others by snatching them from the flames of judgment.
Show mercy to still others, but do so with great caution,
hating the sins that contaminate their lives.

JUDE 1:22-23 NLT

It is right not to force God's Word on anyone, but in our effort to not be pushy, we can sometimes hold back from warning people about the consequences of a weakening faith. When you see a brother or sister who is starting to waver, God asks us to reach out to them in effort to rescue them from the impending fate of turning away from him.

You can approach people with grace and love, just as Jesus' kindness drew you to him. You don't have to condemn people; rather, caution them about sin and then pray that their eyes would be open and their hearts softened to God's grace.

Holy Spirit, give me the wisdom and grace to approach those whom I see wavering in the faith. Let me feel the urgency that you do in saving those who are falling. Let my eyes be open to these opportunities today.

*All glory to God, who is able to keep you from falling away
and will bring you with great joy into his glorious presence
without a single fault.*

JUDE 1:24 NLT

We have a human perspective on sin that can get us into more
danger than the actual sin. We seem to accumulate our sins
in the way you would mark a test—too many crosses mean you
have failed.

When we start believing that we are failures, we are tempted
to give up trying altogether. This is not how Jesus sees your
life. Each time you do something wrong, his grace is there
to cover it. You ask for forgiveness and start again. In this
way, you will be presented without a single fault. It's hard to
accept, but that is the wonder of grace.

*Jesus, it really is amazing that you can see me without a single
fault. Thank you for encouraging my heart tonight. Help me to
encourage others with this perspective.*

Are you tempted to give up because you feel like you have
failed? Who do you know that needs to be reminded of the
wonder of grace?

Omega

"Look, he is coming with the clouds, and every eye will see him, even those who pierced him; and all peoples on earth will mourn because of him. So shall it be! Amen."

REVELATION 1:7 NIV

The sin and sadness of life can make it seem like an endless night where we are continually waiting for the dawn of Christ's return.

There will be a day where all will see his return, even those who mocked him, even those who have chosen not to believe in him. Don't lose heart. He is coming for you. Keep your eyes fixed on him.

God, sometimes I am afraid of eternity and other times I long for it. Help me to endure and even to enjoy today, knowing that my eternity is secure in your hands.

*"I am the Alpha and the Omega," says the LORD God,
"who is, and who was, and who is to come, the Almighty."*

REVELATION 1:8 NIV

We live for the promise of his return. This promise overcomes our pain, our longing, our desperation, and our limits. All things become bearable and light under the assurance of seeing Jesus, embracing him, and gazing on his beauty.

We will be made into a pure and spotless bride. There is nothing more for us but to marvel at him. Glorify him. Believe him. Love him. Thank him. He was at the beginning and he will be at the end.

God, I have been able to get through the day because I know that there is an end to sadness and suffering. Help me to bring your joy into my home, my work, and wherever else I may go. Give me peace as I sleep, knowing that I can face another day with the brightness of a future with you.

What suffering or sadness are you facing in this season? Thank God that there will one day be an end to it.

Lukewarm

"I know your works; you are neither cold nor hot. I wish that you
were either cold or hot. So, because you are lukewarm, and neither
cold nor hot, I am about to spit you out of my mouth."

REVELATION 3:15-16 NRSV

In a life filled with so many other things to work at,
watch, play, buy, and think about, we can easily leave our
Christianity at the back door. We can be so consumed with
this life that we lose our passion for Christ and forget the
eternal home that we are destined for.

God wants your whole heart, either hot or cold in the sense
of being extreme. Apathy will not move you anywhere; it will
make you uncaring and ineffective. Make a point today, of
figuring out if you are pursuing God with your whole heart. Be
hot or be cold, but don't be lukewarm.

*Father God, I love you with my whole heart and I am sorry when
I have become unaffected by the gospel and unwilling to pour my
soul into furthering your kingdom. Give me a renewed sense of
purpose and passion today.*

"You say, 'I am rich, I have prospered, and I need nothing.' You do not realize that you are wretched, pitiable, poor, blind, and naked."

REVELATION 3:17 NRSV

Being comfortable is nice, but it can also lead you into a place of laziness. You know what it is like when you find that nice warm spot in a big comfortable chair at the end of the night – it makes you want to sleep.

Remember that we can't get too comfortable with our faith. We need to experience a certain amount of tension, so we can stay committed to the cause of sharing Christ with a world that desperately needs him.

Jesus, restore my passion to see you working in the world. I want you to use me as much as you can, but I realize that sometimes I don't let you into my busy life. Please enter my heart tonight, and ignite that flame once again.

Are you hot or cold in your relationship with Jesus or are you getting to a comfortable, lukewarm place?

A New Song

They sang a new song, saying, "Worthy are you to take the scroll and to open its seals, for you were slain, and by your blood you ransomed people for God from every tribe and language and people and nation."

REVELATION 5:9 ESV

Jesus was humbled as a man on earth, but it was always promised that he would be elevated back to his rightful place on the throne. At the end of this age, Jesus is the only one who is worthy enough to call the last battle sound. He was perfect in every way and represented the new humanity that he wants to usher in from every tribe, language, people, and nation.

What a beautiful sight to behold—our Lord Jesus Christ—worthy to be praised and glorified.

Thank you, Jesus, that you included all people as part of your plan for humanity. Thank you that this world is made up of so many different people. I praise and worship you because you are so great.

*"You have made them a kingdom and priests to our God,
and they shall reign on the earth."*

REVELATION 5:10 ESV

We are still living in a now-but-not-yet kind of kingdom.
Because of this, we have been placed on earth to reign as we
take our rightful inheritance through the price that Jesus paid
on the cross.

If you are feeling a little low this morning, pick yourself up
with the thought of being a child of the King. He has given you
the inheritance of eternal life! Let that hope be your joy in the
various moments of life, and allow the peace of knowing you
are secure give you rest tonight.

*Jesus, you accomplished so much on the cross for me. Not only did
you win my freedom from sin, but you included me as part of God's
royal family. Thank you that I am a precious child of the King,
who will rule and reign with you forever.*

In what way are you allowing God to reign through you on earth?

First Love

> *"I hold this against you:*
> *You have forsaken the love you had at first."*
>
> REVELATION 2:4 NIV

What does the beginning of your love story with God look like? Was there a song that you can remember falling in love with him to? Maybe there was a verse—a Word from his mouth—that captured your heart. Or is there something about the place you were in when your heart responded to his and you walked away changed?

It's all too easy to lose the initial passion of love. God becomes woven into our lives like a single thread in a tapestry, and like that, though he is part of us, he isn't the whole substance.

Jesus, I remember what it was like when I first knew that I was loved by you. I felt so passionate about you. Return that passion to me. Even in the middle of a busy day, let my gaze rest on you.

"Consider how far you have fallen! Repent and do the things you did at first. If you do not repent, I will come to you and remove your lampstand from its place."

REVELATION 2:5 NIV

Search your heart as you reflect on your day. Have you abandoned the depth of love you had at first? Have you strayed from that place where all you wanted was him and all you needed was his presence?

Take some time to quiet your heart this evening and remember everything about the moment in which you fell in love with God. Sometimes we have to remember how we fell in love to remind ourselves that we are in love.

Lord God, you have been so good to me. I know that you remain faithful, even when I forget to acknowledge that you are the source of my life. Return me to that place of loving you with all that I am.

What will help you remember your love for God in the days to come?

Thirst No More

"They shall hunger no more, neither thirst anymore; the sun shall not strike them, nor any scorching heat."

REVELATION 7:16 ESV

Imagine a marathon with no water stops. A sideline with no giant cooler for the team. Immediately, we picture athletes dropping from dehydration and exhaustion. It's unthinkable.

What is the thirstiest you've ever been? How long had you gone without drinking, and how wonderful did those first few sips taste when your thirst was finally quenched? Perhaps one of Jesus' most audacious promises is to take away our thirst. It's extraordinary. He will be all we need, he tells us.

God, thank you that you will provide me with all my spiritual needs. When I am hungry, you will feed me. When I am thirsty, you will provide me with water. The heat will not burn me. You are a God that takes care of me.

"The Lamb in the midst of the throne will be their shepherd, and he will guide them to springs of living water, and God will wipe away every tear from their eyes."

REVELATION 7:17 ESV

Perhaps today was one of those days where you felt spiritually dry. Maybe you are working through something in your relationship or workplace and you don't have the creativity, time, or energy to put into it.

Go back to your image of the marathon, and picture yourself running strong, completely free from thirst or pain. Ask the Holy Spirit to reveal what this might look like in your life today.

Jesus, wipe away my tears that have come from the pain of hard work. Thank you that while I am running through life, you are there to sustain me with your living water.

What needs can Jesus meet? Thank God for the incredible promise of living water.

Former Things

I heard a loud voice from heaven saying, "Behold, the tabernacle of God is with men, and He will dwell with them, and they shall be His people. God Himself will be with them and be their God."

REVELATION 21:3 NKJV

When terrible things happen in this world, people cry out to God in desperation. They ask how he could have let it happen. How could the One who is in control of everything possibly be good when there is so much hardship?

When we look at the system of heaven, we realize that God never intended for us to have sorrow, pain, or death. All these things only exist as a result of man's sin. When the kingdom of heaven is established on earth, we will live as God intended. All wrong will be righted and all pain will disappear.

God, some days I am faced with these questions of why? On these days, remind me of your promise of the hope that we hold of a good and perfect future. Thank you that your eternal plan for my life is beautiful.

"God will wipe away every tear from their eyes; there shall be no more death, nor sorrow, nor crying. There shall be no more pain, for the former things have passed away."

REVELATION 21:4 NKJV

It is good to live and love with eternity's values in view. On some days, it can be the difference between despair or hope. What kind of day did you have today? Was it filled with hope or filled with hardship?

As a child of God, you know that any pain you have in this life is temporary because your eternal home will be devoid of it all. When the pain and sadness of the world threatens to overwhelm you, cling to the promise of heaven and the hope that one day every tear will be wiped from your eyes.

God, I look forward to the day that there will no longer be struggles and pain around me. Help me to face each night with courage and each day with hope as I live with the expectation of a wonderful future.

What sorrows are you feeling right now? Ask for the hope of eternity to settle in your heart and then pray for those around you.

Promised Peace

"In that day I will make a covenant for them with the beasts of the field, the birds in the sky and the creatures that move along the ground. Bow and sword and battle I will abolish from the land, so that all may lie down in safety."

HOSEA 2:18 NIV

We strive for peace in our countries, cities, workplaces, and homes. It is sad that humans have made so many weapons for the sake of protecting themselves from each other. We want to be safe and yet we fight for our own sense of justice.

What a great day it will be when God can fulfill his promise of bringing true justice and peace to the earth. If you are worried about the strife of today, look expectantly toward the time when all of humanity will once again be at peace. This is his promise to us.

Jesus, it is hard to imagine a world without war and heartbreak, yet I long for that day. Help me to bring a small portion of this peace into my sphere of influence today.

> *"I will betroth you to me forever; I will betroth you in righteousness and justice, in love and compassion. I will betroth you in faithfulness, and you will acknowledge the LORD."*
>
> HOSEA 2:19-20 NIV

Unlike some of the human vows we make, God's promise is forever. When he returns to complete his kingdom on earth, we will experience true righteousness, justice, and the fullness of love. While we are still waiting, God has work for us to do.

God wants to work through you so people can see his heart that is geared toward justice, peace, and love. Were you able to represent some of these things today? Let God speak to you tonight about how you can make a difference in your part of the world.

God, I am passionate about justice and peace. Thank you for creating within me a heart that cares about this world and what happens in it. Give me ideas and energy to contribute toward goodwill on earth.

What actions could you take that can represent God's justice, love, and peace to the world?

Sure as the Sun

*"Let us acknowledge the LORD; let us press on to acknowledge him.
As surely as the sun rises, he will appear."*

HOSEA 6:3 NIV

The weather can be frustratingly unpredictable. A few balmy,
sunny days awaken our senses to the freshness of spring
air and promise the end of winter. We fall into bed after
hours of sunshine and laughter, only to reawaken to a white
blanket covering any evidence of warmth. The sun hides
behind winter clouds that tease us as though they know of our
longing for the great light they cover. When the sun finally
re-emerges, we are bathed in instant warmth.

Jesus is with us in every season. At times we feel the cold of
winter, at times we feel a warm breeze, and still other times
we welcome the freshness of the rain. Jesus is our constant
presence in it all. Whatever the weather is like out there
today, know that he is with you.

*I thank you, Jesus, that you are forever near to me, no matter what
season of life I am in.*

> *"He will come to us like the winter rains,*
> *like the spring rains that water the earth."*
>
> HOSEA 6:3 NIV

Our lives have winters, don't they? We live through seasons where we feel cold, hidden, and trapped. We feel buried under the snow of circumstance with an absence of clarity, warmth, and light. But, if we looked closer, perhaps we could see the rushing of the clouds, the gilded outlines that promise there is hope just past them. And though winter can be long, the moment when the sun returns will be worth it all.

Perhaps you are in the middle of one of life's winters. Remember that for every winter there is a spring. As you press in to him, he will come to you like the sun rushing from behind the clouds. You have only to wait, to hope, and to look for him.

Heavenly Father, your presence has been with me today and will be with me tomorrow. I know that I can trust in you, come what may.

What season of life do you feel you are in now? Can you see Jesus in this season?

Mercy not Sacrifice

"I desire mercy, not sacrifice, and acknowledgment of God rather than burnt offerings."

HOSEA 6:6 NIV

Just as we would not be particularly romanced by someone proving their love by surrendering their belongings, God does not want our sacrifices.

We don't need to make a grand gesture, we just need to sit down and read his Word. He wants us to want him more than anything. He doesn't want our stuff.

God, I want to be with you. Thank you that I don't have to prove my love in grand gestures and that you are pleased with my desire to know you. Help me to know you more even today.

*"As at Adam, they have broken the covenant;
they were unfaithful to me there."*

HOSEA 6:7 NIV

You may think that you haven't proven your interest in God because your day seemed meaningless. You might not have done anything spiritual or particularly worthy of praise.

Right now, however, you have chosen to sit down and think about the Lord. This is what he is after—your heart, right here and right now.

God, I sometimes want to do more spiritual things, thinking that you might be more impressed with that. Thank you that I don't have to impress you. Let me rest tonight in the assurance that all you want is my love.

When you consider the only sacrifice the Lord wants from you is some of your undivided attention, that all you need to offer him is your interest, what happens in your heart? Share this with him tonight.

Put in the Hard Work

I said, "Plant the good seeds of righteousness, and you will harvest a crop of love. Plow up the hard ground of your hearts, for now is the time to seek the Lord, that he may come and shower righteousness upon you."

HOSEA 10:12 NIV

There isn't a lot in life that you get for free without putting hard work into it. We need to work for a living, we need to train to get fit, we need to gather and prepare ingredients to make our meals. The effort that you put into any of these tasks is usually shown in the result.

An advancement in your career, being able to run a much greater distance, or producing delicious, healthy meals all take that extra bit of effort. So it is with your faith. To be righteous you need to spend time with Jesus; to gain wisdom, you need to study his Word. Put the effort in and see what remarkable results will come your way.

Jesus, thank you for this opportunity right now to spend time reading a few Scriptures. Remind me to be more conscious of you throughout the day so I can keep my heart soft toward your will.

"You have cultivated wickedness and harvested a thriving crop of sins. You have eaten the fruit of lies—trusting in your military might, believing that great armies could make your nation safe."

HOSEA 10:13 NIV

How quickly people are to turn to other things to save them. God gives us all the same, simple, strategy. He didn't promise that his ways would be easy work, but he did promise that his ways would bring prosperity.

Have you been tempted to turn to other things that seem like they will bring you better strength, protection, and enjoyment? We can't trust the things of this world to keep us safe. It is God alone who saves, so put your complete trust in him and continue to plant those seeds of righteousness.

Lord God, I am sorry when I have turned my trust toward things of the world. Thank you for reminding me of your power and strength. I know that you are the only thing that is truly reliable in my life. I return to your ways this evening.

What things have you been relying on that you need to submit to God?

A Father's Heart

"It was I who taught Ephraim to walk; I took them up by their arms, but they did not know that I healed them."

HOSEA 11:3 ESV

Have you ever watched a father take his children up into his arms and carry them with ease? A good father looks after his children and directs them in the right way. He keeps them safe and tends to them when they are hurt. It's heartbreaking to think that a child with a father as good as this would not recognize or acknowledge the loving care that has been shown.

This is the anguish that God expresses here. Don't make the same mistake. Consider how your loving Father has carried you through difficult times and acknowledge him for it today.

Loving Father, I thank you so much for caring for me each day. Thank you for the times when I have needed to be picked up and carried by you. Thank you that you have healed me when my heart has been broken.

*"I led them with cords of kindness, with the bands of love,
and I became to them as one who eases the yoke on their jaws,
and I bent down to them and fed them."*

HOSEA 11:4 ESV

Have you seen the Father's kindness and love toward you
today? Have you been grateful for the provision of a home,
food, and transportation? He is a Father that cares enough to
notice when things are getting heavy and he does what he can
to relieve you of your burdens.

As you rest in his presence tonight, let him take the yoke of
heaviness from your shoulders. Let him feed you with the
nourishment of his Word and refresh you with the presence
of his Holy Spirit.

*Father, I acknowledge this evening that you have taken care of me
in so many ways. Thank you for your provision. Help me to rest in
the care that you have for me.*

What do you need from your heavenly Father right now?
Ask him, knowing that he cares for you.

He Will Not Give Up

"Oh, how can I give you up, Israel? How can I let you go? How can I destroy you like Admah or demolish you like Zeboiim? My heart is torn within me, and my compassion overflows."

HOSEA 11:8 NLT

Have you ever experienced love that you didn't want to give up on? It could have been a romantic relationship, or a relative, or even one of your children who has rebelled against you. It doesn't seem to matter how wrong that person has been, your love for them drives you back to that person, again and again.

This is the intense love that God has for his children. Even though they had rejected him, he expresses his unquenchable desire to have them return to him. If you have felt yourself distant from God, remember that he will never give up on you.

God, it is heartbreaking to know that you experience such anguish over your children that have turned their backs on you. I am so grateful that you will never give up on any of us. Thank you for pursuing me with your love. Help me to be loyal to you.

"No, I will not unleash my fierce anger. I will not completely destroy Israel, for I am God and not a mere mortal. I am the Holy One living among you, and I will not come to destroy."

HOSEA 11:9 NLT

Israel didn't deserve to be saved from their sin. They had willingly broken the covenant with God and they knew what the consequence of their sin was. But this is the amazing love that God is all about. His very character won't let him give up on his people. He could have unleashed his anger, he could have destroyed Israel. Instead of destruction, he sought restoration.

If you have been in a place of stubbornness toward God, let his unrelenting love for you cause you to turn to him. Face him with your questions, your pain, and your needs, and allow his compassion to give you peace.

God, I have so many unanswered questions and doubts and I don't always want to show you my frustration and anger. Thank you that you are a God of restoration and that you long for me to return to you. This evening I give you my heart.

What has been in the way of you turning to God? Know that he is not giving up on you.

The Cedar Tree

"My people will again live under my shade. They will flourish like grain and blossom like grapevines. They will be as fragrant as the wines of Lebanon. 'O Israel, stay away from idols! I am the one who answers your prayers and cares for you. I am like a tree that is always green; all your fruit comes from me.'"

HOSEA 14:7-8 NLT

God doesn't just keep us alive, he wants us to be fully alive. When we return to him, he makes us flourish like vines and be as valuable as fine wine.

God doesn't hold back with his restoration for you. Return to him so you can experience the fullness of his grace and love. He will provide for you, he will bring health to you, and he will always be there to protect you, just as a strong cedar tree protects anything underneath it. Stay in his shelter today.

God, thank you for an image of you that reminds me of your power, your strength, your stability, and your protection. Thank you that I can take refuge under your branches today. Help me to become the person that you intended me to be—full of life and love.

> *"Let those who are wise understand these things. Let those with discernment listen carefully. The paths of the LORD are true and right, and righteous people live by walking in them. But in those paths sinners stumble and fall."*
>
> HOSEA 14:9 NLT

Did you feel like you were a flourishing vine or valuable wine when you were out and about today? Sometimes you have to just know that God is working in you, because others may not want to know about the truth that you live by. There are always going to be people who refuse to hear the truth of God's Word.

Although we know the path to righteousness, it will cause those with stubborn hearts to fall. It is important to listen carefully to what God's Word really says and means. Ask God for wisdom when you are unsure, and know that his answers will always be true and right. Don't stray from his Word.

God, I want to walk in your ways. You are holy and righteous and though I can't attain to that in my own strength, I know that I can walk rightly because of the grace that Jesus brought through the cross. Give me answers that I am confident have come from your Word.

Are you seeking answers from the Lord right now? Ask him to help you discern what is true and right.

Return to Me

"Even now," declares the LORD, "return to me with all your heart,
with fasting and weeping and mourning."

JOEL 2:12 NIV

God's grace is always available, always accessible, and yet it is important to remember the sacrifice that he had to offer for your forgiveness. Sometimes we need to take the time to grieve the consequence of wrong actions and attitudes and acknowledge the seriousness of turning away from the Lord.

When we return, we need to do it with all sincerity of heart. As you get ready to go into another day full of all kinds of activities, don't lose your way; stay on the path God has set before you.

God, I don't want to stray from you because I know that it comes with consequences that I don't need in my life. Be a constant reminder to me as I make decisions throughout my day.

Rend your heart and not your garments. Return to the LORD your God, for he is gracious and compassionate, slow to anger and abounding in love, and he relents from sending calamity.

JOEL 2:13 NIV

God doesn't just want us to act like we are remorseful, he wants it to come from the heart. True remorse isn't about whether you can prove that you are sorry, but whether you actually feel a deep longing to make things right.

God does not want you to face calamity, he is ready for your repentance, ready to forgive, and eager to welcome you home.

God, you are slow to anger and abounding in love, which makes me so grateful that I can boldly approach you, knowing that you will forgive me. Keep me in your presence so I will never want to walk away from you.

Do you regret anything that happened today? Be free from your guilt and hand it over to your compassionate God.

Overflowing

*Rejoice, you people of Jerusalem! Rejoice in the L*ORD *your God!*
For the rain he sends demonstrates his faithfulness. Once more
the autumn rains will come, as well as the rains of spring.

JOEL 2:23 NLT

Waking up to a new day can feel like a fresh start, or it can
feel like a here-we-go-again kind of day. Whatever way
your thoughts lean this morning, consider that God doesn't
want you to feel dry and thirsty. He wants to fill you with his
refreshing, living water.

If you are experiencing a season of feeling disheartened, or
not feeling much at all, ask God for the refreshing rain, the
kind that gives you a spring in your step for what lies ahead.

God, I am so glad that you want to water me with your joy this
morning. Help me to come out of my apathy and feel refreshed in
your presence.

The threshing floors will again be piled high with grain,
and the presses will overflow with new wine and olive oil.

JOEL 2:24 NLT

At times we experience feeling completely empty of spiritual motivation. Our lives may not be heading in the direction we had intended, and we wonder where God's plan and timing fits into it all.

Perhaps you are waiting and hoping for long held dreams to come true, or maybe you have begun to feel that God is calling you to something greater. Let God speak to you about his overflowing presence. He wants you to live life in the abundance of his grace and love, so you can step out into those new things.

Jesus, you are the only one who can fill my soul to overflowing. Bring those things into my life that will allow me to experience your abundance of grace and then give me the strength to step out into the new things you are calling me into.

What areas of your life have seemed empty and in need of God's presence?

Spiritual Prophecy

*"I will pour out my spirit on all flesh; your sons and your
daughters shall prophesy, your old men shall dream dreams,
and your young men shall see visions."*

JOEL 2:28 NRSV

Before Jesus came to earth, God revealed himself through
the prophets who spoke his words to his people. God always
planned for there to be a time when he would speak directly
to his children, through the Holy Spirit.

We are part of the other side of this prophesy. We have
received the Holy Spirit and God is able to speak through us.
He will even give us dreams and visions. Have you asked God
for these, believing that he can and will speak to you?

*Holy Spirit, thank you that your presence is for everyone who
believes in the name of Jesus. Help me to hear your voice in my day
today, and let me respond with belief that you are speaking.*

"Even on the male and female slaves,
in those days, I will pour out my spirit."

JOEL 2:29 NRSV

God's Spirit was always intended for everyone. Even though God had chosen Israel as a nation to speak through, his plan has always been for all of humanity. When Jesus came to earth, he showed that his mercy and grace was for all people.

We now know that there is no separation for those who are in Christ Jesus. God is speaking through you and he is speaking through others. Have you been listening?

Holy Spirit, thank you that you do not show favoritism toward any kind of person. I know that you are able to speak through others. At times, I am skeptical about your voice, so please give me the ability to recognize your voice when you speak.

What is the Holy Spirit saying to you tonight?

Our Stronghold

The LORD roars from Zion, and utters his voice from Jerusalem, and the heavens and the earth shake. But the LORD is a refuge for his people, a stronghold for the people of Israel.

JOEL 3:16 NRSV

In times of war, people seek refuge in places that are built and fortified to protect against attacks. These places were called strongholds and the people in that day would have known where to go when they were faced with trouble.

When God says he is the stronghold, he is saying that when trouble comes, he is ready to protect you. If you are feeling uncertainty and perhaps even fear about your day, run to the Lord. He is your refuge today.

God, in those times where I need refuge, I choose to turn to you. Thank you for protecting me from harm when I seek you out.

"You shall know that I, the LORD your God, dwell in Zion,
my holy mountain. And Jerusalem shall be holy,
and strangers shall never again pass through it."

JOEL 3:17 NRSV

You may have come home from a day that felt exhausting
or one that didn't go well because of pressures or even
arguments. Thank God that you have a new day to look
forward to, and that you also have his true rule and reign to
look ahead to.

One day God's kingdom will be fully here and we will live in
peace and safety, never again experiencing a day of fear or
anxiety. Praise God that his promise will come true.

God, I submit my thoughts and feelings about this day to you. Right
now I just need to rest in your presence and to get perspective with
the knowledge that you will make all things right in your time.

What are your current fears and anxieties? Seek out God as
your stronghold in this time.

Punishment for Evil

> *Thus says the LORD: "For three transgressions of Edom, and for four, I will not revoke the punishment; because he pursued his brother with the sword and cast off all pity; he maintained his anger perpetually, and kept his wrath forever."*
>
> AMOS 1:11 NRSV

God is a God of justice and will not let evil go unpunished. There are many days when we ask why God would allow certain things to happen, and although we will never quite understand, it is good to know that God does not tolerate those who show no mercy.

God will not revoke the punishment for those who are evil with no remorse for their actions. If you are faced with questions of justice this week, remember that God longs that his people show mercy.

God, you are a God of mercy and justice. I don't understand a lot of what goes on in this world, and I am sometimes overwhelmed at the thought of evil. But I trust in your goodness and wisdom.

"I will send a fire on Teman,
and it shall devour the strongholds of Bozrah."

Amos 1:12 NRSV

There is nothing that can withstand the power of God.
Although evil may have some temporary hold on the earth,
God will ultimately win this spiritual battle. There is no
refuge in people or places that choose evil over good.

At times we look at our world and wonder why people would
ever get involved in such systems of injustice. These people
have been deceived by the enemy. In time, God will destroy
these strongholds. You don't need to fear evil because you
have been saved and protected by the awesome and powerful
God of all creation.

Jesus, thank you that you rescued me from the power of death and
evil through your demonstration of abundant love on the cross.
Give me the peace of knowing that I am protected in that mighty
love tonight.

Are you holding on to any kind of fear? Let God break down
those strongholds and give you peace instead of anxiety.

Formation

*The LORD is the one who shaped the mountains, stirs up the winds,
and reveals his thoughts to mankind.*

AMOS 4:13 NLT

We often talk about the power and love of God, and indeed
these qualities shape our understanding of him. When we
read and experience all that he has created, we also perceive
him as an intelligent and creative God. To form the splendor
of the mountains and crafted the wind to shape waves on the
ocean are just some of his many visual testimonies of brilliant
creativity.

God has put that creativity in your heart and mind—you
are his image-bearer. Whatever you may be doing today be
encouraged to tap into this resource of imagination.

*God, I don't always see myself as a creative person or a person who
has time to be creative. Open my eyes to see all the different forms
of creativity and help me to use it throughout my day.*

He turns the light of dawn into darkness and treads on the heights of the earth. The LORD God of Heaven's Armies is his name!

AMOS 4:13 NLT

As the light gives way to darkness tonight, think of the Creator of the universe who thought up the whole system of the sun and moon, day and night. It is incredible to think of all that God has imagined for earth, and yet his creativity did not stop there.

God is also the Creator of the known universe and everything in the heavens. Let his greatness overwhelm your mind and heart, knowing with certainty that he is in control of everything.

Heavenly Father, you have created such a wonderful world and I am thankful for all the creation that I have been able to appreciate today. Help me to see your beauty all around me as I go into tomorrow. May I be reminded of your greatness.

How did you notice God's creativity today?

Seek Good, Hate Evil

Seek good and not evil, that you may live; so the Lord *God of hosts will be with you, as you have spoken.*

Amos 5:14 NKJV

We are not always naturally good people; we have to go out of our way to find goodness. There are so many things that tempt us away from our dedication to God, and this is why it can be hard to find the path to goodness. However, it is worth finding the way of the righteous because God promises to be with you and give you fullness of life.

As you go into your day, find the good in people and situations instead of seeking evil. God is with you.

God, thank you that you are a God of all goodness. Help me to walk in this goodness and to do everything that I can to avoid evil. Thank you for being near to me this morning.

Hate evil, love good; establish justice in the gate. It may be that the
Lord God of hosts will be gracious to the remnant of Joseph.

Amos 5:15 NKJV

When we seek out goodness, we begin to love it and then
depend on it. The same is true of evil. That's why it is
important to hate all forms of evil. Don't even go near it.

We need to stand up for the truth of God's Word and at times
that means that you act as a gatekeeper to your heart and to
the community of faith that you are a part of. God wants to
be gracious to you tonight; he wants to restore good things in
place of the difficulties.

*God, help me to be someone who stands up for justice in my
community. Give me ways I can help the cause of those who are
less fortunate or need to know your goodness. Give me strength to
be gracious, just as you are gracious to me.*

What form of justice do you need to stand up for today?

Misfortunes

"Do not gloat over the day of your brother in the day of his misfortune; do not rejoice over the people of Judah in the day of their ruin; do not boast in the day of distress."

OBADIAH 1:12 ESV

When we see people get what we think they deserve, we often feel a sense of satisfaction or relief. It is interesting that we even put ourselves in the position of thinking that we know what other people deserve; it's simply another form of judgment—a right reserved for God alone.

Instead of gloating or rejoicing in the consequences that others are experiencing for their actions, be compassionate toward them. We can hate sin but love the person; this is the way of Christ.

Jesus, I am sorry when I have been glad for others' misfortunes. I know that sometimes this is from jealously or a real dislike for the person, or even because I have hated what they have done. I pray that you would give me a heart of compassion when people experience misfortune or distress.

*"Do not enter the gate of my people in the day of their calamity;
do not gloat over his disaster in the day of his calamity;
do not loot his wealth in the day of his calamity."*

OBADIAH 1:12 ESV

Did you have an opportunity to show compassion toward someone today? Sometimes we are not involved in the downfall of a person, but we can be pretty good at kicking a person while they are down. It might not be anything that you do, but perhaps you have allowed yourself to gossip about that person's pity and revel in the drama of it all.

Be on guard against these behaviors; don't take advantage of others' weaknesses. Do everything that you can to uplift the fallen.

God, I know that you love everyone equally and want the best for all your children. I pray for those who are reaping the consequences of bad decisions or attitudes and ask that they would be drawn toward repentance and a right relationship with you.

When have you rejoiced in the consequence a person has brought on themselves? Ask God to change your heart toward that person.

Blame

Then the sailors said to each other, "Come, let us cast lots to find out who is responsible for this calamity." They cast lots and the lot fell on Jonah. So they asked him, "Tell us, who is responsible for making all this trouble for us? What kind of work do you do? Where do you come from? What is your country? From what people are you?" He answered, "I am a Hebrew and worship the Lord, the God of heaven, who made the sea and the dry land."

JONAH 1:8-9 NIV

We are wired to find someone to blame when things go wrong. When the storms of life come, we want to know who is responsible and who we can complain to or get angry with. Often we will blame God because we know that he is in control and we can't understand why he would allow, or even cause, terrible things to happen.

There's nothing wrong with wondering why things are happening, but we still need to trust that God is in control. If things don't quite go your way today, you have some choices. You can look for someone to blame, or you can trust God to help you figure it out.

Today, God, if things go wrong, I ask that you provide me with self-control, so I can fight the urge to blame someone or to gossip about what others have done wrong. Give me the wisdom to ask you for help when I need it.

This terrified them and they asked, "What have you done?"
(They knew he was running away from the LORD, because he had
already told them so.) The sea was getting rougher and rougher.
So they asked him, "What should we do to you to make the sea
calm down for us?" "Pick me up and throw me into the sea,"
he replied, "and it will become calm. I know that it is my fault
that this great storm has come upon you."

JONAH 1:10-12 NIV

Accepting blame is a humble and honorable thing to do. It is
never easy to admit when you have been wrong and to allow
people to be disappointed in what you have done. In some
cases, it can be so shameful and take many years to walk
through the pain of remorse and regret.

God always wants us to be honest with him and with others.
If you feel like you need to come clean with anything, ask
God for the strength to reply with honesty, as Jonah did. Just
remember that God's grace is always available to you.

Lord Jesus, I am sorry when I have tried to avoid or hide my mistakes.
Help me to be strong and humble enough to admit my mistakes and
show remorse, and then to accept the consequences with dignity.

Is there anything you need to humbly accept blame for
tonight? Repent and be free from it.

Hurled into the Sea

"You hurled me into the depths, into the very heart of the seas, and the currents swirled about me; all your waves and breakers swept over me. I said, 'I have been banished from your sight; yet I will look again toward your holy temple.'"

JONAH 2:3-4 NIV

It doesn't matter whether you feel like you are drowning because you have intentionally walked away from God or whether circumstances have simply overwhelmed you. Expressing how you feel about being distant from God or grace is important.

If you feel like this today, tell God. In the same way that you express your sorrow, be intentional about directing your words and heart toward God. Look toward his holy temple, not away from it. God is near and will answer your cries.

God, at times I do feel like I am drowning. I feel stressed or anxious about everything that I have to get done today. Although I may feel distant from you, I choose to look toward you and trust you for answers.

"The engulfing waters threatened me, the deep surrounded me; seaweed was wrapped around my head. To the roots of the mountains I sank down; the earth beneath barred me in forever. But you, Lord my God, brought my life up from the pit."

JONAH 2:5-6 NIV

You can probably remember times in your life where you felt like you hit rock bottom. Perhaps today has been one of those days you didn't feel like you could sink any lower. We all have those days, or those seasons, in our lives and they can feel lonely, desperate, and discouraging.

Think of Jonah tonight and how he must have felt. There are people throughout history and there are people right now who have been in the deepest of pits—you are not alone. Let your life be a testimony that God does indeed bring you out of the pit. Rejoice in the fact that God will always rescue his children.

God, as I reflect tonight on those low points in my life, I know that you were with me, hearing my cries for help. Thank you for providing a way out and being my strength and source of life while I was going through it. May I always testify to your mercy and help.

Do you remember the moments when God has lifted you from those pits of life? Rejoice and praise him for those times.

A Quick Response

"Let people and animals be covered with sackcloth. Let everyone call urgently on God. Let them give up their evil ways and their violence. Who knows? God may yet relent and with compassion turn from his fierce anger so that we will not perish."

JONAH 3:8-9 NIV

We are trained to respond quickly when we hear warnings of impending danger. If an alarm sounds for fire, we have an exit plan and know to leave the premises immediately. If the media issues a storm warning, we take cover. When Jonah delivered the message of God's wrath on the people of Nineveh, the king was quick to react. He called for everyone to repent, give up their ways and throw themselves at the mercy of God.

Could you say that you would respond so quickly if told to repent? As you get ready for the day ahead, be prepared to act quickly when God speaks to you.

Holy Spirit, be my guide today. Help me to always be ready for those important divinely inspired opportunities. Help me to know your voice and to be quick to respond.

*When God saw what they did and how they turned from
their evil ways, he relented and did not bring on them
the destruction he had threatened.*

JONAH 3:10 NIV

God is also quick to respond to your cries for forgiveness.
When we recognize our failures and mistakes and ask for
God's mercy, he is waiting to tell you that you are loved and
accepted.

God sent Jesus into this world to ensure that the consequence
of humanity's sins had been erased. In doing so, he released
us from the destruction of our ways. Accept his grace tonight
and begin to live in the freedom of knowing that you are
worthy in his kingdom.

*Father, I turn from my own ways tonight. I know that I often
choose to pursue the wrong things, but I thank you that you love
me enough to gently warn me when I am going astray. I come back
to you this evening and rest in your merciful arms.*

Is God speaking to you about repentance tonight?

I Knew It

This was very displeasing to Jonah, and he became angry. He prayed to the L ORD and said, "O L ORD! Is not this what I said while I was still in my own country? That is why I fled to Tarshish at the beginning; for I knew that you are a gracious God and merciful, slow to anger, and abounding in steadfast love, and ready to relent from punishing."

JONAH 4:1-2 NRSV

We can be pretty good judges of character, especially when we know someone well enough and have seen repeat behaviors and actions from them. This is why Jonah was so upset with God. He couldn't see the point in declaring destruction on a people when he knew that the character of God was to be merciful.

Instead of being glad that God was proving true to his good and loving character, Jonah was mad that God had made him do a seemingly pointless job. This morning, God might ask you to speak words on his behalf. Don't worry about the outcome; just be obedient.

Holy Spirit, speak to me right now so I can be confident of the things that you want me to say today. Give me the ability to know when to speak, and help me to have a heart attitude that wants restoration not retribution.

"Now, O Lord, please take my life from me, for it is better for me to die than to live." And the Lord said, "Is it right for you to be angry?"

JONAH 4:3-4 NRSV

One can only imagine that Jonah wanted to die because he felt so humiliated. After all, he had been preaching doom and destruction, and instead the people of Nineveh got restoration and healing.

You may never understand the way God works, but hopefully you know in your heart that God is forever pursuing the lost and even in his frustration and anger, he still chooses compassion and mercy over wrath. It is not your right to be angry about the way God acts; instead, in humility, submit your feelings to him and acknowledge his authority.

God, I can get so frustrated with what I see going on around me and I don't know why you let it happen. But forgive my anger, because I know it is really just ignorance and lack of having your knowledge. Replace my anger with peace as I go to sleep tonight.

What are you angry with God about? Share your heart with him tonight.

In the Shade

"Everyone shall sit under his vine and under his fig tree,
And no one shall make them afraid;
For the mouth of the Lord of hosts has spoken."

MICAH 4:4 NKJV

If you have ever been in a hot dry place during the middle of the day, you will know how much even a small amount of shade is sought after. When you find that shade you feel relieved and immediately better out of the scorching sun.

God has put in the heart of his people a longing to be in the shade of his presence. He is the one that protects us and nourishes us. This morning, you may have a lot of work to do and it might be hard. Look forward to those moments when God provides you with his shade of rest and revival.

God, I ask for endurance to get through this day. Help me to find moments of rest and joy, knowing that you have me covered.

> *"All people walk each in the name of his god,*
> *But we will walk in the name of the* LORD *our God*
> *Forever and ever."*
>
> MICAH 4:5 NKJV

There is a big difference between you and those who do not know God. It might feel like we are just ordinary people, but we are walking on an entirely different path from those who don't believe in the saving grace of Jesus.

You have chosen to walk in the name of the one true God and this gives you the hope of eternity. You may be feeling insignificant or discouraged after a long day, so take some time to dwell on the hope you have through Christ. Think about how you can share this light with the world, so they too may walk in the hope of the one true God.

God, tonight I see that although my days might seem insignificant, I am walking in your path and it is lighting my way. Help me to reach others with your light.

How can you see that your life is different from unbelievers?

What Is Required

With what shall I come before the Lord and bow down before the exalted God? Shall I come before him with burnt offerings, with calves a year old? Will the Lord be pleased with thousands of rams, with ten thousand rivers of olive oil? Shall I offer my firstborn for my transgression, the fruit of my body for the sin of my soul?

MICAH 6:6-7 NIV

We can try so hard to earn the favor of God. You might be involved in serving at church, going to the local mission, or spending dedicated time each day in his presence. These are really remarkable things to do for God... as long as you remember that he doesn't require this of you in order to please him.

God loves you and his entire creation so much. As you reflect on his great love for you today, think of what he would want the most from you.

God, thank you that I don't have to earn your acceptance or do anything to make you love me more. I dedicate this day to you, spending time with you not because you require it of me, but because I love you.

He has shown you, O mortal, what is good. And what does the LORD require of you? To act justly and to love mercy and to walk humbly with your God.

MICAH 6:8 NIV

Have you been able to reflect on what God requires of you today? He doesn't need your sacrifice, or even the best of your best. He wants you to show the world what he is like, and that is to act with justice and mercy.

You won't have all the answers but you can trust that God will give you enough wisdom and love to treat others with kindness, respect, and forgiveness. He also wants to walk with you and has given his Holy Spirit to guide you in all truth. Take a hold of his hand tonight.

Lord God, thanks for making it simple for me. I know I can complicate things by trying to figure out what you want from me, so I am glad to be reminded that you just want me to walk with you in humility and to love others the way you do. Give me a fresh chance to do this tomorrow.

What things are you striving to please God with?

Trouble Will Pass

This is what the LORD says: "Although they have allies and are numerous, they will be destroyed and pass away. Although I have afflicted you, Judah, I will afflict you no more."

NAHUM 1:12 NIV

Some days we wake up feeling like there are too many things that will be against us. The weather is terrible, you're running late, you are not going to meet your deadline, and there's that relationship issue to sort out. It can feel like all those afflictions have arrived at your doorstep at once.

God knows when you are overwhelmed, and he is there to walk you through it. Live in the moment and do the best you can, knowing that one day there will be no more suffering or troubles coming your way.

Jesus, I look forward to the day when you take all these troubles away and when those things coming up against me will be destroyed. Until then, grant me patience and peace to get through one day at a time.

> *"I will break their yoke from your neck*
> *and tear your shackles away."*
>
> NAHUM 1:13 NIV

God is the great liberator of humankind. He never intended for us to be oppressed by sin and all the troubles of the world. Humanity put this on itself, and yet God provided a way out; he gave his only Son to win back our freedom.

You don't have to live like you are in slavery anymore; he has lifted your burden and removed the shackles from your feet. Dance, shout, and sing, for he has saved you and brought you into the fullness of truth.

Holy God, give me perspective tonight as I think about those things that are weighing me down. Release me of my troubles and take the shackles off me so I can live with a sense of freedom in my heart and mind.

What are your burdens tonight? Acknowledge that the Lord wants to lift these off you.

Future Promise

*"This vision is for a future time. It describes the end,
and it will be fulfilled. If it seems slow in coming, wait patiently,
for it will surely take place. It will not be delayed."*

HABAKKUK 2:3 NLT

Habakkuk was a great prophet of God, known for his
complaints. Many times he cried out to God for the end to evil
and war. Wherever he looked he saw violence and injustice
and he didn't see God answering his prayers for help.

We know too well what this is like. You only have to turn
on the news or read things on social media to feel like God
has deserted this world and left evil to run its course. Don't
be discouraged today. Wait patiently, trusting that God's
promises will come true. It may seem slow in coming, but it
will surely happen.

*God, I continue to cry out for your promises of peace and goodness
to be evident in this world. There is so much suffering, but I praise
you that you are working. Give your people patience as we do what
we can to bring goodness to your wonderful creation.*

"Look at the proud! They trust in themselves, and their lives are crooked. But the righteous will live by their faithfulness to God."

HABAKKUK 2:4 NLT

Have you been tempted to give up on God's promises and just live for yourself? Many do not have the patience or understanding to hold on to God's promises and therefore turn from God's ways. These are proud people, trusting in themselves, and it never ends well for them.

Be encouraged as you remain faithful to God and his Word that you will live in the fullness of his love and mercy. Your faith will lead you to his promises. One day you will see an end to suffering and be welcomed into the glory of eternal life.

God, it seems like it is taking a long time for you to make all things right again. Thank you that we now have the promise of your kingdom, seen in your Son, Jesus Christ. Help me to rest in the knowledge of the truth of your return tonight.

What are you discouraged about in the world tonight? Declare your trust and faithfulness to God in the middle of these frustrations.

Yet I Rejoice

Even though the fig trees have no blossoms, and there are no grapes on the vines; even though the olive crop fails, and the fields lie empty and barren; even though the flocks die in the fields, and the cattle barns are empty, yet I will rejoice in the LORD! I will be joyful in the God of my salvation!

HABAKKUK 3:17-18 NLT

Life is full of disappointments, and sometimes there are seasons when nothing goes your way. You may have an illness that you are still battling, you might have lost a job, or seen your children go through some hard times. You could replace this Scripture with your own words of sorrow. The difference between you and those who do not have Jesus, is that you have an internal peace and joy that goes beyond your circumstances.

You may be unwell, but you can still be grateful, you may have gone through hardships, but you still believe in God's provision. You may have lost much, but know that your treasure is in heaven. There is a lot to rejoice in the Lord for. May your life today be a witness of the hope of Christ within you.

Jesus, thank you so much for the salvation that you freely gave to me. I choose today to be joyful in the God of my salvation.

The Sovereign LORD *is my strength! He makes me as surefooted as a deer, able to tread upon the heights.*

HABAKKUK 3:19 NLT

A deer is a beautifully swift animal, able to navigate the toughest of terrains. This is our testament as his children—that even when things get steep and tricky, he makes our feet swift and nimble, giving us strength and surety as we walk through the hardships into the successful heights of the mountaintops.

Whether you are trying to navigate those difficult times, or have reached a mountaintop, praise the God who gives you strength and skill.

God, thank you so much for being my strength and giving my feet a sure place to land every time I need your help. I praise you for helping me through and bringing me to mountaintops.

Are you trying to walk through some difficult and intense times right now, or are you able to testify to the strength that God has given you to reach the other side?

Escaping Wrath

*Gather together, gather, O shameless nation, before you are driven
away like the drifting chaff, before there comes upon you the fierce
anger of the LORD, before there comes upon you the day
of the LORD's wrath.*

ZEPHANIAH 2:1-2 NRSV

It can be hard to hear about the anger or wrath of God when
we also know about his unending mercy and unfailing love.
We can, however, see God's mercy in the warnings that he
sent with the prophets.

God cannot tolerate evil; therefore, he gives people a chance
to turn away from their sin. This is his mercy. Ultimately,
we know that God provided a way out for the world, through
Jesus' life, death, and resurrection. God is good and will
always provide you with a way out.

*God, thank you for the day ahead of me. I know that you are not
an angry and vengeful God, so I choose to see your warnings as a
gracious act for humanity to turn away from wrong. Let me hear
your warnings clearly today.*

Seek the LORD, all you humble of the land, who do his commands;
seek righteousness, seek humility; perhaps you may be hidden on
the day of the LORD's wrath.

ZEPHANIAH 2:3 NRSV

We don't know what God's final judgment is going to look
like, but we don't need to fear it. When your heart remains
humble before your Creator, and you do your best to live in
his ways, you are surely covered from judgment.

Even when you stumble and make mistakes, God has made a
way, through Jesus, to not count those things against you. So,
lift your head high tonight, knowing that God will judge you
favorably.

Jesus, I am really thankful that I know you have saved me from
the consequences of sin. Provide me with peace as I rest in your
presence this evening.

Are you worried about God's judgment or wrath? Remember
Christ's saving grace and let your heart be at peace.

Fear Not

The Lord has taken away the judgments against you; he has cleared away your enemies. The King of Israel, the Lord, is in your midst; you shall never again fear evil. On that day it shall be said to Jerusalem: "Fear not, O Zion; let not your hands grow weak."

ZEPHANIAH 3:15-16 ESV

Fear can be crippling and seems to present itself in all kinds of different scenarios, from physical heights, work presentations, and tests, to waiting on medical news from the doctor. When we are full of fear, our bodies prepare us for flight or fight mode, but if neither of those kick in, the feeling of weakness or becoming faint is the next response.

Fear of enemies would have been a very real experience for the Israelites, and it would have meant such freedom for them to know that they would never again have to experience the fear of evil. The same promise can be for you today. God is in your midst and he says, "Fear not."

God, I bring my fears and anxieties to the foot of the cross, knowing that you have given me freedom from these troubles. Thank you that one day all evil will be gone, and I will have nothing to fear.

"The LORD your God is in your midst, a mighty one who will save; he will rejoice over you with gladness; he will quiet you by his love; he will exult over you with loud singing."

ZEPHANIAH 3:17 ESV

After the busyness of a full day, a little quiet time can go a long way. We have so many things coming at us—demands, discussions, decisions, distractions—it can be difficult to think straight or know where your emotions are.

As you think back over your day, see God in the middle of your situations. He is your rescuer and can quiet your spirit with the simple truth of knowing that you are loved. Your Creator rejoices over you simply because he loves you. Let the other things slip away as you focus on this truth.

Lord God, you are mighty and wonderful. Thank you that you know just what I need tonight, and that you are here with me to provide me with love and joy to quiet and refresh my soul.

What things of your day do you need to submit to Jesus, so he can quiet you with his love?

For the Outcast

"Behold, at that time I will deal with all your oppressors. And I will save the lame and gather the outcast, and I will change their shame into praise and renown in all the earth."

ZEPHANIAH 3:19 ESV

When your heart is moved by seeing people in poverty, or having experienced abuse of any form, or watching someone being treated as less than others, you are experiencing a small measure of the compassion that God has for those who have been oppressed. God cares immensely for the suffering that happens in this world, and one day he will restore everything to those who have suffered and experienced shame.

Today, if you see or experience some form of oppression, be someone who stands against it. Allow God's compassion in you to reach out to the outcast.

Jesus, I care deeply about people who have experienced being an outcast for any reason. Give me a chance to show compassion and considerate love to someone today.

"At that time I will bring you in, at the time when I gather you together; for I will make you renowned and praised among all the peoples of the earth, when I restore your fortunes before your eyes," *says the* Lord.

Zephaniah 3:20 esv

Did you take note of the oppressed or outcast today? God wants us to see people as he does, and to be as concerned as he is about injustice.

Don't just feel sorry for people, be someone who makes a change. It doesn't have to be a huge social action; simply start with making one person feel better about themselves. God is seeking restoration for these people and we don't need to wait until the final day. His kingdom is here and he is ready to use you.

God, give me eyes that see those who are feeling oppressed, lonely, and outcast. Give me wisdom to know how to help these people.

What opportunities do you have this week to dedicate to seeking justice or showing compassion for those who have been downtrodden or outcast?

God's House

"Why are you living in luxurious houses while my house lies in ruins?" This is what the Lord of Heaven's Armies says: "Look at what's happening to you! You have planted much but harvest little. You eat but are not satisfied. You drink but are still thirsty. You put on clothes but cannot keep warm. Your wages disappear as though you were putting them in pockets filled with holes!"

HAGGAI 1:4-6 NLT

The economy of God runs a whole lot different than our society's systems. It should be that when you gather enough money for yourself then you will be satisfied with a great house, plenty of clothes, and glorious food. This is the falsity of the world: that money is what offers you comfort and prosperity. In reality, God is the source of all these things.

Instead of hoarding money for yourself, be generous and build God's house. We don't need fancy church buildings, but we need a healthy church body. As you prepare for your day, think of ways you can bless others.

Father God, I am sorry when I have thought only of myself in terms of my earthly possessions. Help me to see beyond my circumstances today and look toward being able to bless the body of Christ.

This is what the LORD of Heaven's Armies says: "Look at what's happening to you! Now go up into the hills, bring down timber, and rebuild my house. Then I will take pleasure in it and be honored," says the LORD.

HAGGAI 1:7-8 NLT

We have no shortage of renovation shows on television because we all like to see something go from shoddy to beautiful. Are there ways that God might be calling you to help re-build his church?

God needs the church as a witness to his light and life and it is important that his presence can be shared through the body of believers. This is how you can honor him in this life: do whatever you can to encourage, uplift, serve, and love his house.

Jesus, I pray for your church, your precious bride, tonight. Encourage those who are leading these communities of faith; bring unity within congregations, and bring revival to your house. Remind me to continually encourage your people so your name will be glorified.

Is the Lord taking pleasure in how you are rebuilding his church?

Relentless Pursuit

"Sing and rejoice, O daughter of Zion! For behold, I am coming and I will dwell in your midst," says the Lord. "Many nations shall be joined to the Lord in that day, and they shall become My people. And I will dwell in your midst. Then you will know that the Lord of hosts has sent Me to you."

ZECHARIAH 2:10-11 NKJV

God never gave up on his people. Though they forgot him and scattered to other lands and served other gods, he pursued them with all his heart.

If you have woken up this morning, wondering if God wants to be near you, trust in the truth of his heart, which is shown so clearly in his Word. He is pursuing your heart and will not stop until you accept his love. Sing and rejoice: he is coming for you.

Heavenly Father, thank you for pursuing me until I have no choice but to surrender to the wonder of your love. Give me a day full of the knowledge that you want to surround me with your presence.

"The Lord will take possession of Judah as His inheritance in the Holy Land, and will again choose Jerusalem."

ZECHARIAH 2:12 NKJV

Again, and again, and again. This is our God. The One who goes out of his way to find the lost. The One who restores the broken to wholeness. The One who gave us back our fullness of life.

God is coming to reestablish his kingdom, started in the birth, death, and resurrection of Jesus. This kingdom will be even better than anyone could ever imagine.

God, thank you that your promises never fail. You are a God of mercy and love, and you have pursued your people so they would turn back to you. I need you to fill my life, in this moment, and heal my brokenness so I can live in your fullness of life.

Do you need God's restoration in your life? Give him your brokenness so he can make you whole.

Heart Motivations

*The word of the Lord Almighty came to me: "Ask all the people of
the land and the priests, 'When you fasted and mourned in the
fifth and seventh months for the past seventy years, was it really
for me that you fasted? And when you were eating and drinking,
were you not just feasting for yourselves? Are these not the words
the Lord proclaimed through the earlier prophets when Jerusalem
and its surrounding towns were at rest and prosperous, and the
Negev and the western foothills were settled?"*

ZECHARIAH 7:4-7 NIV

We can go through all the right Christian expectations: going
to church, fasting, tithing, and serving. We can help out with
missions and take communion or recite liturgy. All these
things are excellent Christian disciplines, but we need to
examine our heart motivations for why we are doing them.

If we seek these things for praise from others, or because it
somehow fills our own expectations, then they aren't worth
a whole lot to God. He wants you to be motivated to do things
for him because you love just as he does.

*God, as I go into my day I pray you would help me to examine
my heart and why I am doing the various things that I am doing.
Give me the same love that you have for others, so my actions truly
come from my heart.*

> *The word of the LORD came again to Zechariah:*
> *"This is what the LORD Almighty said: 'Administer true*
> *justice; show mercy and compassion to one another. Do not*
> *oppress the widow or the fatherless, the foreigner or the poor.*
> *Do not plot evil against each other.'"*

ZECHARIAH 7:8-10 NIV

While our efforts to live a disciplined Christian life are good and honorable, it is always wise to examine whether these disciplines are leading toward compassion for others.

If your daily prayers, fasting, and service to the church is resulting in justice for the oppressed, mercy for the sinner, and provision for the poor, then this is something worth celebrating.

Father, I take this time tonight to examine my heart motivations behind all the Christian works that I do. Show me areas that are affected by the wrong motivation and encourage me to keep doing those things that are closest to your heart.

What Christian discipline do you have in place that is producing true justice? Keep it up.

The Faithful City

The LORD says: "I am returning to Mount Zion, and I will live in Jerusalem. Then Jerusalem will be called the Faithful City; the mountain of the LORD of Heaven's Armies will be called the Holy Mountain." This is what the LORD of Heaven's Armies says: "Once again old men and women will walk Jerusalem's streets with their canes and will sit together in the city squares. And the streets of the city will be filled with boys and girls at play."

ZECHARIAH 8:3-5 NLT

It is a scene that is played out in movies, books, and even in our imaginations. People sitting together, talking and enjoying one another's company. Children playing games in the streets, completely safe, laughing, and relishing in the freedom of life.

These ideals of life are exactly how God wants us to look forward to his kingdom. He wants us to know that one day there will be conversations, peace, fun, laughter, and connectedness. Allow yourself to dream a little as you prepare for the day.

God, thank you for giving me a beautiful picture to enter my day with. Thank you that I see glimpses of your kingdom happening even now and that this reminds me that your kingdom is here on earth. I pray we would see the fullness of that kingdom soon.

*This is what the L*ord *of Heaven's Armies says: "All this may seem impossible to you now, a small remnant of God's people. But is it impossible for me?" says the L*ord *of Heaven's Armies.*

Zechariah 8:6 nlt

We can approach the newness of a day with hope and vision for the future, but somehow by the end of the day we can start to doubt and despair. It seems impossible sometimes to think that one day everything will be perfect and beyond our wildest dreams.

God anticipates that we will feel this way. Perhaps the edge has been taken off your hope by the worries of the day. Listen to him say to you, "Is it impossible for me?" The answer is, of course not. We are weak, but he is strong.

Jesus, thank you that nothing is impossible for you and when you say that this world is going to be perfect and complete, I should believe it. Renew and invigorate my heart with your promises tonight.

What do you need to believe God for this evening?

Punishment to Protection

This is what the LORD of Heaven's Armies says: "I was determined to punish you when your ancestors angered me, and I did not change my mind," says the LORD of Heaven's Armies. "But now I am determined to bless Jerusalem and the people of Judah. So don't be afraid."

ZECHARIAH 8:14-15 NLT

We see the wrestling between God's mercy and love all throughout the Old Testament. God calls his people to turn back to him and do it his way, they disobey, they are punished. Yet, so many times, God turns from punishing to protecting. His heart was always to bless his people, not destroy them.

If you are wondering this morning whether God is trying to punish you for something, remember his words to his people. He is determined to bless you, so don't be afraid.

God, sometimes I feel like you should be angry with me for all my selfish ways. Thank you for your astounding love that leads you to be merciful to me. Help this love to get rid of any fear that is in my heart.

"'This is what you must do: Tell the truth to each other. Render verdicts in your courts that are just and that lead to peace. Don't scheme against each other. Stop your love of telling lies that you swear are the truth. I hate all these things," says the LORD.

ZECHARIAH 8:16-17 NLT

God's mercy should lead us to righteousness. He freely gives his grace, and yet he expectantly hopes that you will begin to walk in his ways. He wants truth, and peace, and unity between people.

When you start to think that he is a vengeful God, look at his instructions to his people and understand that he wants goodness to reign in the hearts of his people so love will spread to the ends of the earth.

Lord Jesus, I know that you want honesty and truth, so I ask that the Holy Spirit would illuminate those areas of my life where I am not being completely honest. Give me the boldness to ask for forgiveness if I have caused others harm with false words.

Are there areas of your life where you can see that you have been dishonest? Do you need to release truth into those situations?

On That Day

On that day there shall be no light, cold, or frost. And there shall be a unique day, which is known to the LORD, neither day nor night, but at evening time there shall be light.

ZECHARIAH 14:6–7 ESV

Have you ever been to a country where the light shines all the way through the night? It is a strange sensation to be able to go outside as if it is day and yet it is actually midnight.

It will indeed be a unique day when Jesus returns, but it isn't something to fear; it is something to look forward to. As you go through your day, watching the temperature get warmer and the sky get darker, remember the hope you have for your eternal future.

God, I marvel at what the day is going to be like when you return once again. I know I cannot even begin to imagine the beauty of your light, but I thank you for a glimpse into the beauty of that day.

On that day living waters shall flow out from Jerusalem, half of them to the eastern sea and half of them to the western sea. It shall continue in summer as in winter. And the LORD will be king over all the earth. On that day the LORD will be one and his name one.

ZECHARIAH 14:8-9 ESV

We spend our lives thinking about vacations in the sun; we must be wired to want to live in warmth and light. The picture of waters forever flowing, not freezing up in the winter, is a sign of God's eternal reign.

You may have had a long and tiring day and feel drained of all energy. This is our experience on earth, but it will not be our experience when God sets up his kingdom once and for all. He will be King over all the earth. Look forward to that day.

Holy Spirit, remind me of the future glory that we will all have one day. Give me peaceful dreams tonight as I rest in the thoughts of your warm, light, and refreshing eternal kingdom.

What areas of your life feel like they need God's living waters to flow into them?

In Awe

"My covenant with him was one of life and peace, and I gave them to him. It was a covenant of fear, and he feared me. He stood in awe of my name. True instruction was in his mouth, and no wrong was found on his lips. He walked with me in peace and uprightness, and he turned many from iniquity."

MALACHI 2:5-6 ESV

We have experienced God as a personal and loving God, and so, at times, it is harder to revere him in the way that we should. The Israelites were able to recall and recount the miraculous signs and wonders they experienced, and these acts of God were able to give them a respect for his power and authority.

When you experience God in this way, either through reading of his miracles or experiencing his power in your own life, let it encourage you to be someone who walks with God in uprightness and turns others from their sins.

Father, today I am grateful for your power and your presence. I am in awe of your name. I pray that my holy respect for you would be a witness to those around me—that they would only hear truth from my lips.

*"The lips of a priest should guard knowledge,
and people should seek instruction from his mouth,
for he is the messenger of the LORD of hosts."*

MALACHI 2:7 ESV

God gave us all the privilege of being priests when he sent
Jesus to claim the ultimate title of the High Priest. The role
of the priest was to mediate between God and man. Jesus
fulfilled that role and became the true mediator.

Because Christ is within us, we are now able to have
direct communication with God. Were you able to feel the
awesomeness of God's presence with you today? You are a
messenger of God, so seek him with all your heart to hear his
instruction.

*God, you are awesome, powerful, and too supreme for words.
Thank you for sending Jesus to be the true mediator between
yourself and humanity. I seek you this evening, and await your
instruction.*

What instructions do you need to hear from God, right now?

Enough for Everyone

*"Bring the full tithe into the storehouse, that there may be food in
my house. And thereby put me to the test," says the LORD of hosts,
"if I will not open the windows of heaven for you and pour down
for you a blessing until there is no more need."*

MALACHI 3:10 ESV

We like to hold tight to the hard-earned money that we make;
it seems that we never have very much to spare. Consider,
however, that everything you have—your skills, ability to
learn, opportunities, and the job that you have now—is a
blessing from God. None of us did anything in our own effort
to give us these privileges; therefore, we need to acknowledge
God's blessing.

When God asks for a small portion of our income to give
to the church or to those who are doing God's work in the
world, it shouldn't be a hard decision for us to make. If you're
holding back from giving a little extra, consider how you
might be putting that burden of responsibility onto others. A
little from all of us will go a long way.

*God, thank you for the challenge to give more to further your work
on earth. I'm sorry when I have neglected my responsibility of
giving back to you. Thank you for the abundant blessings in my
life. Let me be a blessing to others today.*

"I will rebuke the devourer for you, so that it will not destroy the fruits of your soil, and your vine in the field shall not fail to bear," says the LORD of hosts. "Then all nations will call you blessed, for you will be a land of delight," says the LORD of hosts.

MALACHI 3:11-12 ESV

Giving more doesn't seem to equate with getting more, yet God almost challenges us to test this theory. The way God works is not the way the world works, and his Word promises that you will have plenty when you give plenty.

Why not try it out this week? See what joy and abundance God can bring into your life when you offer more of yourself to do God's work.

God, I know that I could give more toward those serving in ministry. Help me to respond to the challenge and the prompting of your Holy Spirit, and encourage me with the blessing that comes from giving.

In what ways are you challenged to give more this week?